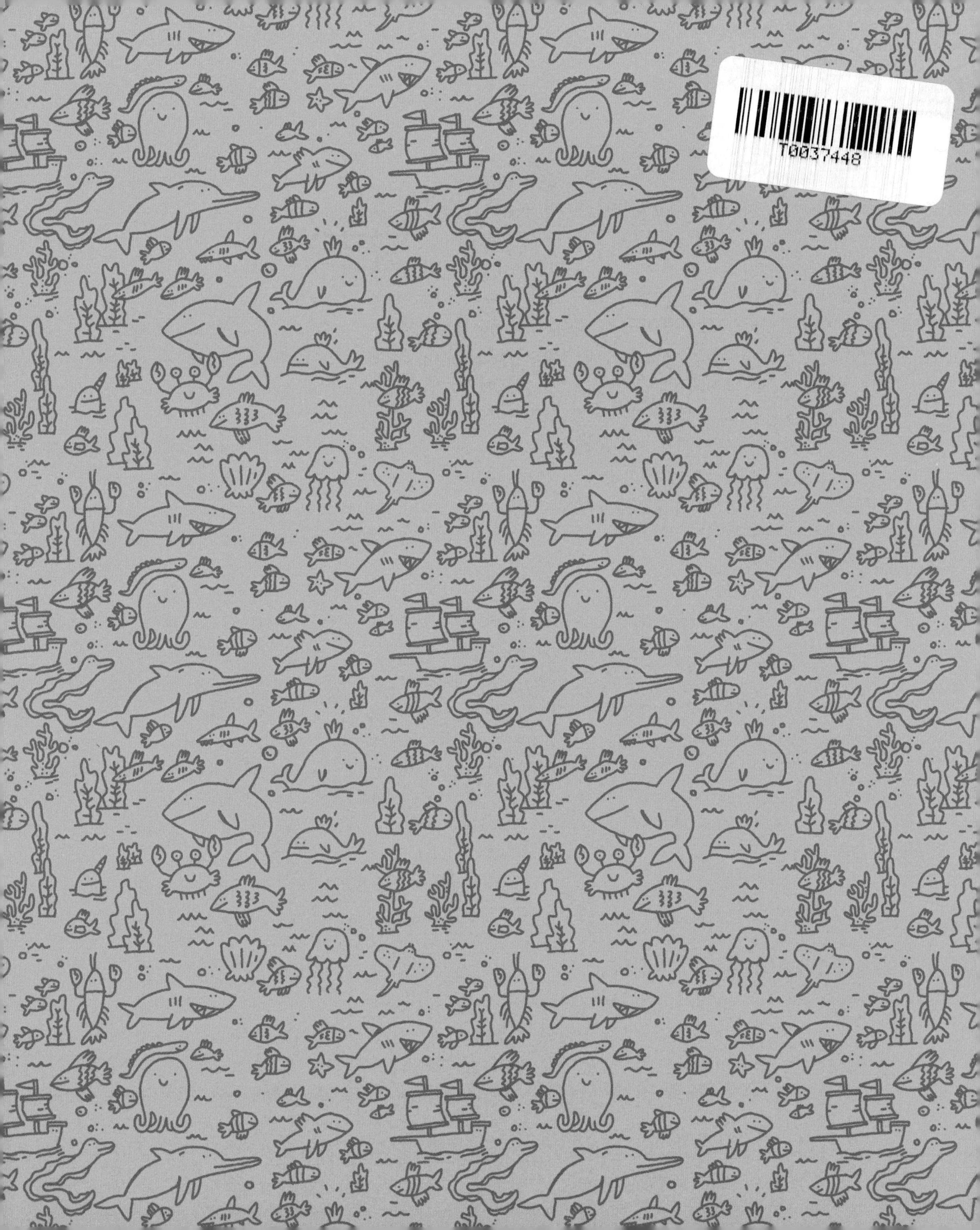

For Steve M. and Liza B., who helped make this series of weird
and awesome books happen!

—M.L.

Copyright © 2020 by Mike Lowery

Special thanks to Dr. Christopher Lowe, Professor and Director of the CSULB Shark Lab, for his guidance and expert
verification of the information included in this book.

Library of Congress Cataloging-in-Publication Data available
ISBN 978-1-338-35973-2
10 9 8 7 6 5 4 3 2          22 23 24
Printed in China     62 • First edition, October 2020
The text type was set in Gotham.
The display type was hand lettered by Mike Lowery.
Book design by Doan Buu

# EVERYTHING AWESOME

# AWESOME

## ABOUT

# SHARKS

## AND OTHER

## UNDERWATER

## CREATURES!

WRITTEN AND ILLUSTRATED BY

## MIKE LOWERY

Orchard Books
New York
An Imprint of Scholastic Inc.

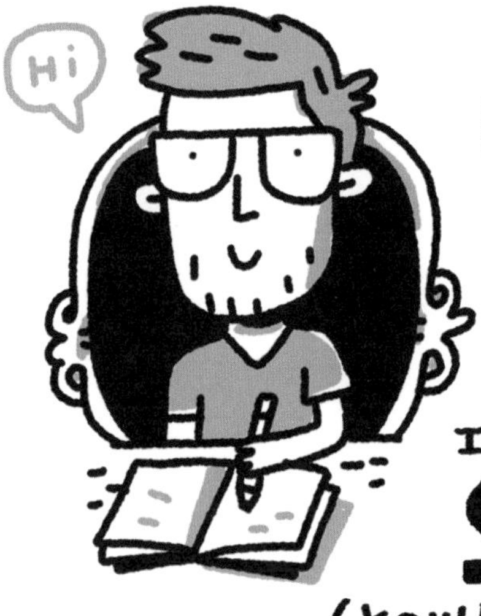
HI

# OH, HELLO.

I'M MIKE LOWERY

AND I'D LIKE TO SHOW YOU SOMETHING.

IT'S A GIANT BOOK ABOUT

# SHARKS!

(YOU'RE HOLDING IT RIGHT NOW!)

IT'S TOTALLY LOADED WITH INFO, WEIRD FACTS, AND JOKES THAT WILL KEEP YOU HOOKED!

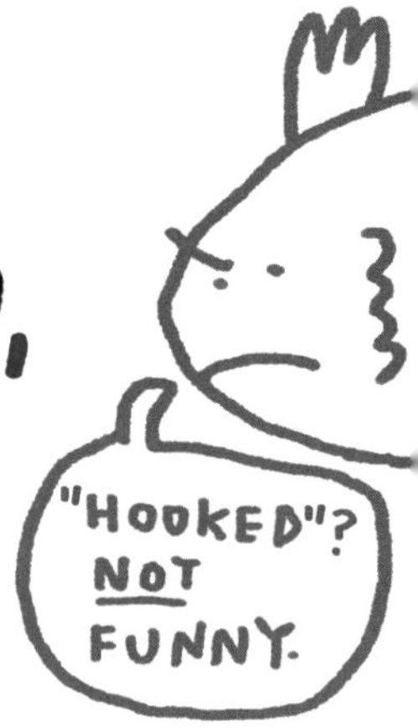
"HOOKED"? NOT FUNNY.

WHY SHARKS? THEY ARE SOME OF THE COOLEST, MOST EXCITING CREATURES EVER!

BUT SHARKS AREN'T THE ONLY TOTALLY AMAZING THINGS THAT LIVE UNDERWATER.

INSIDE YOU'LL LEARN ABOUT:

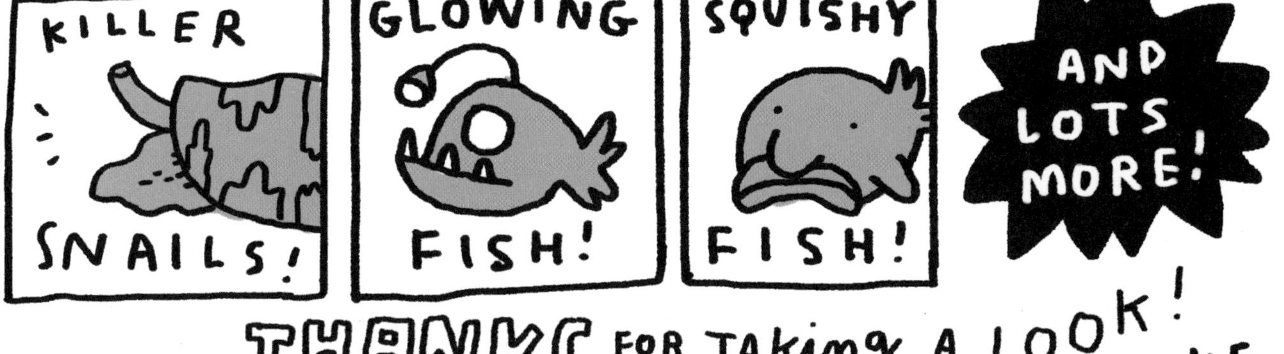
KILLER SNAILS!
GLOWING FISH!
SQUISHY FISH!
AND LOTS MORE!

THANKS FOR TAKING A LOOK!

-MIKE

# TABLE of CONTENTS

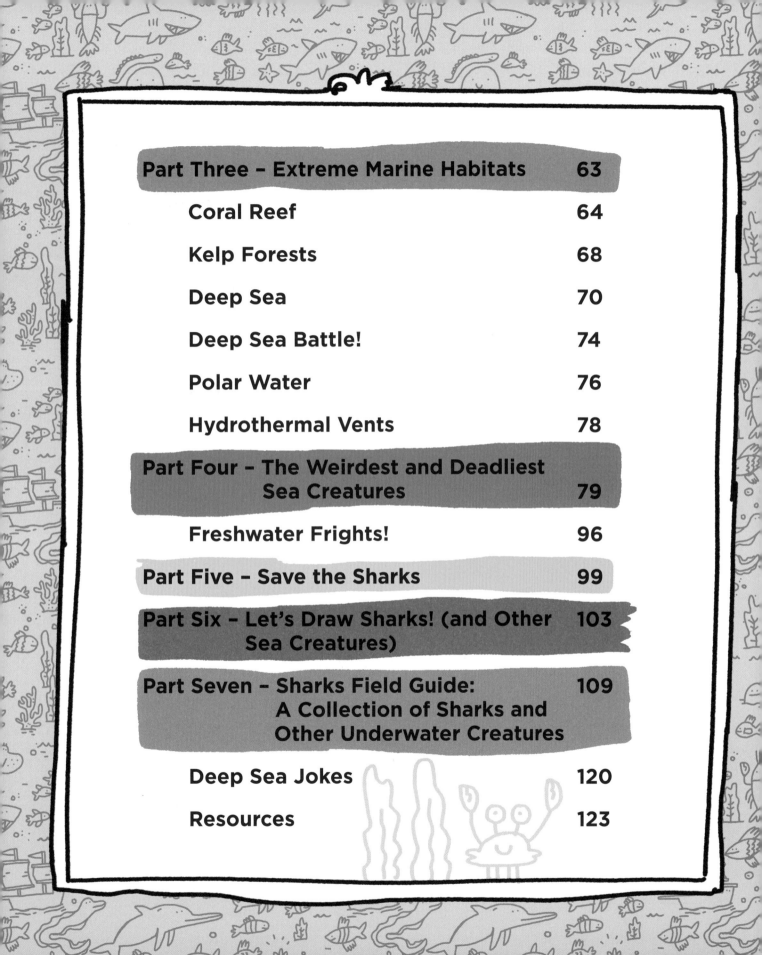

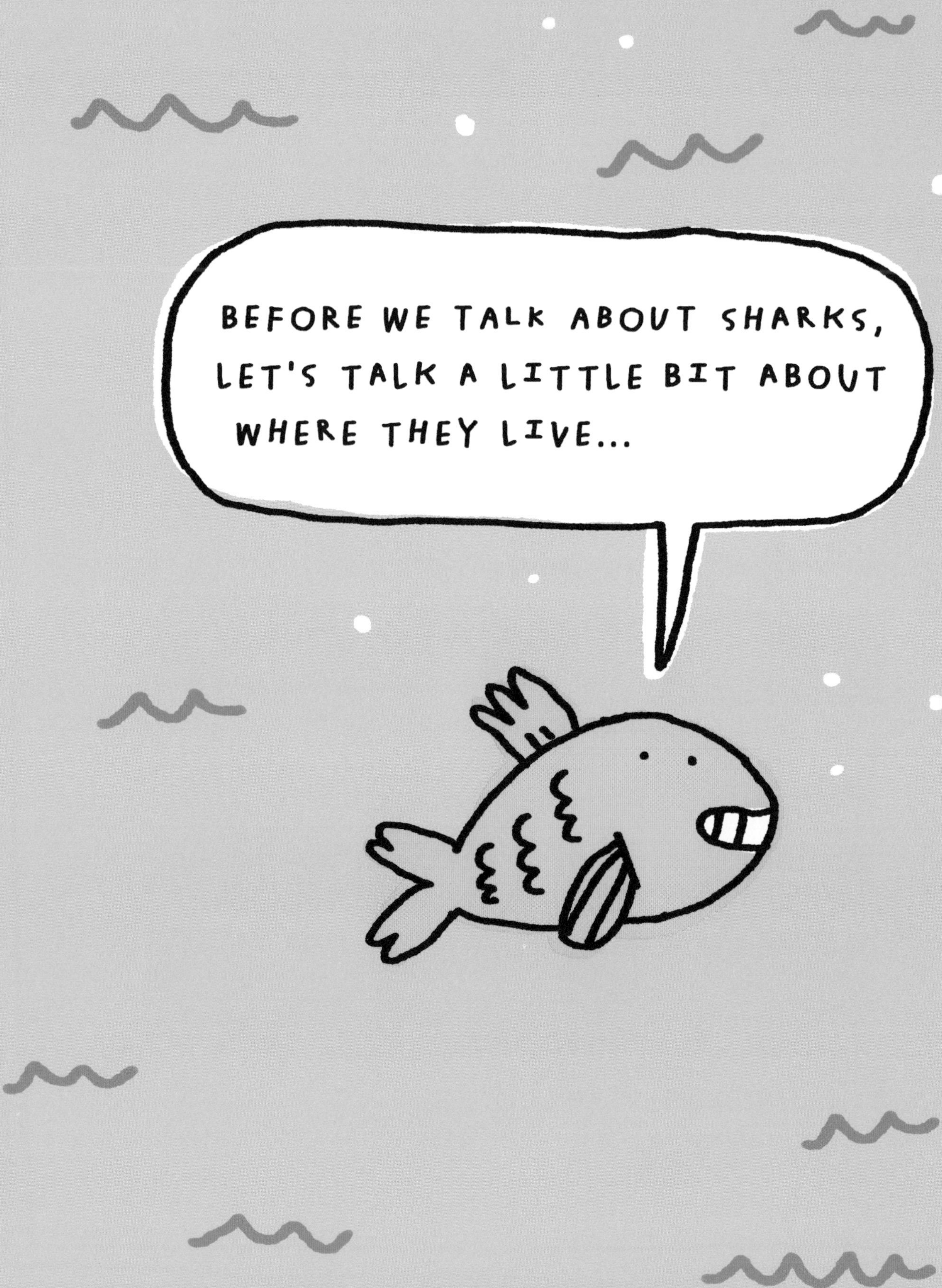
BEFORE WE TALK ABOUT SHARKS, LET'S TALK A LITTLE BIT ABOUT WHERE THEY LIVE...

# PART ONE

# OUR AMAZING OCEANS!

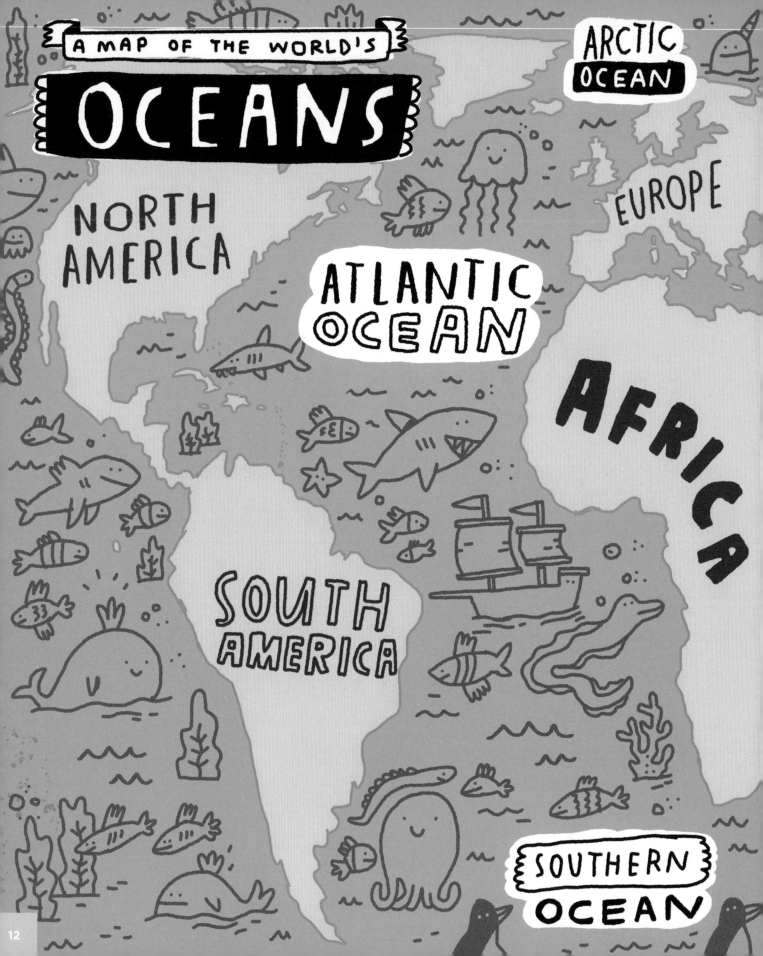

A MAP OF THE WORLD'S

# OCEANS

ARCTIC OCEAN

NORTH AMERICA

EUROPE

ATLANTIC OCEAN

AFRICA

SOUTH AMERICA

SOUTHERN OCEAN

MOST OF THE WATER ON OUR PLANET IS CONNECTED AMONG FIVE OCEANS. THEY COVER MORE THAN 70% OF THE EARTH'S SURFACE AND THEY'RE FULL OF AWESOME LIVING CREATURES (LIKE SHARKS)!

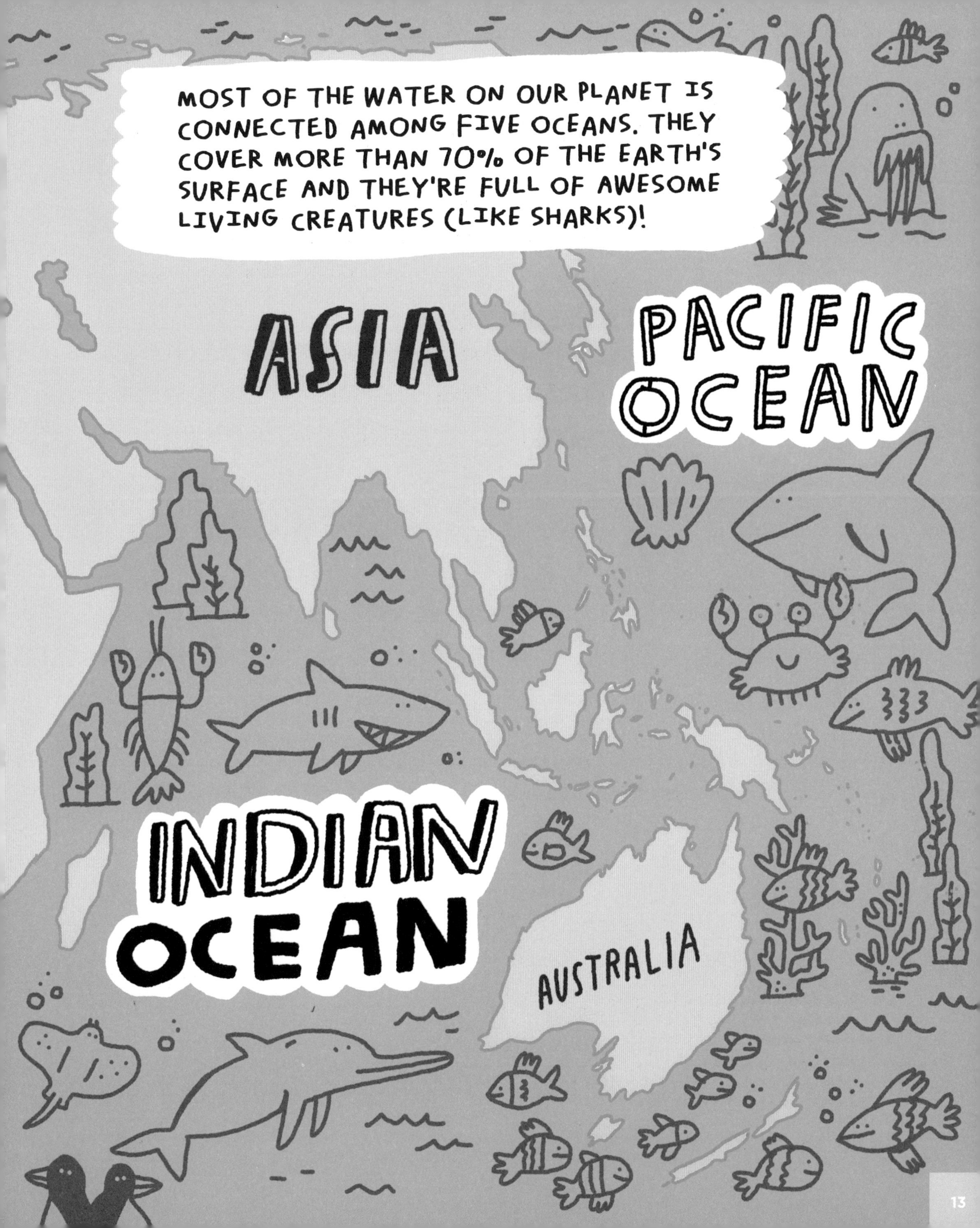
ASIA
PACIFIC OCEAN
INDIAN OCEAN
AUSTRALIA

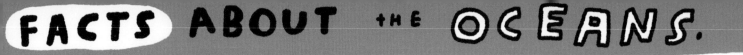

# FACTS ABOUT THE OCEANS.

## 1 THE ATLANTIC OCEAN

GREEN-LAND
NORTH AMERICA
EUROPE
AFRICA
SOUTH AMERICA

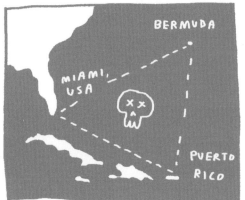

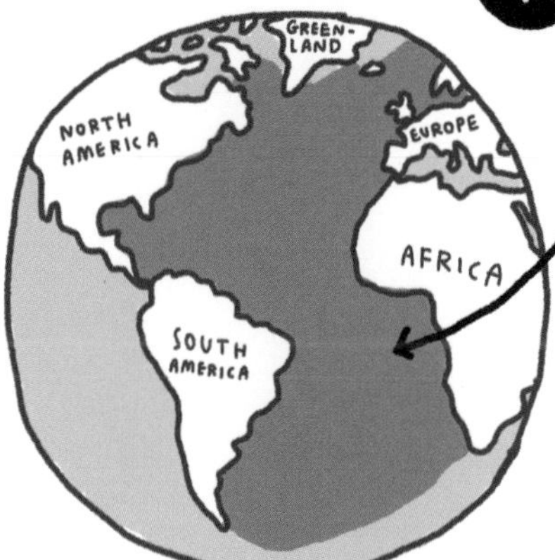

ITS NAME COMES FROM GREEK MYTHOLOGY FOR "THE SEA OF ATLAS."

- COVERS 1/5 OF THE SURFACE OF THE EARTH.
- MOST MAJOR RIVERS (MISSISSIPPI, THE AMAZON, THE CONGO) DRAIN INTO IT.
- HAS THE HIGHEST TIDES OF ANY OCEAN.

BERMUDA
MIAMI, USA
PUERTO RICO

It's also home to

### THE BERMUDA TRIANGLE!

This triangle between Miami, Bermuda, and Puerto Rico is said to be a spot where boats and airplanes...just disappear! Some people have even claimed that there are aliens that like to visit here and an ancient city beneath the waves (the Lost City of Atlantis)! But scientists don't really think that's true.

## 2 THE INDIAN OCEAN

EUROPE
ASIA
AFRICA
AUSTRALIA

- IT'S THE third LARGEST OCEAN.

* Hidden beneath the Indian Ocean is the Kerguelen Plateau, a submerged continent that is almost three times the size of Japan.

**WEIRD FACT:** EVERY YEAR the INDIAN OCEAN GROWS ABOUT 7.8 INCHES! THIS HAPPENS BECAUSE OF MELTING POLAR ICE CAPS AT THE NORTH AND SOUTH POLES.

HOME TO SEVERAL ENDANGERED SPECIES, LIKE THE DUGONG.

Can grow up to 10 feet and up to 1,100 pounds

# 3 THE SOUTHERN OCEAN

• THE YOUNGEST OCEAN.
(IT'S ONLY 30 MILLION YEARS OLD.)

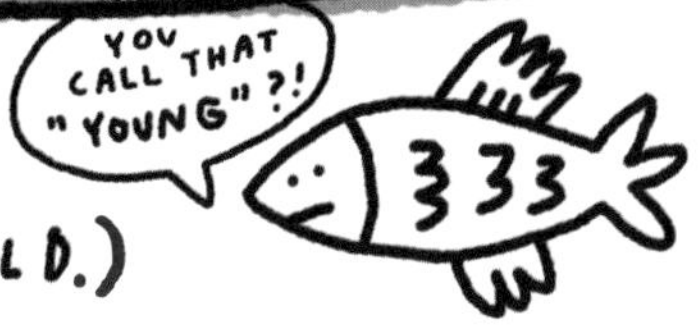
YOU CALL THAT "YOUNG"?!

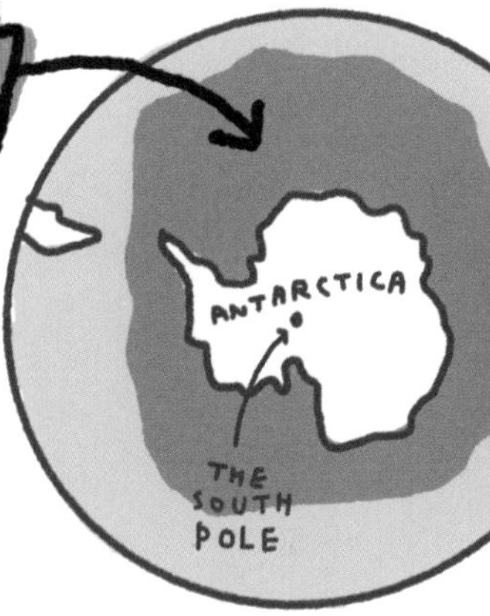
ANTARCTICA
THE SOUTH POLE

## THE MOST DANGEROUS OCEAN!

During winter months, there are big sheets of ice that float on the water off the coast of

ANTARCTICA

When big pieces of ice break off, they become icebergs.

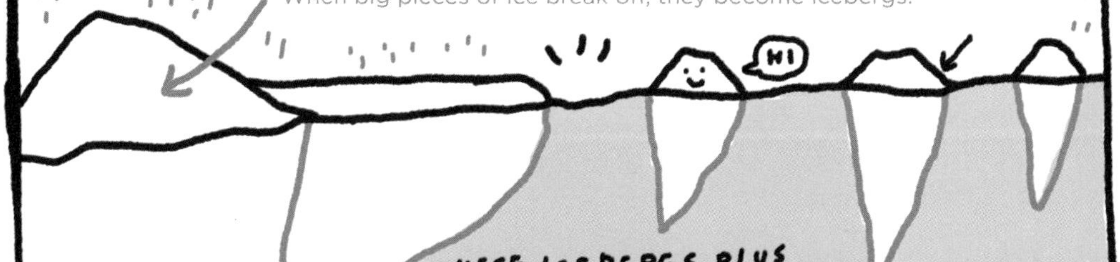
HI

THESE ICEBERGS, PLUS TERRIBLE STORMS AND GIANT WAVES, MAKE THIS A SCARY PLACE FOR BOATS.

### DID YOU KNOW?

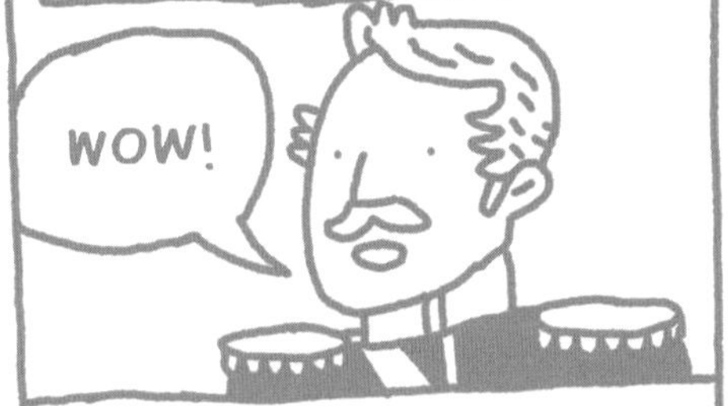
WOW!

Antarctica wasn't seen by a human until 1820, when it was spotted by Russian explorer Fabian Gottlieb von Bellingshausen.

AND AT THE VERY TOP OF THE WORLD IS

# 4 THE ARCTIC OCEAN

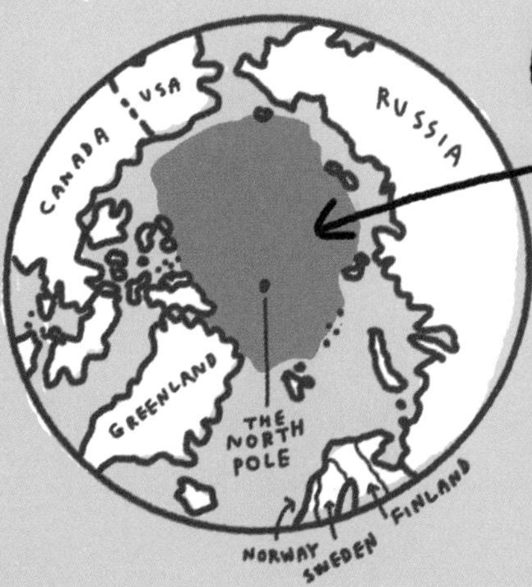
USA
CANADA
RUSSIA
GREENLAND
THE NORTH POLE
NORWAY
SWEDEN
FINLAND

• SMALLEST AND SHALLOWEST OCEAN

• IT'S USUALLY COVERED IN "ICE".

GETS ITS NAME FROM THE GREEK WORD "ARKTIKOS," WHICH MEANS "NEAR THE BEAR."

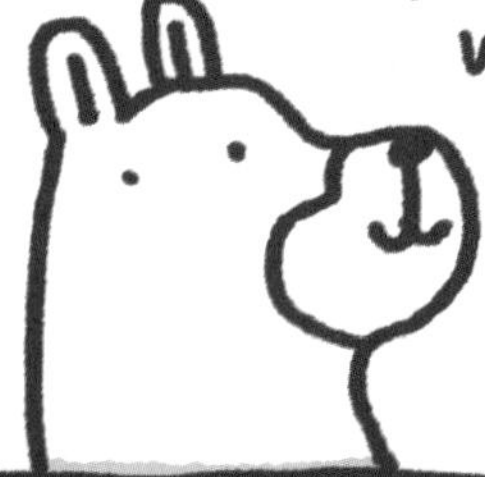

EVEN THOUGH IT'S REALLY COLD, ANIMALS STILL LIVE HERE, LIKE:

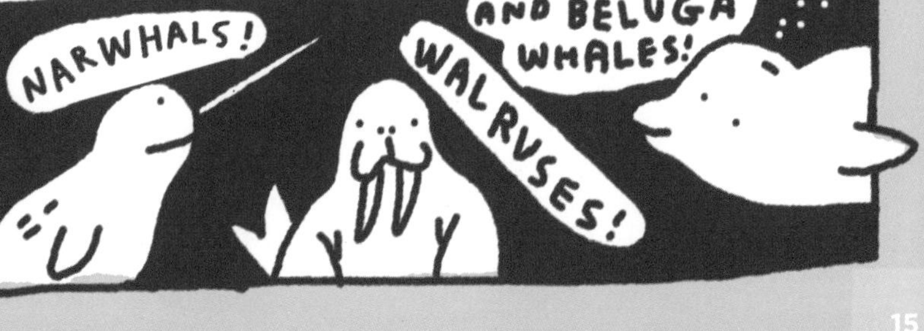
NARWHALS!
WALRUSES!
AND BELUGA WHALES!

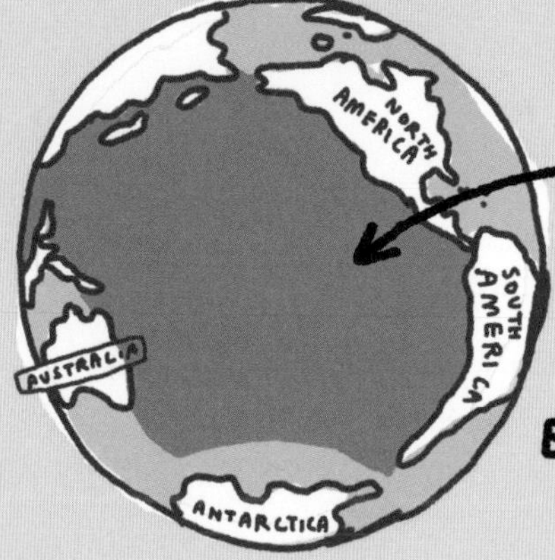
NORTH AMERICA
SOUTH AMERICA
AUSTRALIA
ANTARCTICA

# 5 THE PACIFIC OCEAN

IN 1521, THE PORTUGUESE EXPLORER FERDINAND MAGELLAN CALLED IT

**MAR PACIFICO**

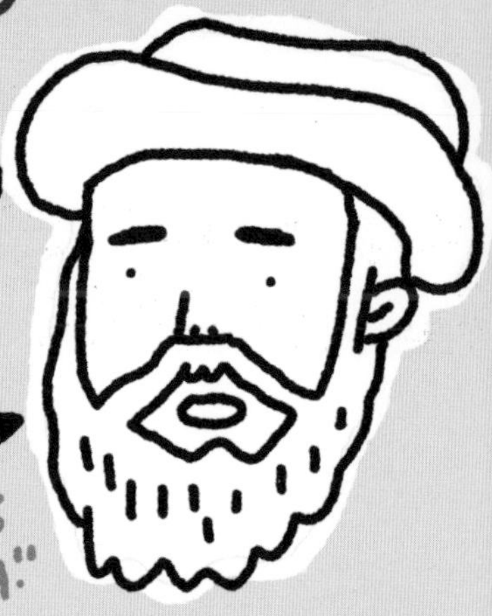

WHICH MEANS "PEACEFUL SEA."

BY FAR THE BIGGEST OCEAN. It COVERS

**1/3**

OF THE ENTIRE SURFACE OF THE EARTH!

IT'S BIGGER THAN ALL OF THE CONTINENTS IF THEY WERE SMASHED TOGETHER!

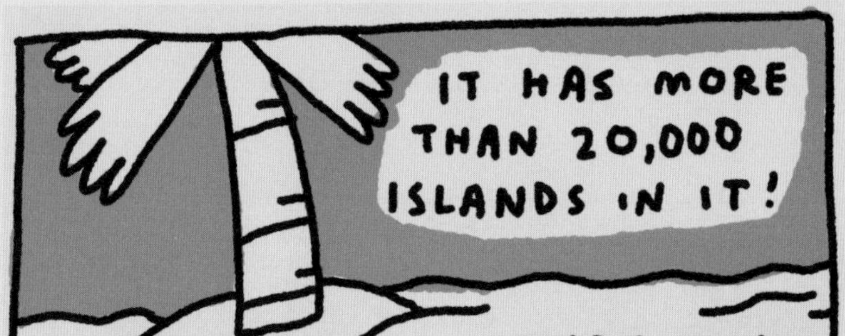

IT HAS MORE THAN 20,000 ISLANDS IN IT!

THAT'S MORE ISLANDS THAN ALL THE OTHER OCEANS COMBINED.

## HOME OF THE GREAT BARRIER REEF

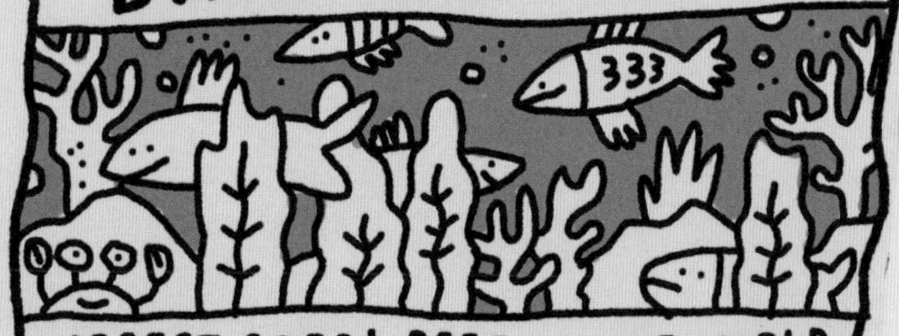

LARGEST CORAL REEF IN THE WORLD

ALSO HOME OF THE MARIANA TRENCH, THE DEEPEST KNOWN SPOT ON THE PLANET.

# THE LONELIEST PLACE ON EARTH

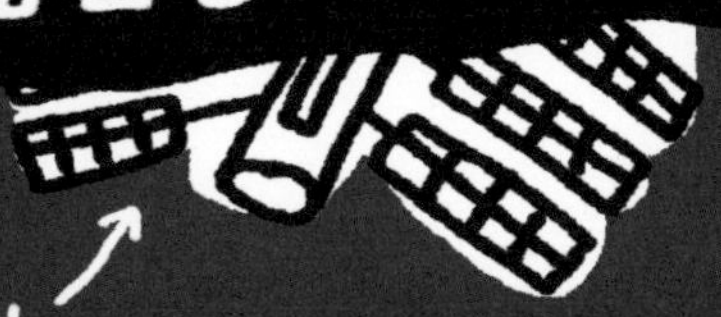

SPACE STATION


# POINT NEMO

NOT NAMED AFTER A MISSING FISH!

NAMED AFTER THE SUBMARINE CAPTAIN IN 20,000 LEAGUES UNDER THE SEA.

There's a spot in the South Pacific that is so far from any land that at points the closest humans are astronauts on the International Space Station. It's surrounded by more than 1,000 miles of ocean in every direction, and the space station is usually around 258 miles from Earth.

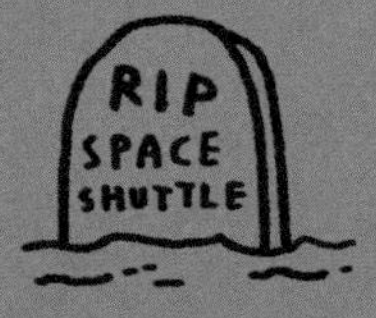

RIP
SPACE
SHUTTLE
X


## It's also a SPACECRAFT GRAVEYARD!

When spaceships that are unmanned return to Earth, they can't handle reentry into the Earth's atmosphere and they usually burn up. So scientists selected this spot as their place to land to be sure they were as far away from people as possible so folks wouldn't get hit by falling space junk! There are 161 sunken spaceships here.

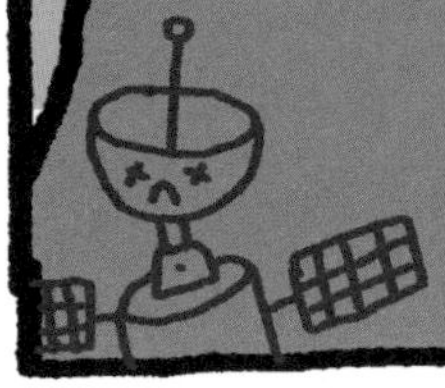

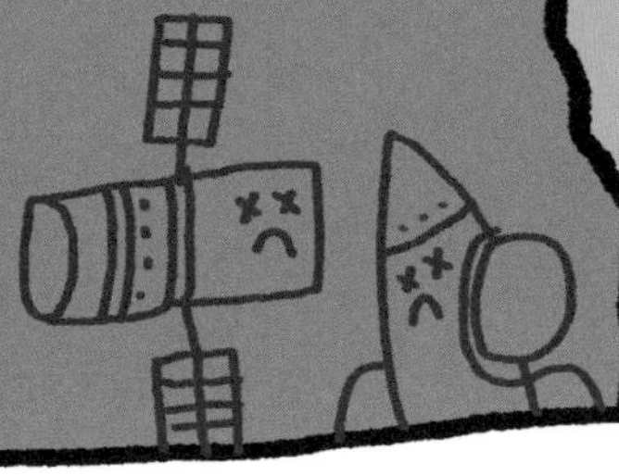

# HOW OUR OCEANS WERE FORMED!

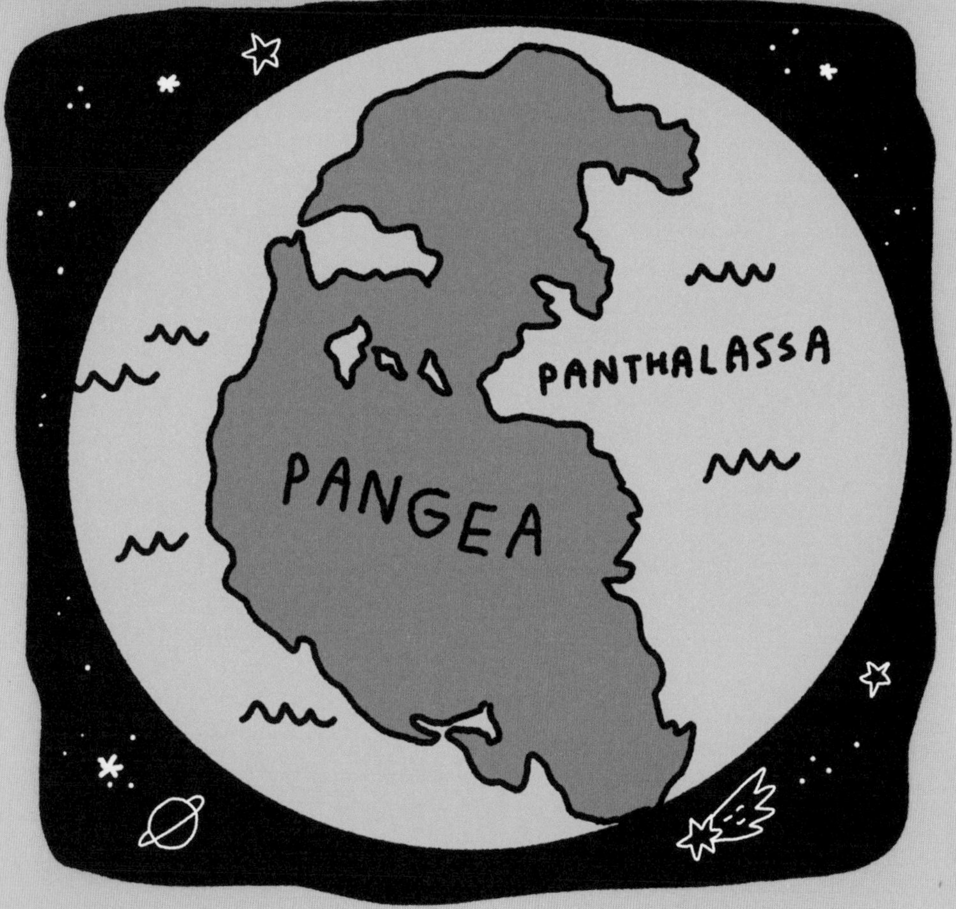
PANTHALASSA
PANGEA

A long time ago (actually, 250 MILLION years ago), there was just one big ocean called

**PANTHALASSA**

and all of the continents were grouped together into one big mass called

**PANGEA.**

160 million years ago, that giant cluster of continents started to break up and the pieces began to drift away from each other.

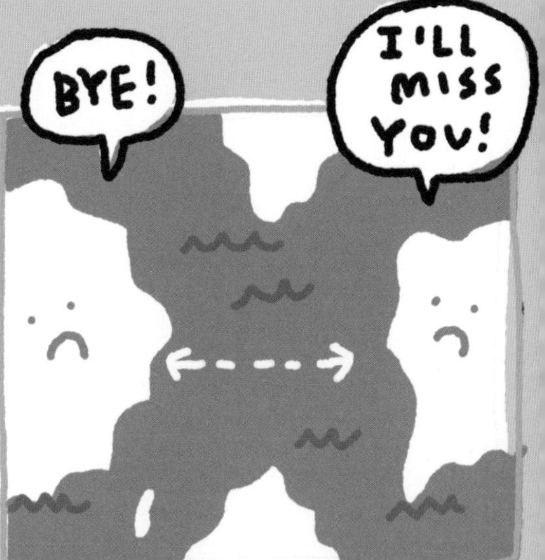
BYE!
I'LL MISS YOU!

## PLATE TECTONICS

This theory says that the outer layer of Earth is made up of rock plates that are constantly (but very slowwwwwly) moving. On top of these plates is all of the land and water on the planet. These moving plates not only helped form our planet's oceans and continents, but also cause earthquakes and even volcano eruptions.

# THE PACIFIC RING OF FIRE

There's a path in the Pacific Ocean that's 24,900 miles long that's called the Pacific Ring of Fire (or the Circum-Pacific Belt) because it's home to more than

**450 VOLCANOES!**

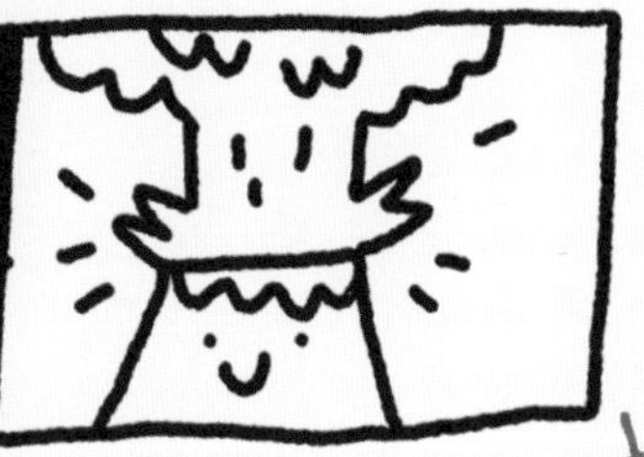

THAT'S MORE THAN **75%** OF THE WORLD'S VOLCANOES!

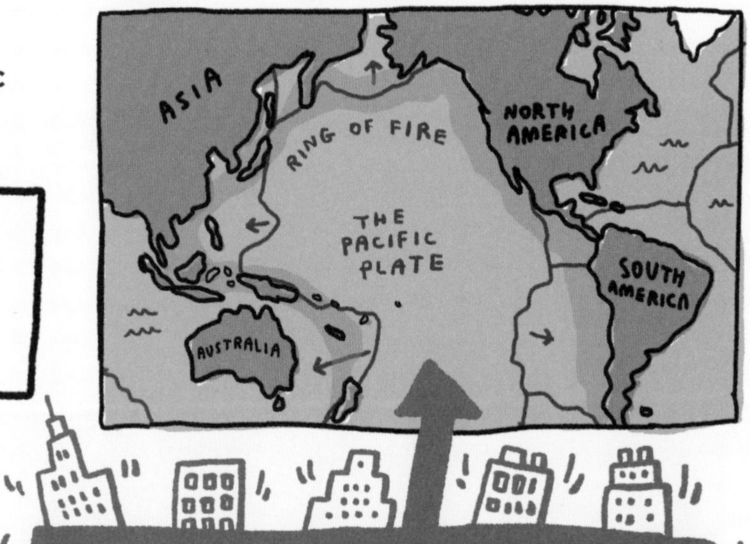
ASIA
RING OF FIRE
NORTH AMERICA
THE PACIFIC PLATE
SOUTH AMERICA
AUSTRALIA

It's also where 90% of earthquakes happen. All of these volcanoes and earthquakes are the result of Earth's largest plate (the Pacific plate) pushing up against the plates that are around it.

## TSUNAMIS

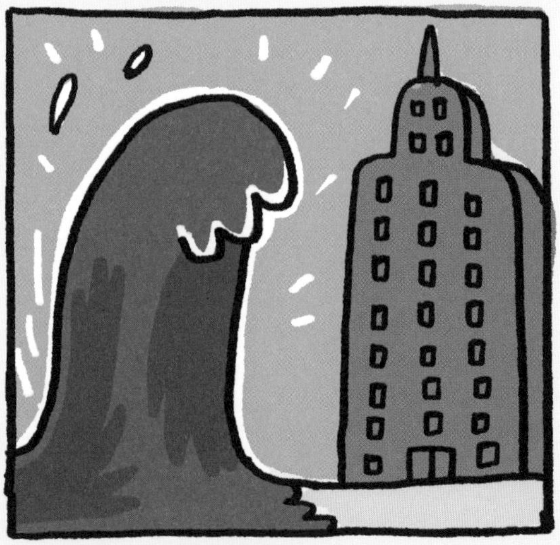

Earthquakes under the ocean can also lead to tsunamis, which are huge waves of water that can be up to 100 feet high (that's about the size of a TEN-STORY building). They can also move at up to 500 mph, which is as fast as a jet. These waves sometimes make it to shore and can cause a lot of damage.

### HOW TO SPOT AN INCOMING TSUNAMI

**EARTHQUAKE!**

IF YOU'RE NEAR THE OCEAN AND FEEL THE GROUND SHAKE, IT MIGHT MEAN THAT A TSUNAMI COULD HAPPEN.

**SUDDEN CHANGE IN WATER LEVEL.**

IF THE OCEAN RUSHES OUT QUICKLY, GO TO HIGH GROUND JUST IN CASE!

**Tsunamis are a series of waves, not always just one big one, and sometimes the first waves aren't the most dangerous.**

# THE OCEAN'S ZONES!

Water absorbs and diffuses sunlight, which means the deeper you go down into the ocean, the darker it gets! Once you hit 3,300 feet deep there's no light at all. The ocean is divided into different zones, depending on how much sunlight they get from the surface.

## SUNLIT ZONE
### (SURFACE–660 FEET)

This layer gets lots of sunlight, which means plants and little organisms like plankton and algae love it here. Small fish hang out at this plant buffet, and some end up becoming food for bigger marine life like tuna, dolphins, and lots of other stuff. Actually, most of the animals that live in the ocean live in this zone!

## TWILIGHT ZONE
### (660–3,300 FEET)

This layer is almost completely dark, but there's still a little bit of a glow from the surface. For all of the humans reading this book right now, it would be complete darkness. No plants grow here, but there are still some residents like jellyfish, octopuses, and squid.

I CAN STILL SEE A LITTLE.

## MIDNIGHT ZONE
## AKA THE DARK ZONE
### (3,300–13,300 FEET)

Way down here there's no light at all except for the occasional little bit from some animals that can glow in the dark, like the viperfish and anglerfish! It's also really cold! It's almost freezing! Also, many of the animals in this layer are black or red because of the absence of sunlight. Some whales can dive down to this region in search of food.

I LIKE IT DOWN HERE.

## ABYSSAL ZONE
## AKA THE ABYSS
### (13,000–20,000 FEET)

Its name comes from a loose translation from Greek for "no bottom."

Around 75% of the floor of the ocean is in this zone.

## HADAL ZONE
### (ANYTHING BELOW 20,000 FEET)

The very last zone is the hadal zone, which can be found in deep trenches in the bottom of the ocean. This zone was named after the Greek mythological realm of Hades, which is a very dark place where souls of the dead would end up!

All that water on top of you makes the pressure impossible for humans to take without a super-specialized submarine. It's 1,100 times the pressure on the surface. That would be as much pressure as 50 airplanes on top of you!

# HOW DEEP IS THE OCEAN?

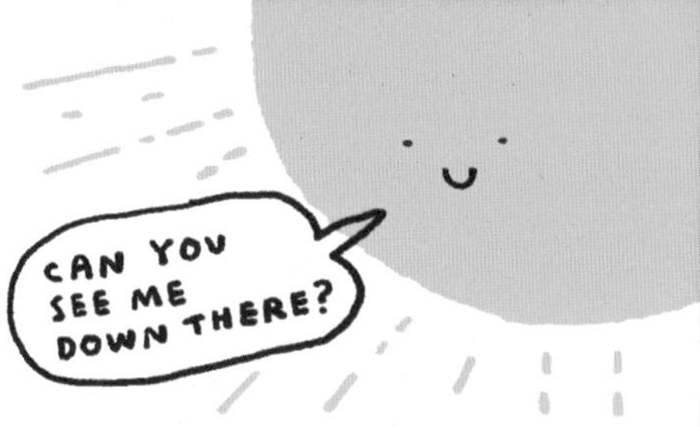
CAN YOU SEE ME DOWN THERE?

**• 131 FEET**
Deepest recreational scuba diving depth.

**• 328 FEET** This is where diving can get dangerous for humans because of the pressure.

**• 702 FEET**
Deepest freedive record. Herbert Nitsch swam all the way down with just one breath!

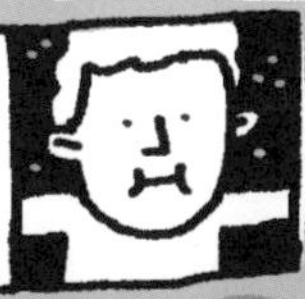

**• 1,089 FEET**
Deepest scuba dive.

**• 1,453 FEET**
Height of the Empire State Building.

**• 2,717 FEET**
Height of Burj Khalifa (the tallest building in the world).

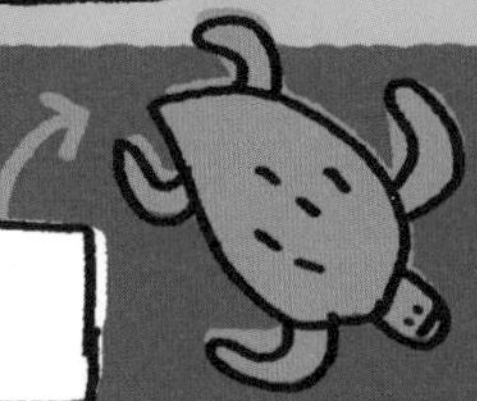

**• 4,199 FEET**
Maximum depth a leatherback turtle will dive.

## DID YOU KNOW?

## SCUBA

**IS AN ACRONYM.**

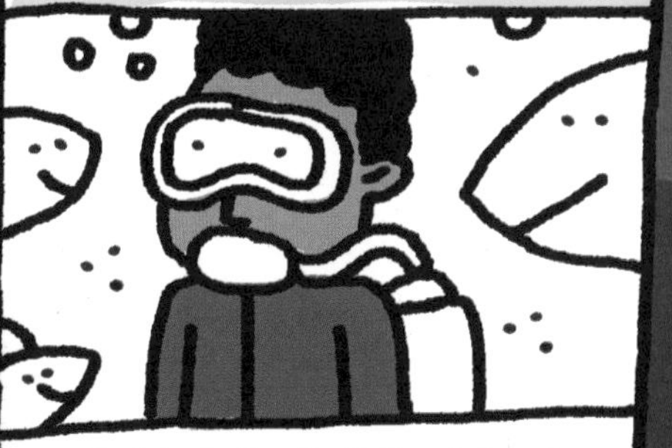

**It stands for Self-Contained Underwater Breathing Apparatus!**

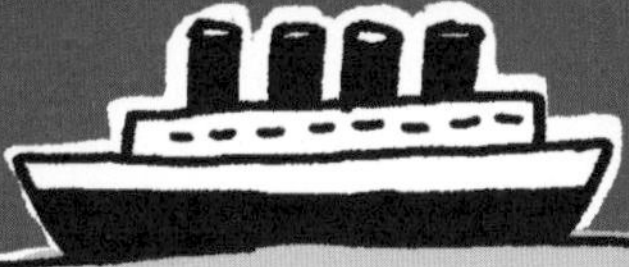

**• 12,467 FEET**
This is where the wreckage of the *Titanic* is.

IT KEEPS GOING!

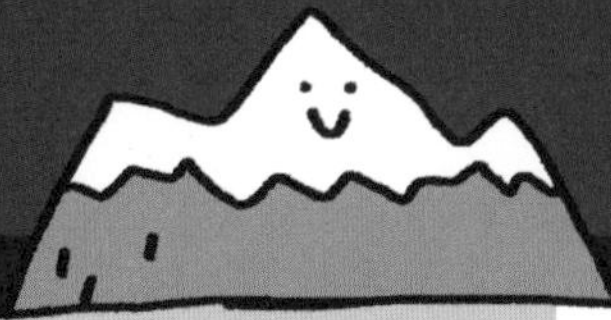

**• 29,028 FEET**
Height of Mount Everest if it were upside down in the water.

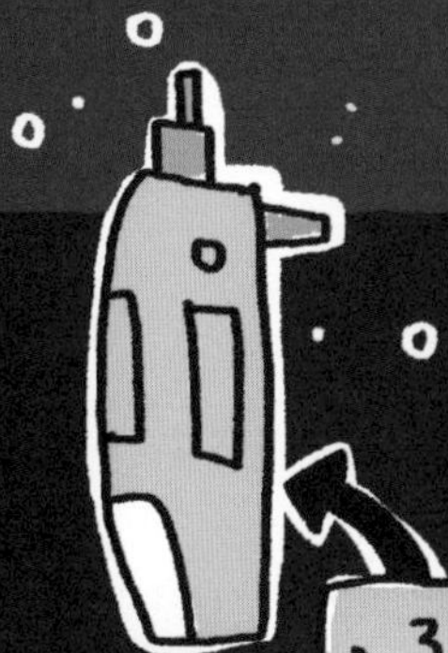

**• 35,787 FEET**
Depth of dive for James Cameron's (director of *Titanic*, *The Abyss*, and *Avatar*) *Deepsea Challenger* mission.

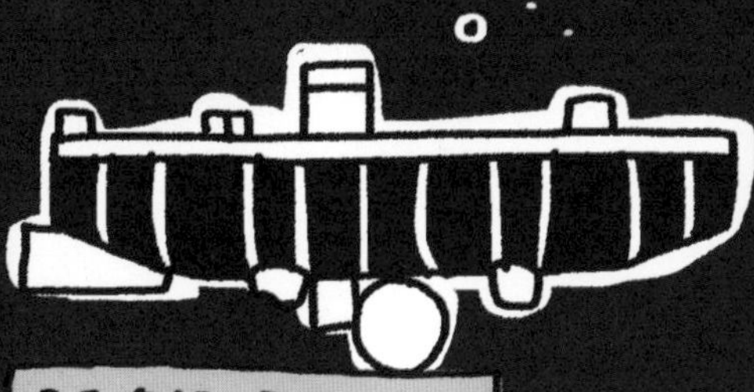

**• 35,813 FEET**
Don Walsh and Jacques Piccard traveled to this depth in a submarine in 1960. It took 5 hours! Unfortunately, the crew only stayed 20 minutes before having to return to the surface after a window started to crack!

# CHALLENGER DEEP!

The deepest known part of the ocean is the Challenger Deep, which is in the Mariana Trench. It's more than 36,000 feet deep! That's deeper than Mount Everest is tall! Mount Everest is 29,028 feet tall, and it's the tallest mountain in the world.

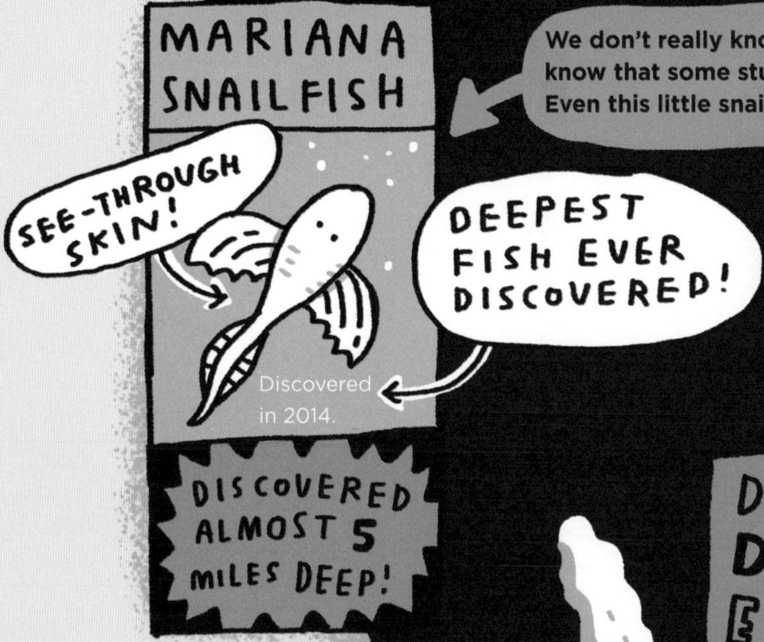

MARIANA SNAILFISH
SEE-THROUGH SKIN!
DEEPEST FISH EVER DISCOVERED!
Discovered in 2014.
DISCOVERED ALMOST 5 MILES DEEP!


We don't really know much about life in the trench, but we do know that some stuff does live down there, like microorganisms. Even this little snailfish was discovered down there.

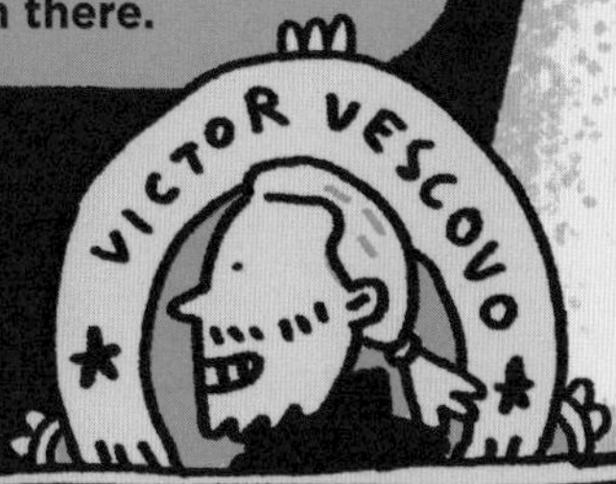

VICTOR VESCOVO


For years, the record for deepest solo dive was held by film director James Cameron, but in 2019 his record was beaten by billionaire Victor Vescovo, who traveled 35,853 feet to the bottom of the Mariana Trench in a submarine.

He saw life way down there but sadly also saw a plastic trash bag.

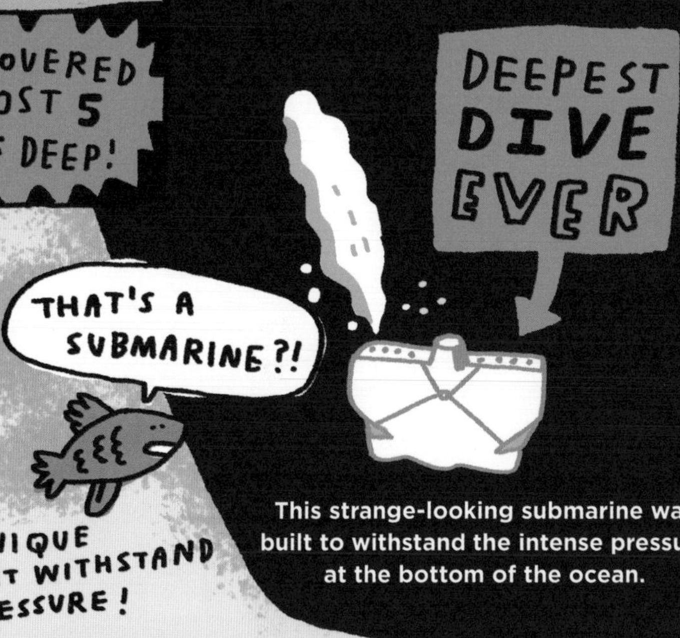

DEEPEST DIVE EVER
THAT'S A SUBMARINE?!
YEP! ITS UNIQUE SHAPE HELPS IT WITHSTAND THE PRESSURE!


This strange-looking submarine was built to withstand the intense pressure at the bottom of the ocean.

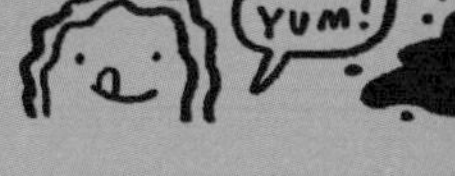

YUM!


Down in the trench, scientists have discovered a group of hydrogen-degrading bacteria. **THAT MEANS THIS BACTERIA EATS OIL.** This finding might lead to a better way of cleaning up oil spills!

# MORE AWESOME OCEAN STUFF

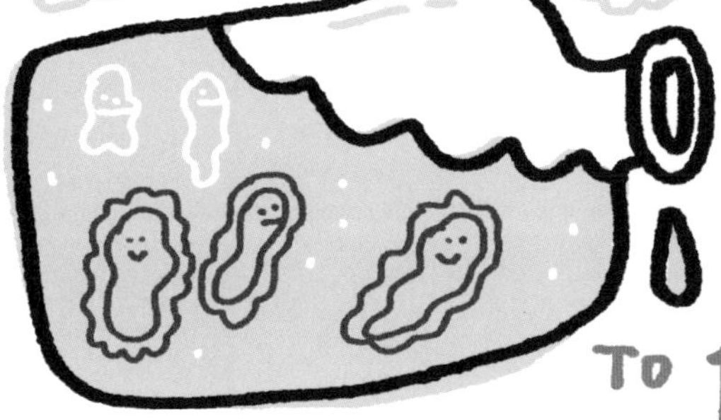

## OCEAN WATER IS FULL OF LIFE.

JUST ONE DROP CONTAINS UP TO 1 MILLION VIRUSES.

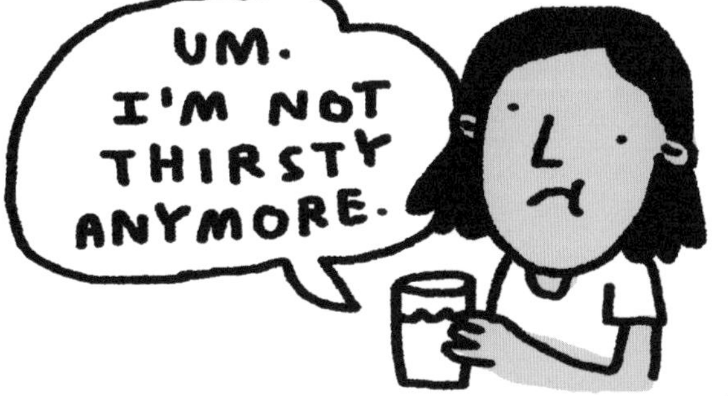
UM. I'M NOT THIRSTY ANYMORE.

DON'T WORRY! MOST OF THEM ARE HARMLESS!

## CHECK THIS OUT!

It's estimated that up to

**80%**

of all life on this planet is in the

OCEAN.

AND scientists believe that only around 9% of all marine life has been classified! What will we discover next??

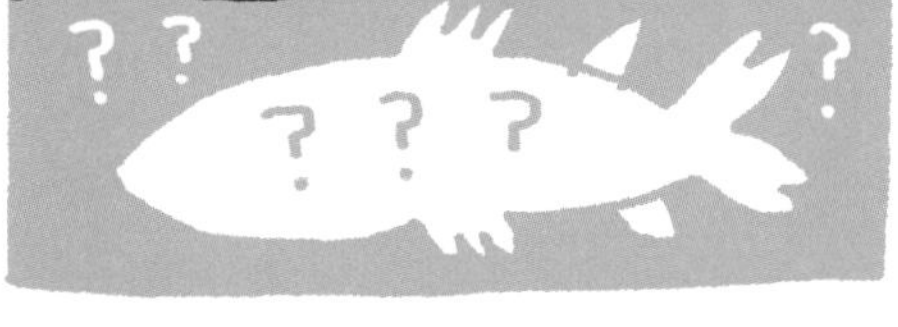
? ? ? ? ? ?

## SECRET MOUNTAINS!

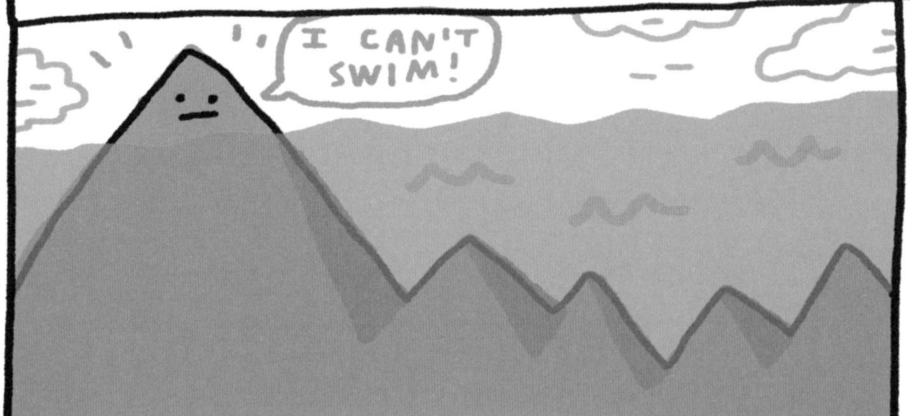
I CAN'T SWIM!

The largest mountain range in the world is almost completely underwater. It's called the mid-oceanic ridge and it's more than 40,000 miles long and has peaks higher than the Alps! Explorers didn't go down to visit the ridge until 1973, which was 4 YEARS after men walked on the moon.

# THE BLOOP!

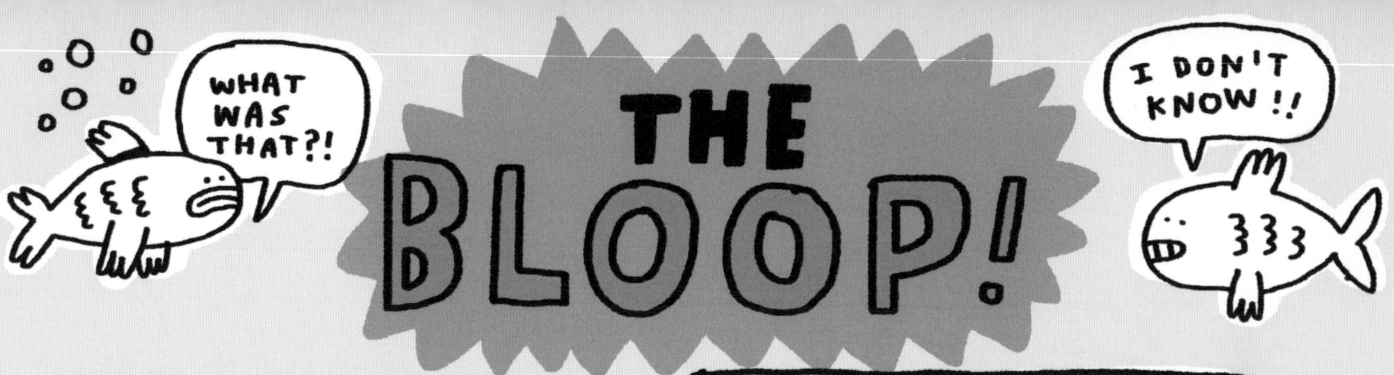
WHAT WAS THAT?!
I DON'T KNOW!!

In 1997 underwater microphones recorded one of the loudest sounds ever heard in the ocean. They started calling it "THE BLOOP." The sound was heard by researchers roughly 3,000 miles away from each other. **It was louder than any known animal and it wasn't believed to be man made.**

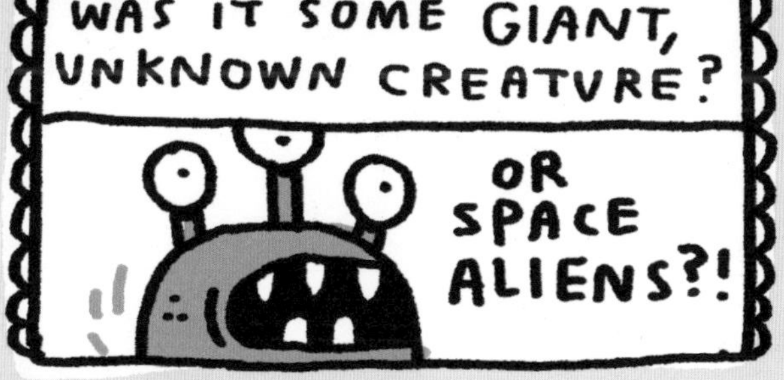
WAS IT SOME GIANT, UNKNOWN CREATURE?
OR SPACE ALIENS?!

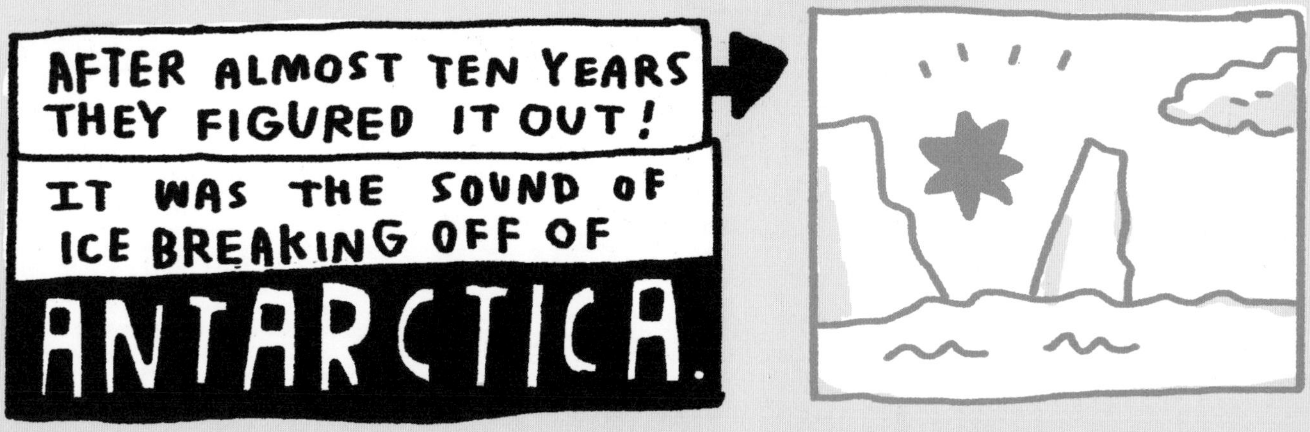
AFTER ALMOST TEN YEARS THEY FIGURED IT OUT!
IT WAS THE SOUND OF ICE BREAKING OFF OF
ANTARCTICA.

## UNDERWATER... WATER?!

**This might seem a little strange, but there are areas underwater where the water is even denser than other parts of the ocean. This creates underwater lakes and waterfalls! In some cases the lakes even have their own waves.**

**Weirder yet, the world's biggest waterfall is underwater. It's 11,500 feet tall and carries 175 million cubic feet of water with it PER SECOND. That's 2,000 times more water than Niagara Falls carries.**

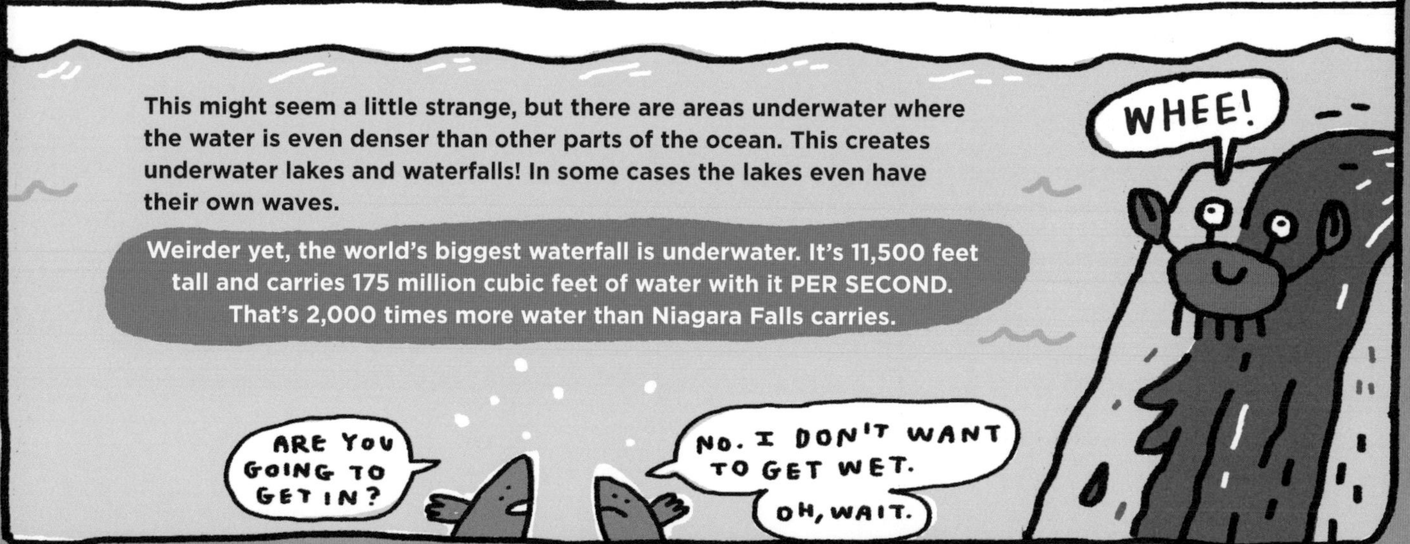
WHEE!
ARE YOU GOING TO GET IN?
NO. I DON'T WANT TO GET WET.
OH, WAIT.

# FEELING BLUE?

Have you ever noticed that stuff looks blue or greenish blue under ocean water? That's because the water can absorb the other colors in sunlight. The light that is reflected through the water also does this, which is why ocean water near the surface usually looks blue. However, this only works if the water is really clean. For example, creek water looks brown because it has bits of mud floating in it, which ends up reflecting the light.

I GOT THE BLUES!

# WAVES OF GOLD

There's about 20 million tons of totally FREE gold just floating in the ocean. However, it's in little bits so small that there's no way of getting it out.

DAGNABBIT! I WANT THAT GOLD!

**How much is all that gold WORTH?**
Well, 1 ton is worth about 41.5 million dollars. So, multiply that by 20 million and you've got…ummm… A LOT OF MONEY!

# LOST BOMBS!

**Stuff gets lost in the ocean all the time. Boats, people…and HYDROGEN BOMBBBBSS.**

**Several nuclear weapons have been lost over the years. One was lost only 80 miles off the coast of some Japanese islands. It rolled off the deck of the USS *Ticonderoga* when the aircraft carrier was attacked. It's now 16,000 feet underwater.**

**Another was lost over the Mediterranean Sea in 1956. A jet carrying two nuclear weapons disappeared in very thick clouds 14,500 feet in the air. It just vanished! The plane and crew (and those bombs!) were never seen again.**

MISSING

HAVE YOU SEEN THIS BOMB?

THIS KIND OF BOMB!

# WEIRD STUFF THAT'S BEEN FOUND IN THE OCEAN

## THE LOST CITY OF HERACLEION!

Discovered off the coast of Egypt, these ancient ruins are from a 2,300-year-old civilization and include: 64 ships, 700 anchors, a huge temple, lots of gold coins, and even 16-foot-tall statues.

## AN ARMY OF RUBBER DUCKS!

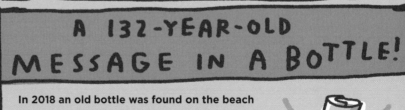

When 28,000 rubber ducks fell off a cargo ship, it wasn't great for the company who made them, but scientists have been using them to study the currents in the ocean. When one is discovered somewhere on the planet, we can see how the current carried it to that spot.

## A GIANT LEGO MAN!

For more than 10 years, giant LEGO men have been washing up on shores all over the world. The LEGO company didn't make them, and they all have a mysterious message on their chests: "NO REAL THAN YOU ARE." (Which doesn't make sense!)

I JUST NEEDED A VACATION!

NO REAL THAN YOU ARE!

## SNOWBALLS!

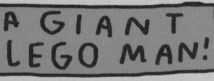

Okay, so this wasn't found IN the ocean, but it came from the ocean. In 2011, thousands of snowballs washed ashore on a beach in Siberia. They were all over the 11-mile beach and some were the size of tennis balls, while others were up to 3 feet wide. It turns out it was just a natural (but rare) phenomena caused by ice rolled around by wind and water, creating the little spheres.

## A 132-YEAR-OLD MESSAGE IN A BOTTLE!

In 2018 an old bottle was found on the beach in western Australia. Inside was a letter that had been dropped in the Indian Ocean by a German sailor in 1886. How did they know where it had been dropped? The letter listed the coordinates!

# PART TWO

# SHARKS!

THIS IS MY FAVORITE SECTION!
GULP! NOT MINE!

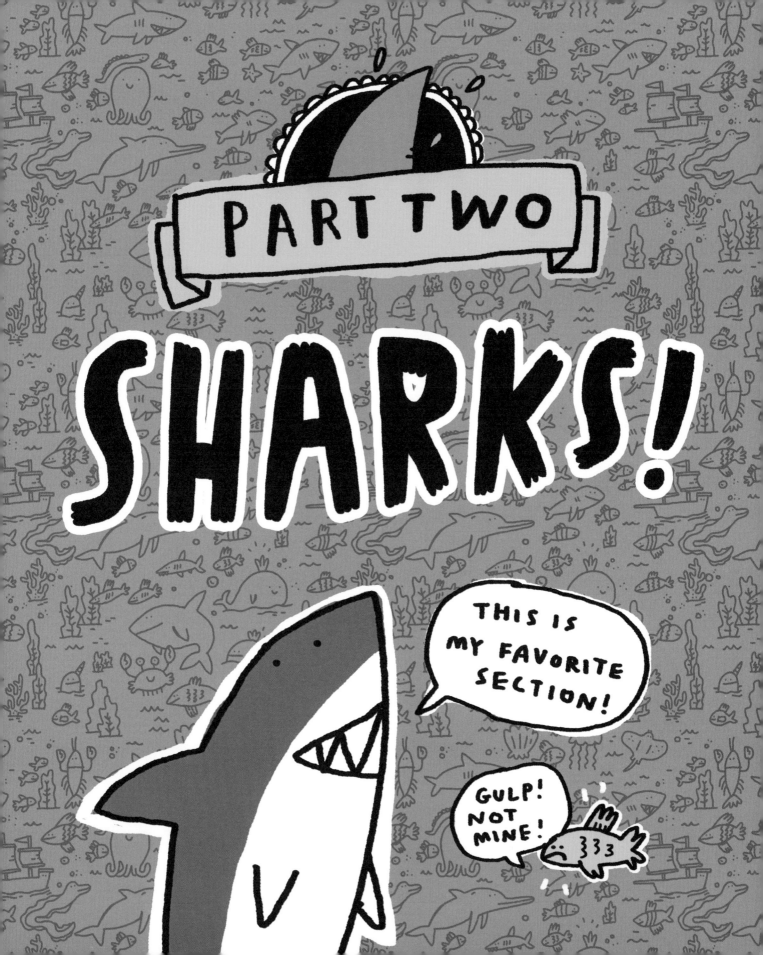

# WHAT IS A SHARK?

Now that we've had a chance to look at our amazing oceans, let's get to the main attraction:

# SHARKS!

BUT BEFORE WE DO, WE HAVE TO TALK ABOUT **FISH**.

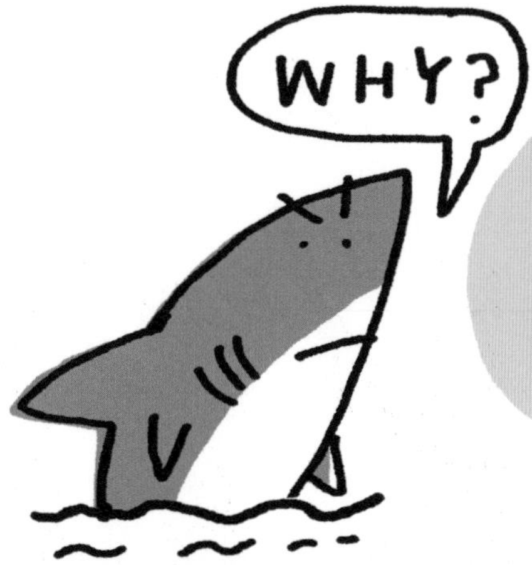
WHY?

BECAUSE A **SHARK** IS A FISH!

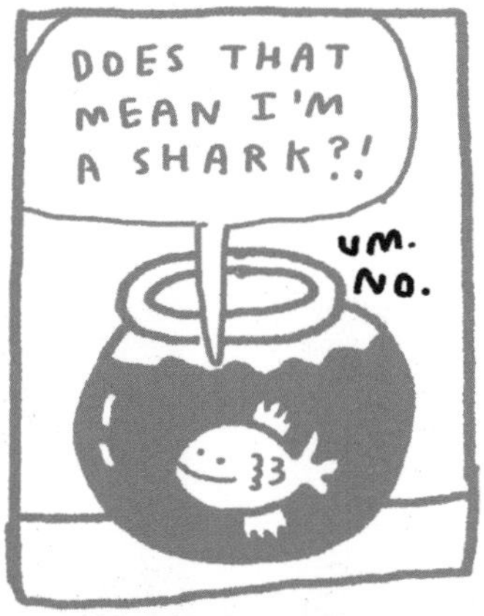
DOES THAT MEAN I'M A SHARK?!
UM. NO.

## A FEW FAST FISH FACTS:

The branch of zoology that focuses on studying fish is called "ichthyology" and is sometimes called

**FISH SCIENCE.**

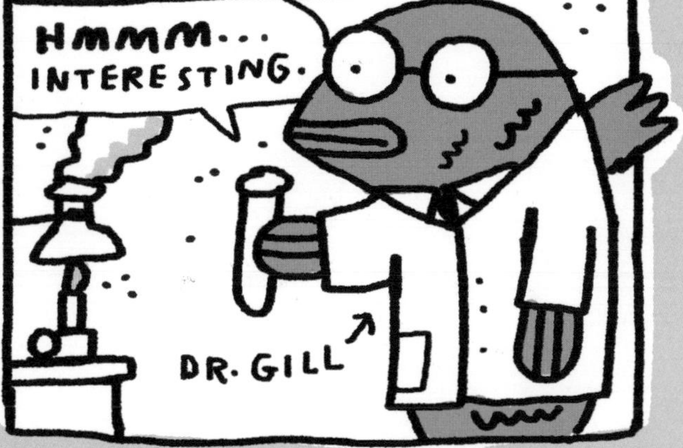
HMMM... INTERESTING.
DR. GILL

## FISH OR FISHES?

What's the correct plural form of fish? Is it FISH or FISHES? FISH is definitely the most common way of referring to multiple fish. But let's get picky! If you're talking about more than one of the SAME type of fish (like six tuna), you HAVE TO say "FISH"! If you're talking about different types of fish in one group, you CAN say "FISHES"!

# WHAT MAKES A FISH A FISH?!

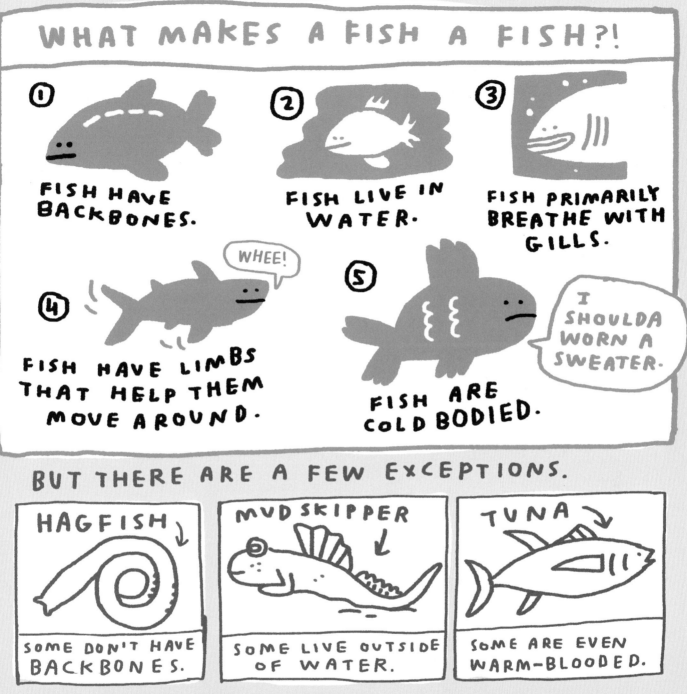

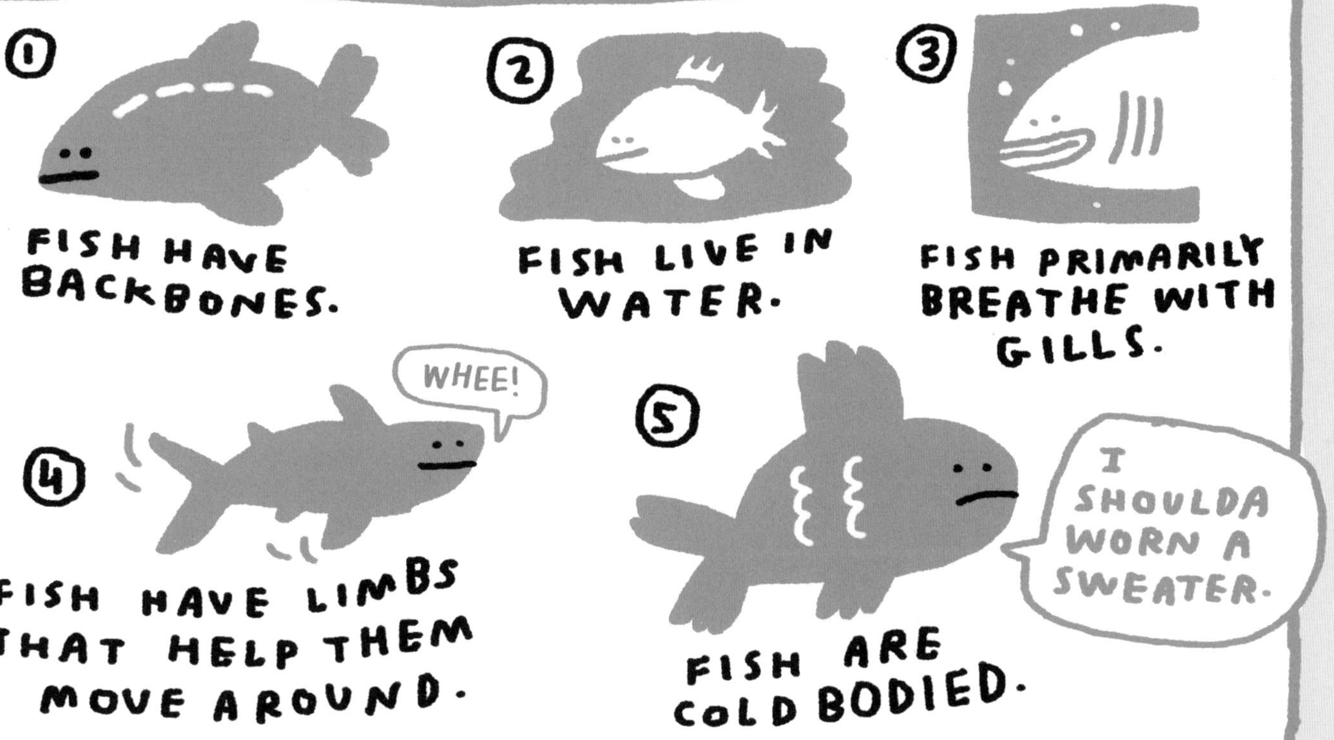
1
FISH HAVE BACKBONES.
2
FISH LIVE IN WATER.
3
FISH PRIMARILY BREATHE WITH GILLS.
WHEE!
4
FISH HAVE LIMBS THAT HELP THEM MOVE AROUND.
5
I SHOULDA WORN A SWEATER.
FISH ARE COLD BODIED.

## BUT THERE ARE A FEW EXCEPTIONS.

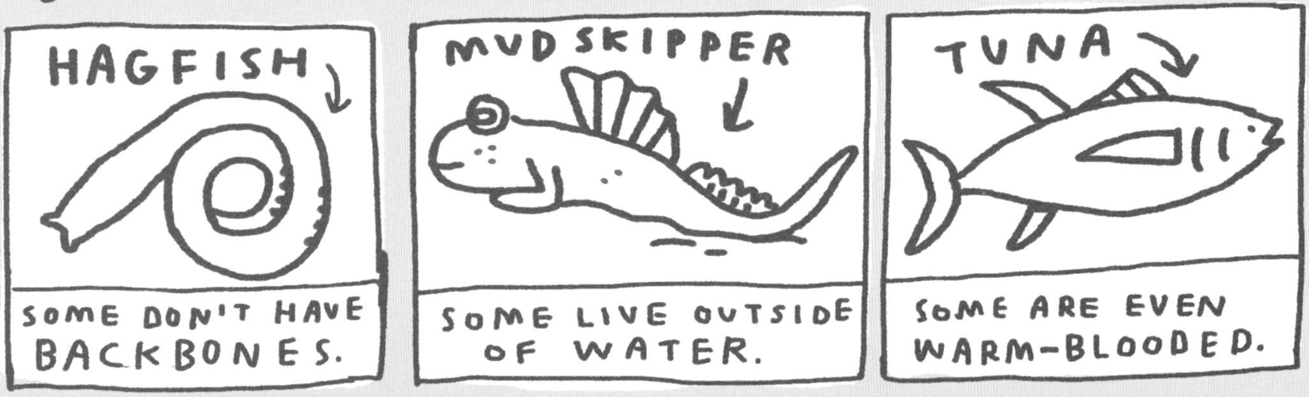
HAGFISH
SOME DON'T HAVE BACKBONES.
MUDSKIPPER
SOME LIVE OUTSIDE OF WATER.
TUNA
SOME ARE EVEN WARM-BLOODED.

Turns out that the term "fish" is really just a word that's used as an easy way to classify different types of aquatic animals, but it's not really a scientific classification term like "mammal."

## WHAT ARE GILLS?

Animals need to take in oxygen to live. We do this with our lungs, which turn oxygen in the air into energy for our bodies and then the lungs turn oxygen into carbon dioxide. Fish do it with their gills, which take in oxygen from water. They also use their gills to get rid of waste!

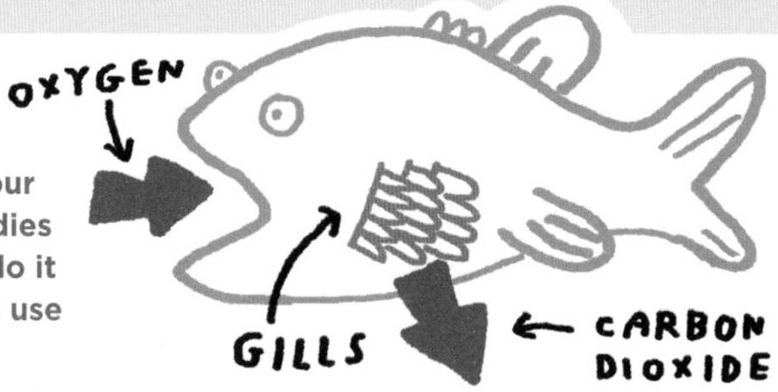
OXYGEN
GILLS
CARBON DIOXIDE

# NOW THAT WE'VE TALKED ABOUT FISH, WE CAN FOCUS ON SHARKS!

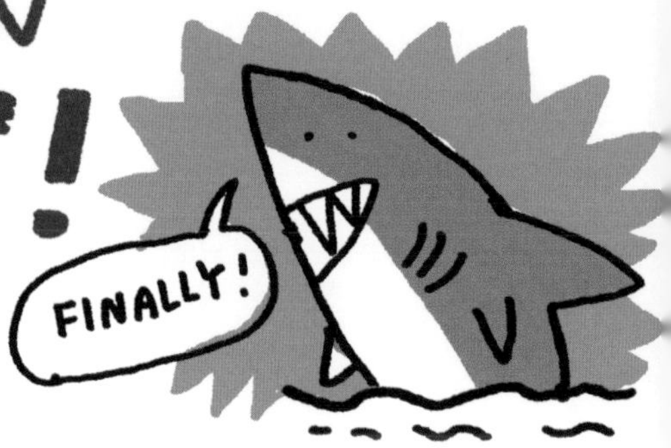
FINALLY!

Most sharks have long bodies and a fin on the end of their tail that they use to propel through the water quickly.

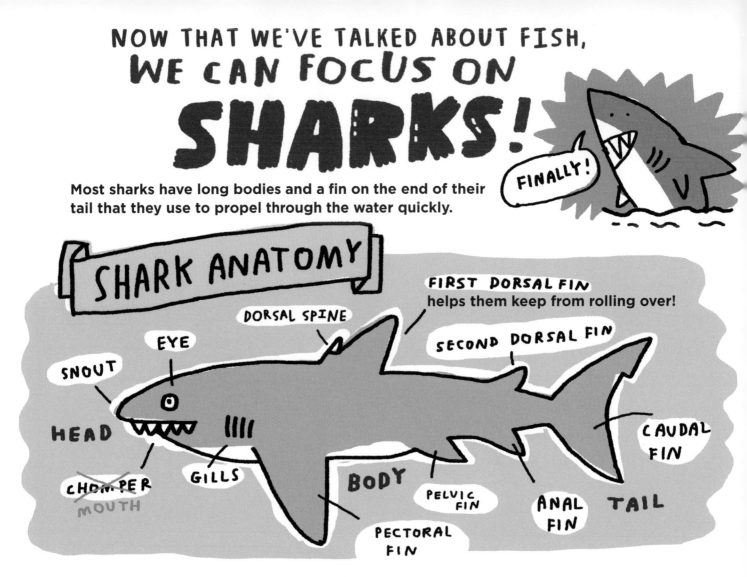

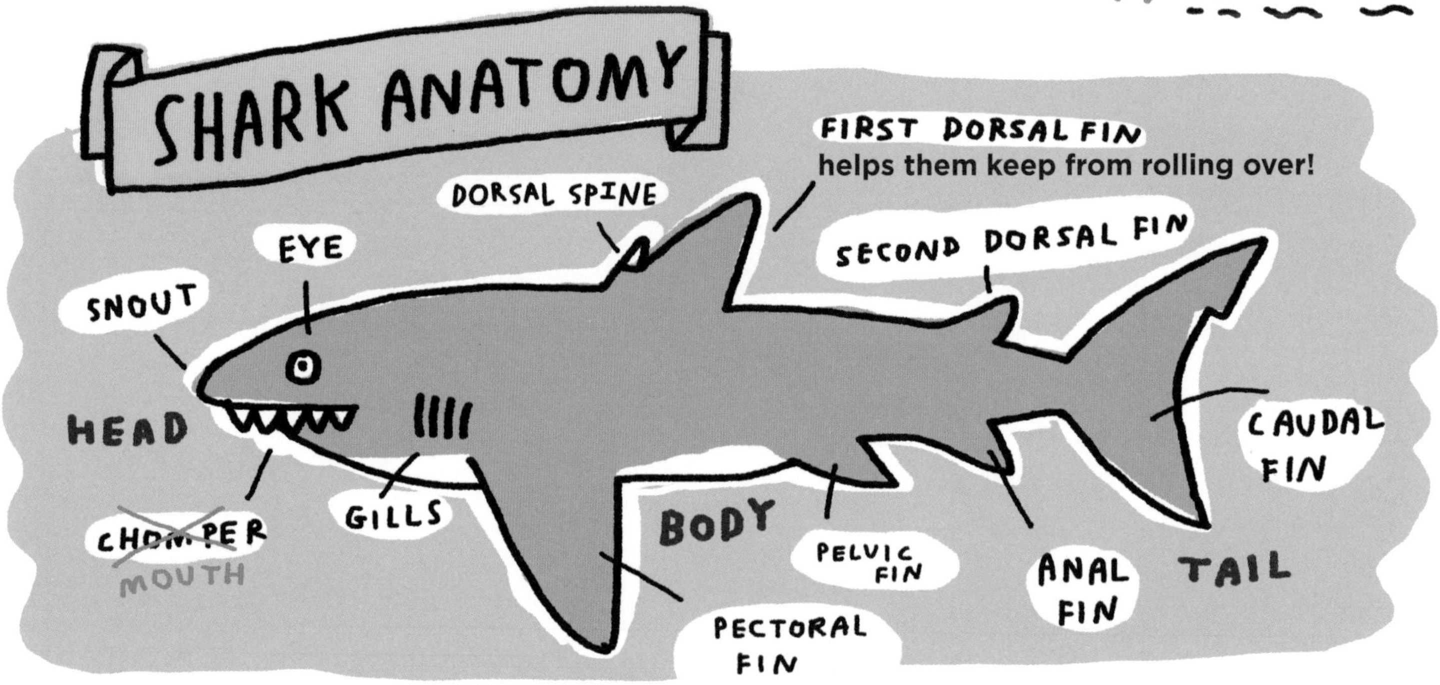
SHARK ANATOMY
FIRST DORSAL FIN
helps them keep from rolling over!
DORSAL SPINE
EYE
SECOND DORSAL FIN
SNOUT
HEAD
CAUDAL FIN
CHOMPER
MOUTH
GILLS
BODY
PELVIC FIN
ANAL FIN
TAIL
PECTORAL FIN

Most sharks have around 8 fins. 2 dorsal fins, 2 pectoral fins, 2 pelvic fins, 1 anal fin, and a big one for the tail called a caudal fin. These fins help them balance, speed through the water to catch prey (or if they're late to an appointment), and move in different directions.

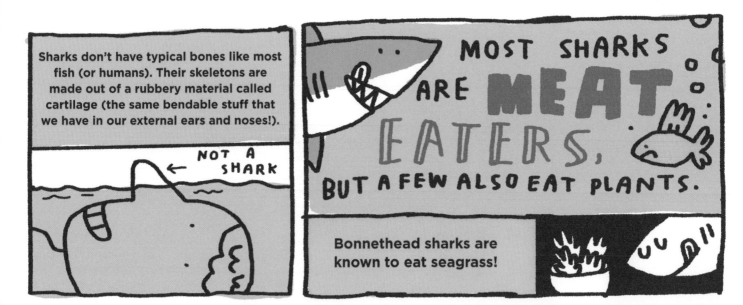

Sharks don't have typical bones like most fish (or humans). Their skeletons are made out of a rubbery material called cartilage (the same bendable stuff that we have in our external ears and noses!).

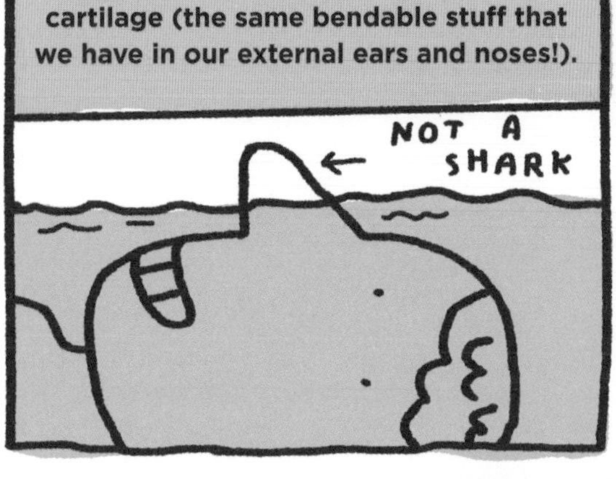
NOT A SHARK

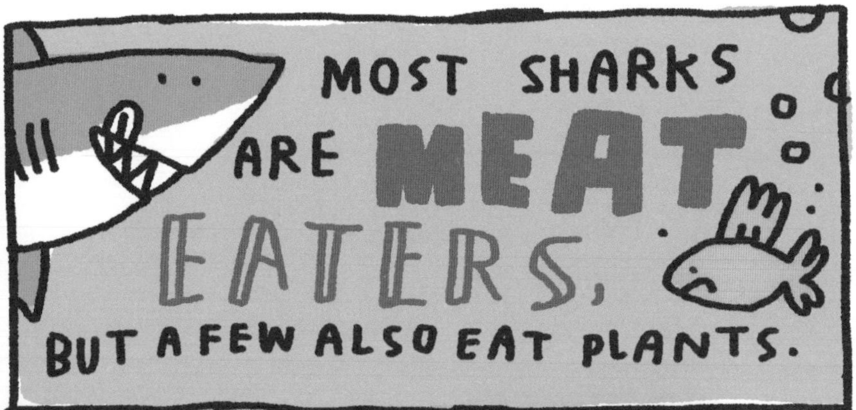
MOST SHARKS ARE MEAT EATERS,
BUT A FEW ALSO EAT PLANTS.

Bonnethead sharks are known to eat seagrass!

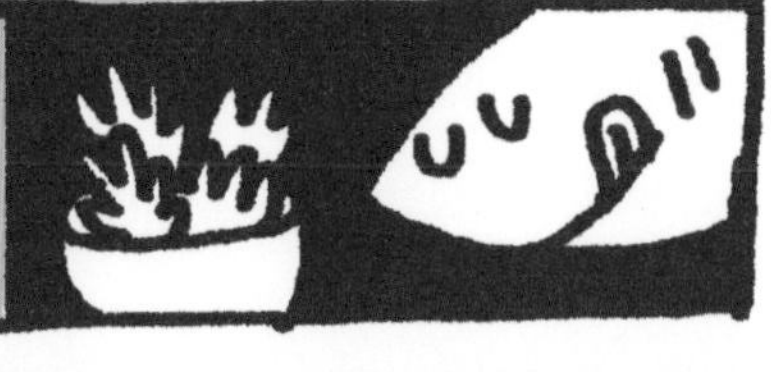

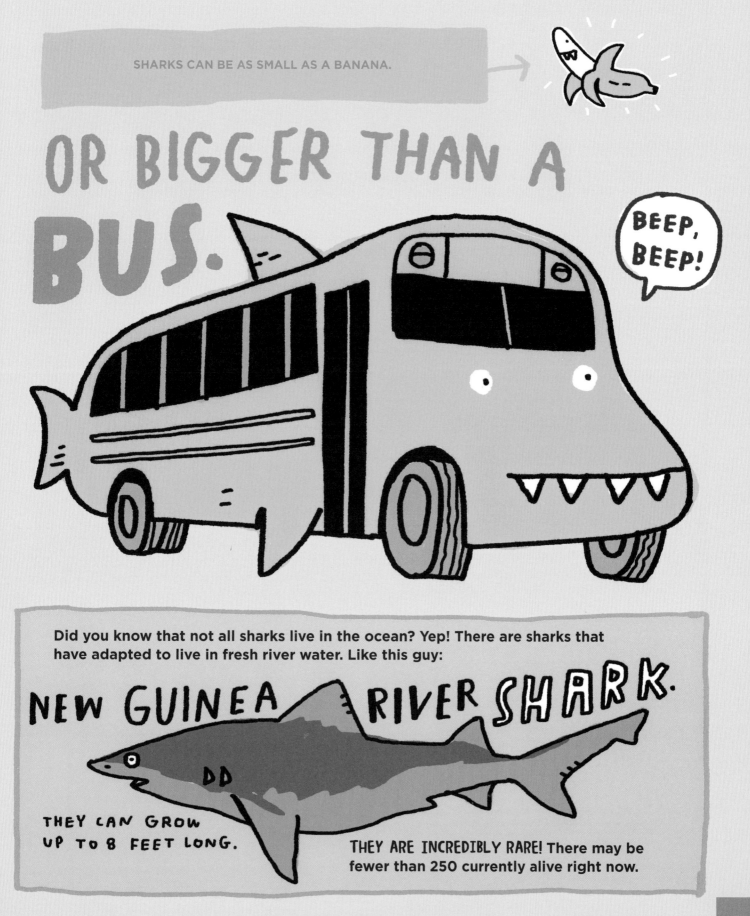

SHARKS CAN BE AS SMALL AS A BANANA.

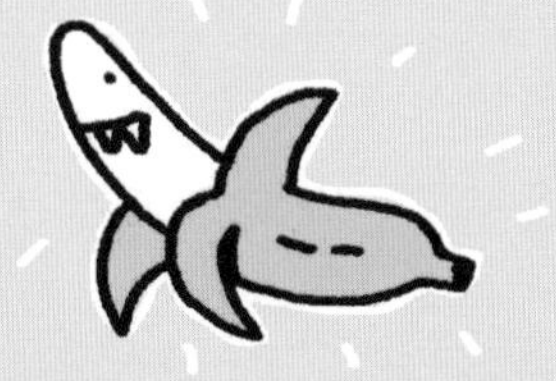

# OR BIGGER THAN A BUS.

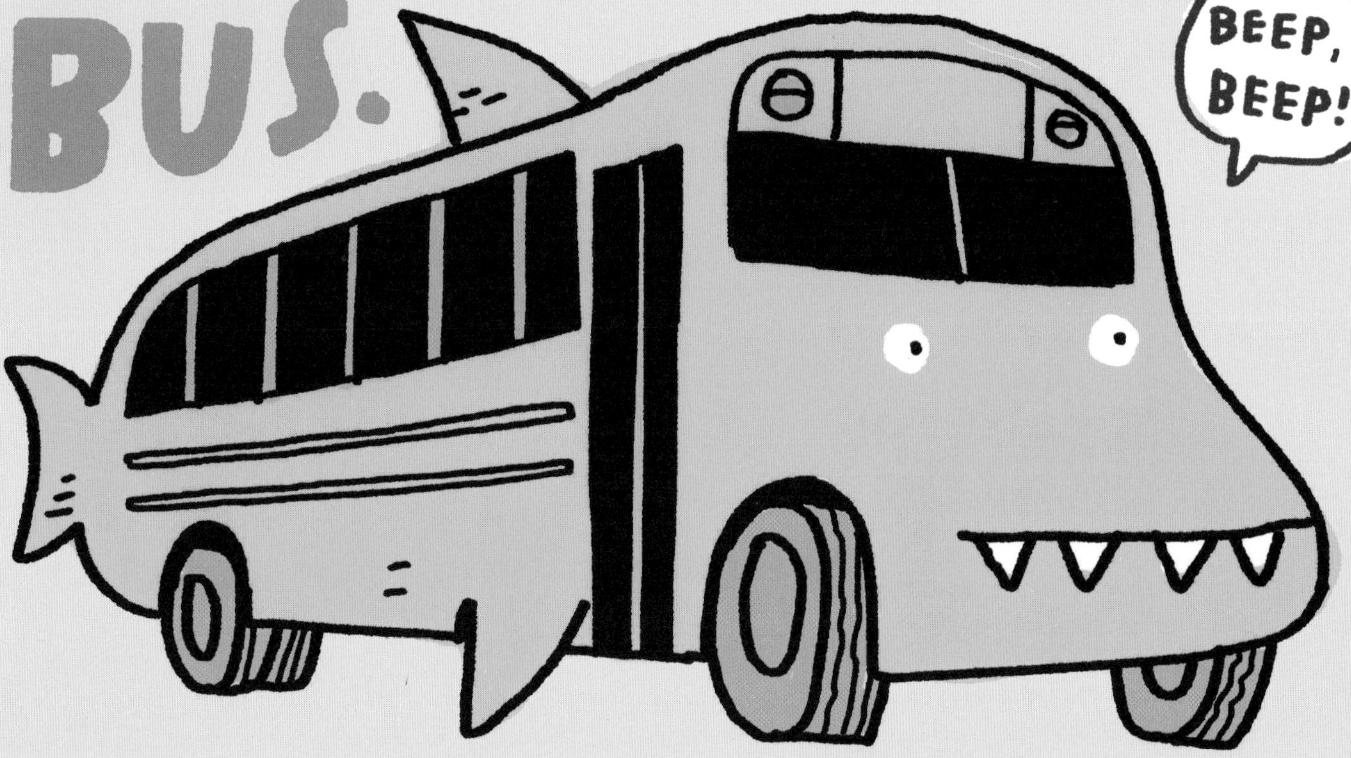
BEEP, BEEP!

Did you know that not all sharks live in the ocean? Yep! There are sharks that have adapted to live in fresh river water. Like this guy:

## NEW GUINEA RIVER SHARK.

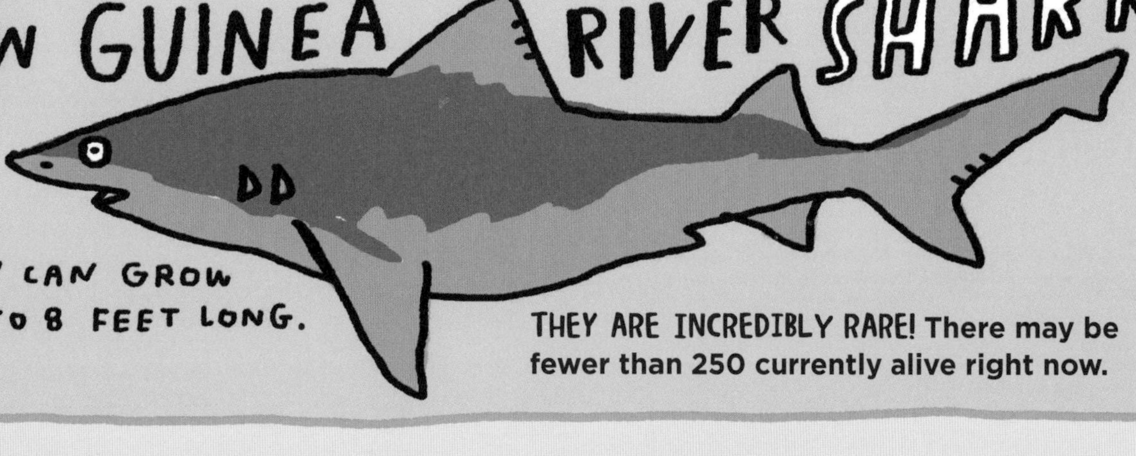

THEY CAN GROW UP TO 8 FEET LONG.

THEY ARE INCREDIBLY RARE! There may be fewer than 250 currently alive right now.

# SHARK SUPERPOWERS!

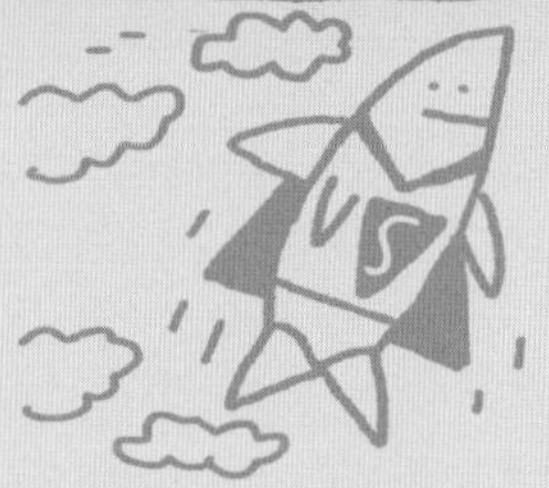

Sharks are pretty amazing. Wait, no, they're better than amazing—they're AWESOME. And they have some pretty AWESOME superpowers! Don't believe me? Check this out.

## 1. SUPER SKIN!

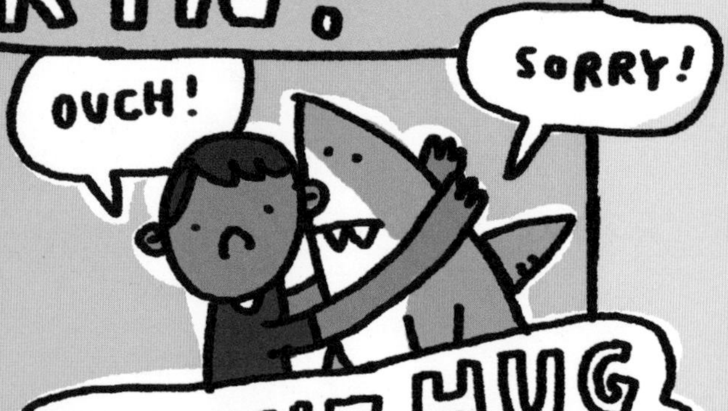
OUCH!
SORRY!

Sharks don't have scales like other types of fish. If you look at a picture of them, it might look like they've got soft, rubbery skin like a wetsuit... You probably want to snuggle with that soft shark, right?! No way. Shark skin is NOT soft. And it's not rubbery. It's super rough, like sandpaper.

DON'T HUG A SHARK!

IT'S ACTUALLY MADE UP OF MILLIONS OF LITTLE **TOOTHLIKE** BUMPS CALLED **DENTICLES.**

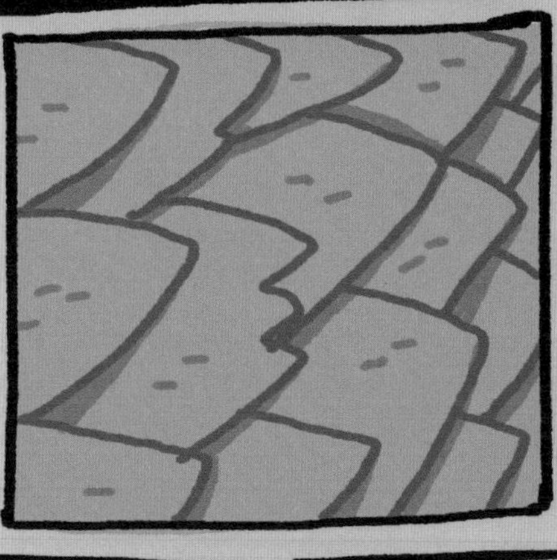

"Denticle" actually means "little tooth," and they overlap like shingles on a roof. If you were to pet them from head to tail, they would feel sort of smooth, but run your hand the other way and it feels really rough. Some swimmers have even gotten scratched up pretty bad by shark skin. *Which is probably better than what COULD'VE happened to them!*

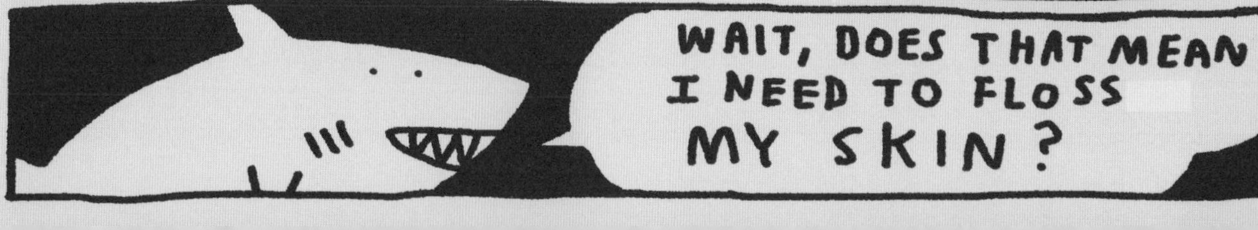
WAIT, DOES THAT MEAN I NEED TO FLOSS MY SKIN?

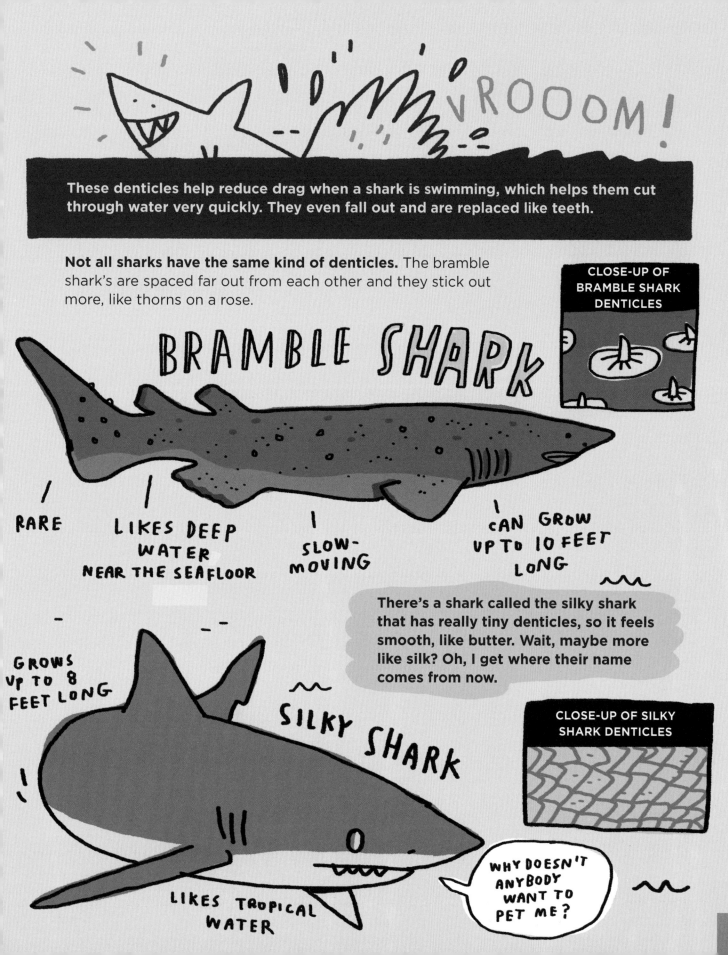

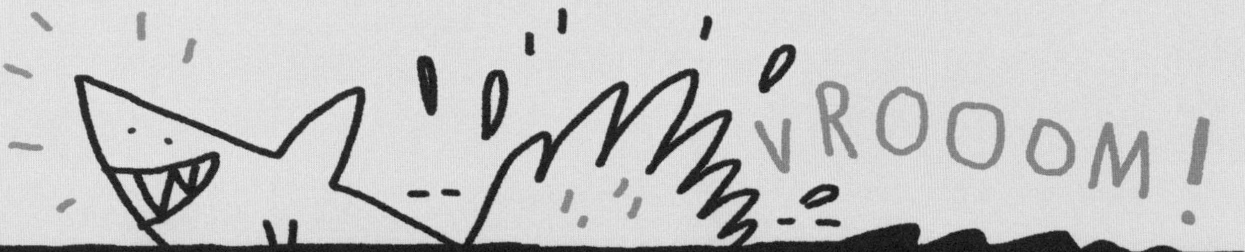
VROOOM!

**These denticles help reduce drag when a shark is swimming, which helps them cut through water very quickly. They even fall out and are replaced like teeth.**

**Not all sharks have the same kind of denticles.** The bramble shark's are spaced far out from each other and they stick out more, like thorns on a rose.

**CLOSE-UP OF BRAMBLE SHARK DENTICLES**

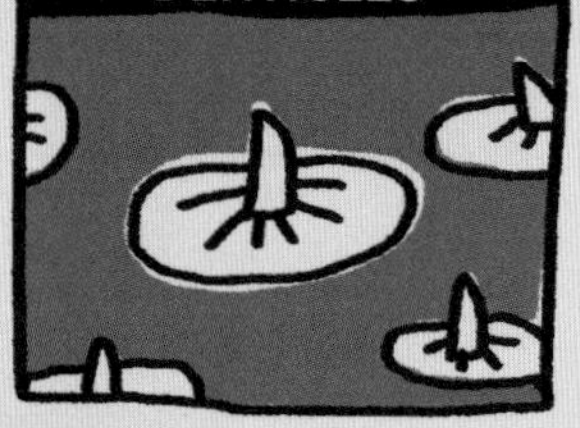

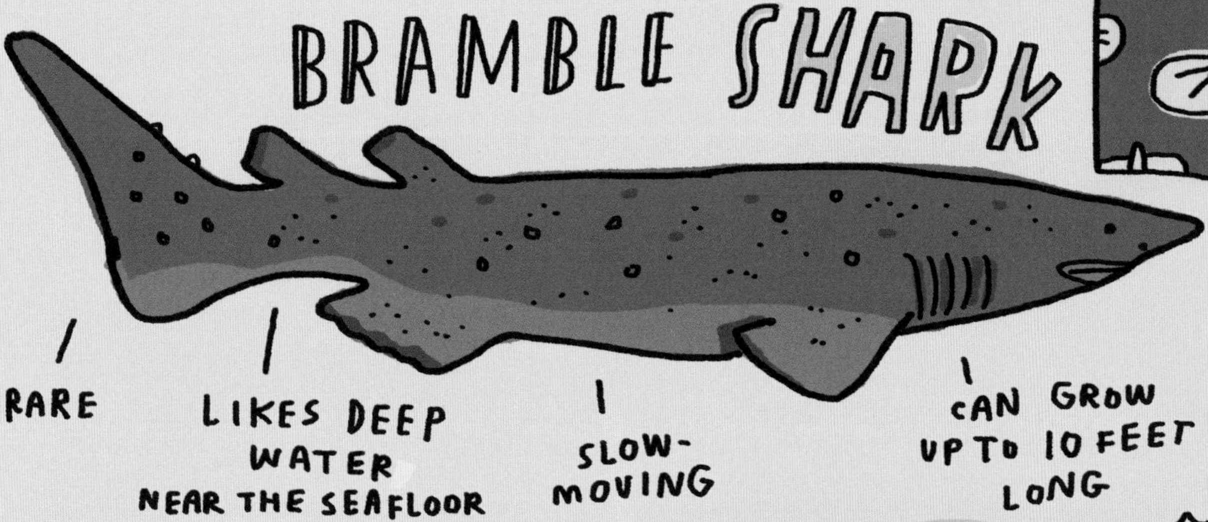
BRAMBLE SHARK
RARE
LIKES DEEP WATER NEAR THE SEAFLOOR
SLOW-MOVING
CAN GROW UP TO 10 FEET LONG

**There's a shark called the silky shark that has really tiny denticles, so it feels smooth, like butter. Wait, maybe more like silk? Oh, I get where their name comes from now.**

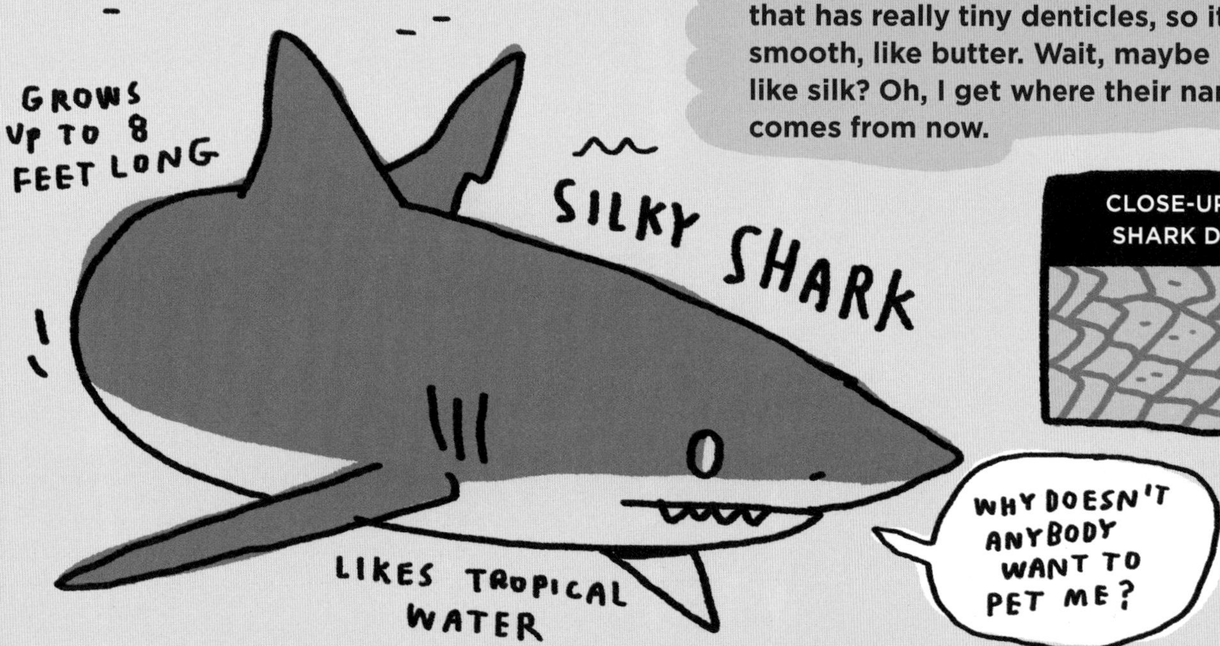
GROWS UP TO 8 FEET LONG
SILKY SHARK
LIKES TROPICAL WATER
WHY DOESN'T ANYBODY WANT TO PET ME?

**CLOSE-UP OF SILKY SHARK DENTICLES**

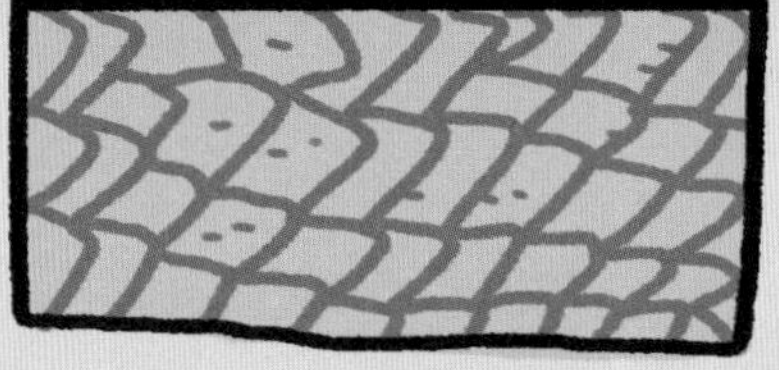

# 2. SUPER SMELL!

Up to two-thirds of a shark's brain is used to process information about the smells in the water around it. And because water is constantly flowing into a shark's snout, sharks have an incredible ability to smell when blood is in the water. Remember that they use their gills for breathing, so their nostrils are just for smelling!

JOKE TIME!

WHY DON'T SHARKS WEAR PERFUME?

BECAUSE THEY SMELL GOOD!

## BOGUS FACT!

You might've heard people say that sharks can smell a drop of blood a mile away, but that's not really true. Some sharks have been known to detect blood up to a quarter of a mile away, but it's not quick (like when you smell bread baking) and it doesn't necessarily mean they're going to charge off and find where it's coming from. BUT! Their sense of smell is still hundreds of times better than a human's.

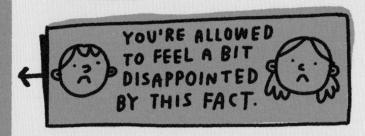

YOU'RE ALLOWED TO FEEL A BIT DISAPPOINTED BY THIS FACT.

# 3. SUPER EYES!

Ocean water can be pretty dark, and sharks have adapted to have pretty great eyesight. Like a cat, their eyes are more sensitive to light than a human's, which gives them NIGHT VISION. Shark's eyes are ten times more sensitive to light than human eyes!

## EXTRA EYELID!

They also have a translucent extra eyelid called a nictitating membrane that can cover their eye to protect it, while still letting them see.

OPEN

CLOSED

# 4. SUPER SIXTH SENSE!

**Sharks have a sixth sense called ELECTRORECEPTION. Small black spots on their faces are openings to special organs called ampullae of Lorenzini that can detect electric and magnetic fields in the water. All living animals emit a very weak electro-chemical charge, and sharks use their "sixth sense" to detect this! It helps them find prey that their other senses would miss, like rays buried in the sand.**

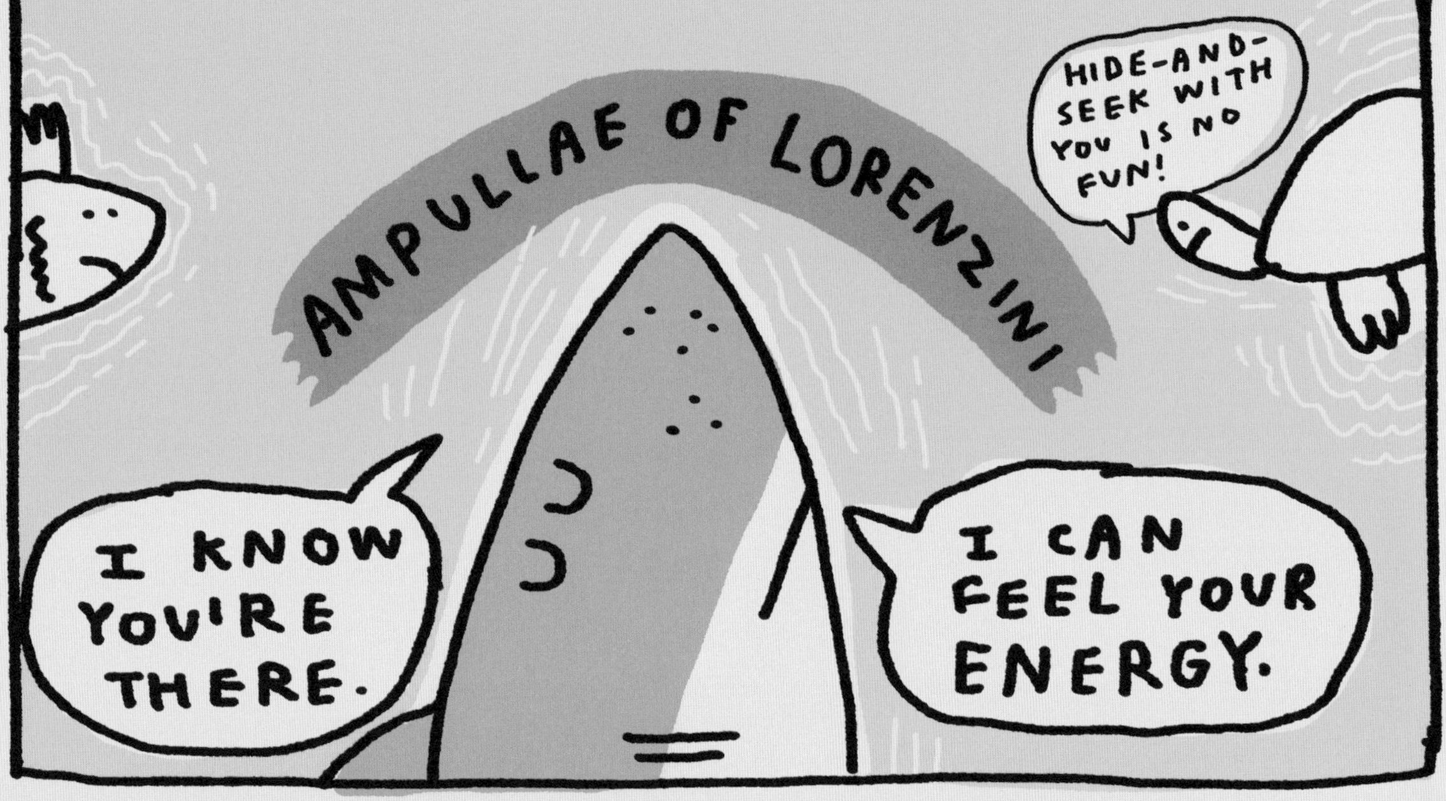

AMPULLAE OF LORENZINI
HIDE-AND-SEEK WITH YOU IS NO FUN!
I KNOW YOU'RE THERE.
I CAN FEEL YOUR ENERGY.


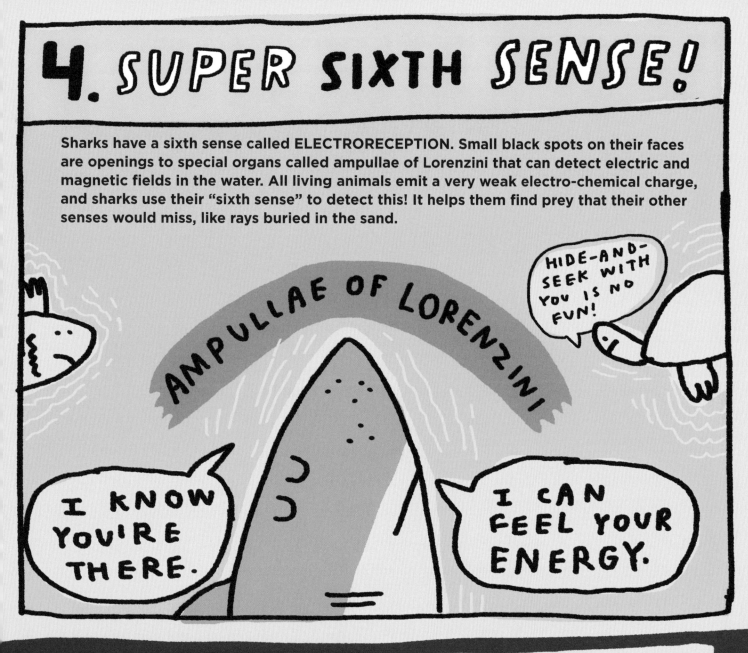

# DO SHARKS SLEEP?

Lots of people think that sharks don't sleep at all, but it's just not true. Some sharks have to be moving constantly, so they've adapted to swim while they're sleeping. They do this because they need water to always be moving over their gills so they can get oxygen.

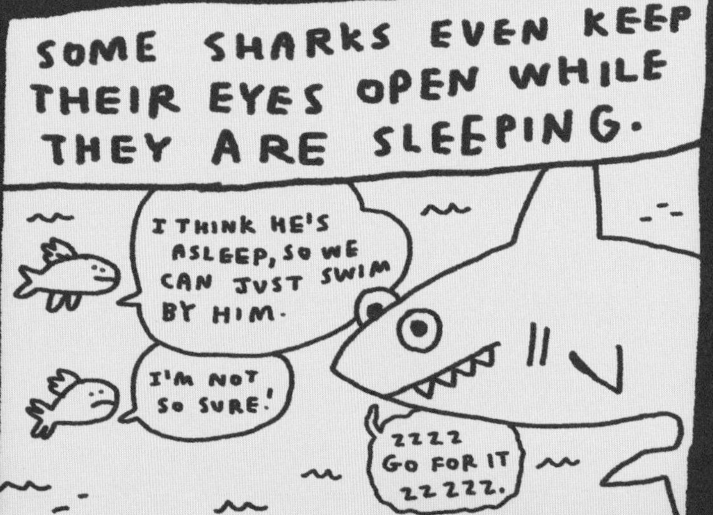

SOME SHARKS EVEN KEEP THEIR EYES OPEN WHILE THEY ARE SLEEPING.
I THINK HE'S ASLEEP, SO WE CAN JUST SWIM BY HIM.
I'M NOT SO SURE!
ZZZZ GO FOR IT ZZZZZ.

BUT THAT'S NOT ALL OF THEIR POWERS! LET'S NOT FORGET...

# 5. SUPER TEETH!

SOME SHARKS HAVE MORE THAN ONE ROW OF TEETH! LIKE THIS:

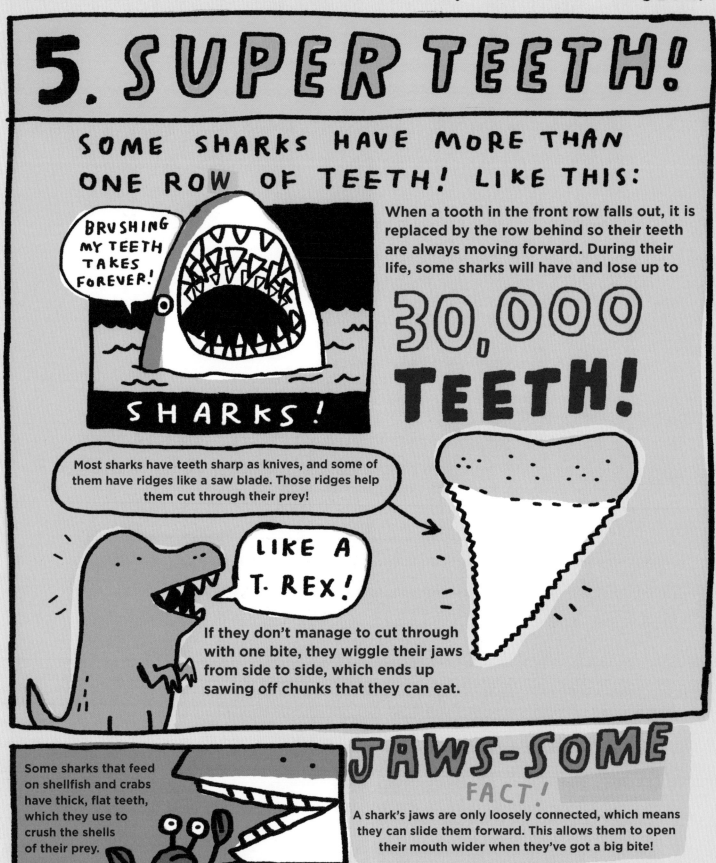

BRUSHING MY TEETH TAKES FOREVER!
SHARKS!


When a tooth in the front row falls out, it is replaced by the row behind so their teeth are always moving forward. During their life, some sharks will have and lose up to

## 30,000 TEETH!

Most sharks have teeth sharp as knives, and some of them have ridges like a saw blade. Those ridges help them cut through their prey!

LIKE A T. REX!


If they don't manage to cut through with one bite, they wiggle their jaws from side to side, which ends up sawing off chunks that they can eat.

Some sharks that feed on shellfish and crabs have thick, flat teeth, which they use to crush the shells of their prey.

## JAWS-SOME FACT!

A shark's jaws are only loosely connected, which means they can slide them forward. This allows them to open their mouth wider when they've got a big bite!

# LET'S MEET THE SHARKS!

## PREHISTORIC SHARKS

BACK IN MY DAY, WE SWAM 60 MILES TO SCHOOL AND PLANKTON ONLY COST ONE SAND DOLLAR...

SIGH.

SHARKS HAVE BEEN AROUND FOR ABOUT **450 MILLION YEARS,** WHICH MEANS THEY'RE ROUGHLY **150 MILLION** YEARS OLDER THAN **DINOSAURS!** THEY'RE EVEN OLDER THAN TREES!

HERE ARE A FEW OF THE MOST AWESOME PREHISTORIC SHARKS (THAT ARE NOW EXTINCT).

## XENACANTHUS

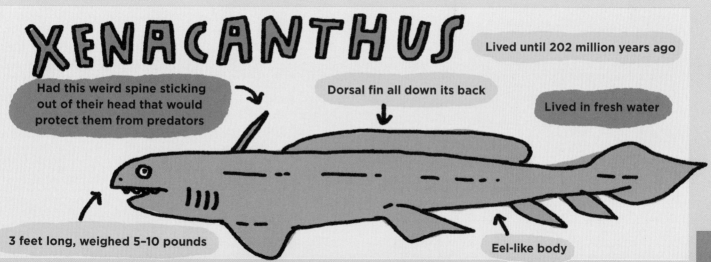

Lived until 202 million years ago

Had this weird spine sticking out of their head that would protect them from predators

Dorsal fin all down its back

Lived in fresh water

3 feet long, weighed 5–10 pounds

Eel-like body

LOOK OUT! IT'S THE MIGHTY

# MEGALODON

**Lived until 2.6 million years ago**

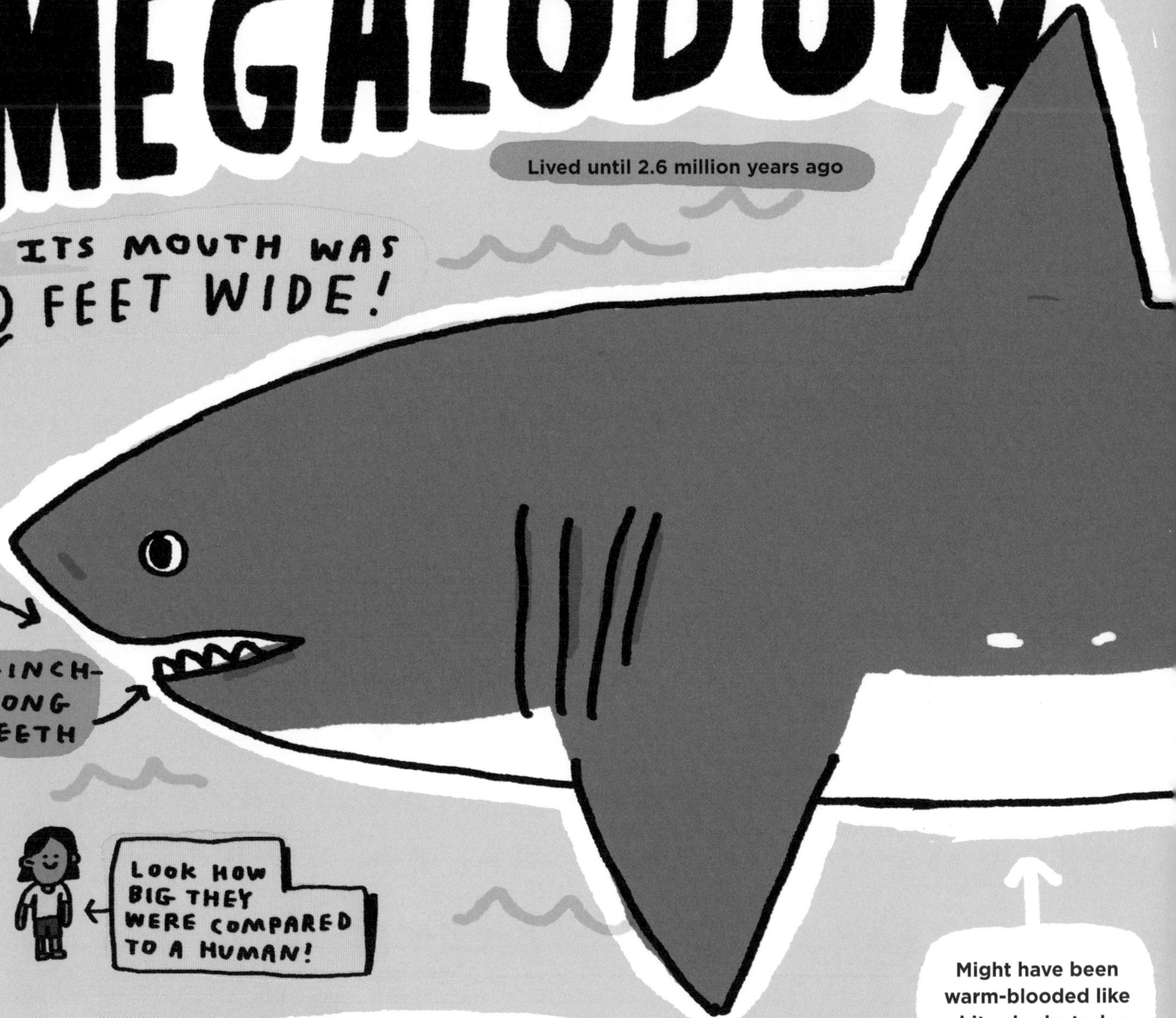

ITS MOUTH WAS 10 FEET WIDE!

7-INCH-LONG TEETH

LOOK HOW BIG THEY WERE COMPARED TO A HUMAN!

**Might have been warm-blooded like white sharks today, which would have made it possible for them to swim in colder water.**

## 3 TIMES BIGGER THAN WHALE SHARKS (WHICH ARE THE BIGGEST SHARKS ALIVE TODAY)!

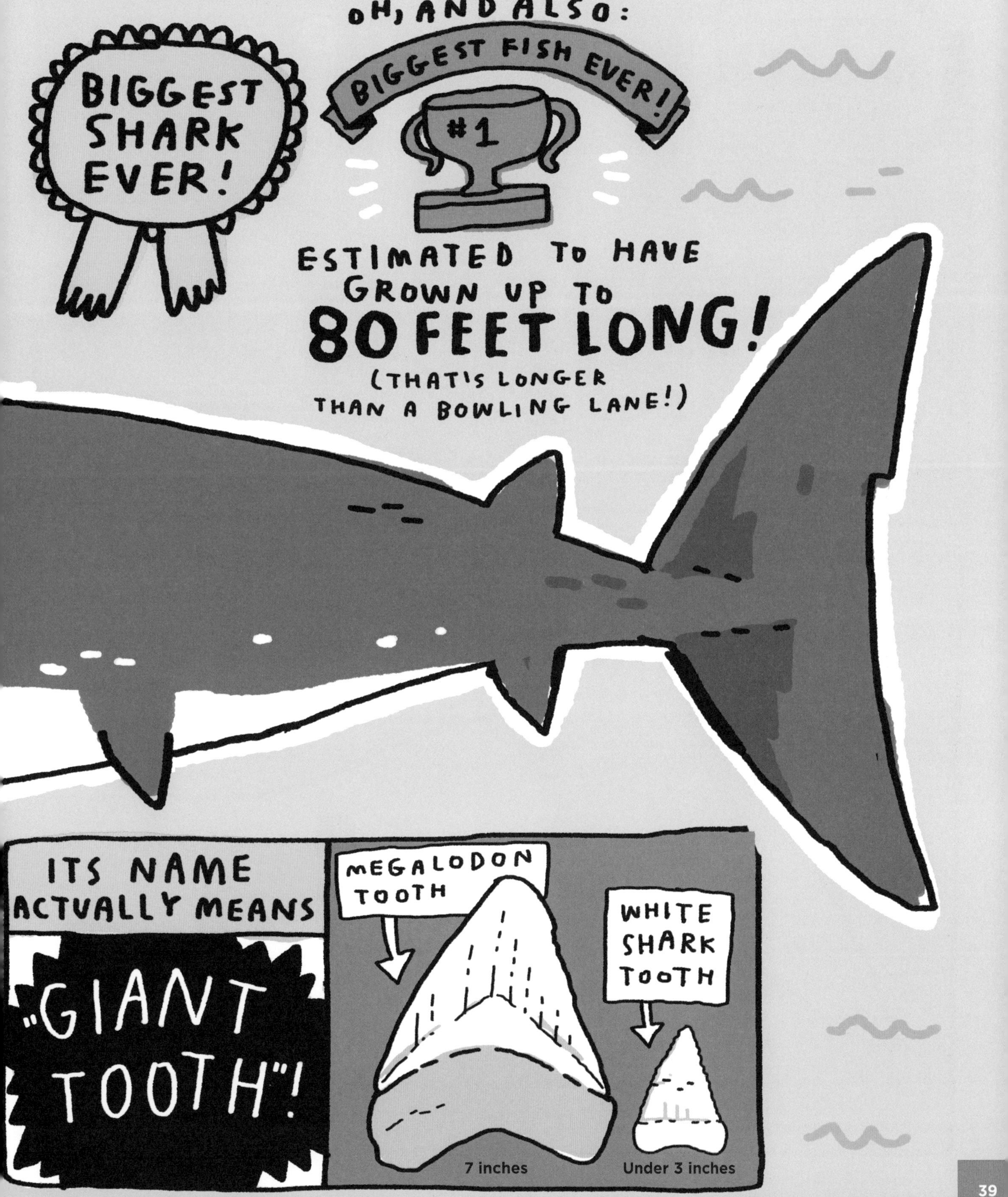
BIGGEST SHARK EVER!
OH, AND ALSO:
BIGGEST FISH EVER!
#1
ESTIMATED TO HAVE GROWN UP TO
80 FEET LONG!
(THAT'S LONGER THAN A BOWLING LANE!)
ITS NAME ACTUALLY MEANS
"GIANT TOOTH"!
MEGALODON TOOTH
WHITE SHARK TOOTH
7 inches
Under 3 inches

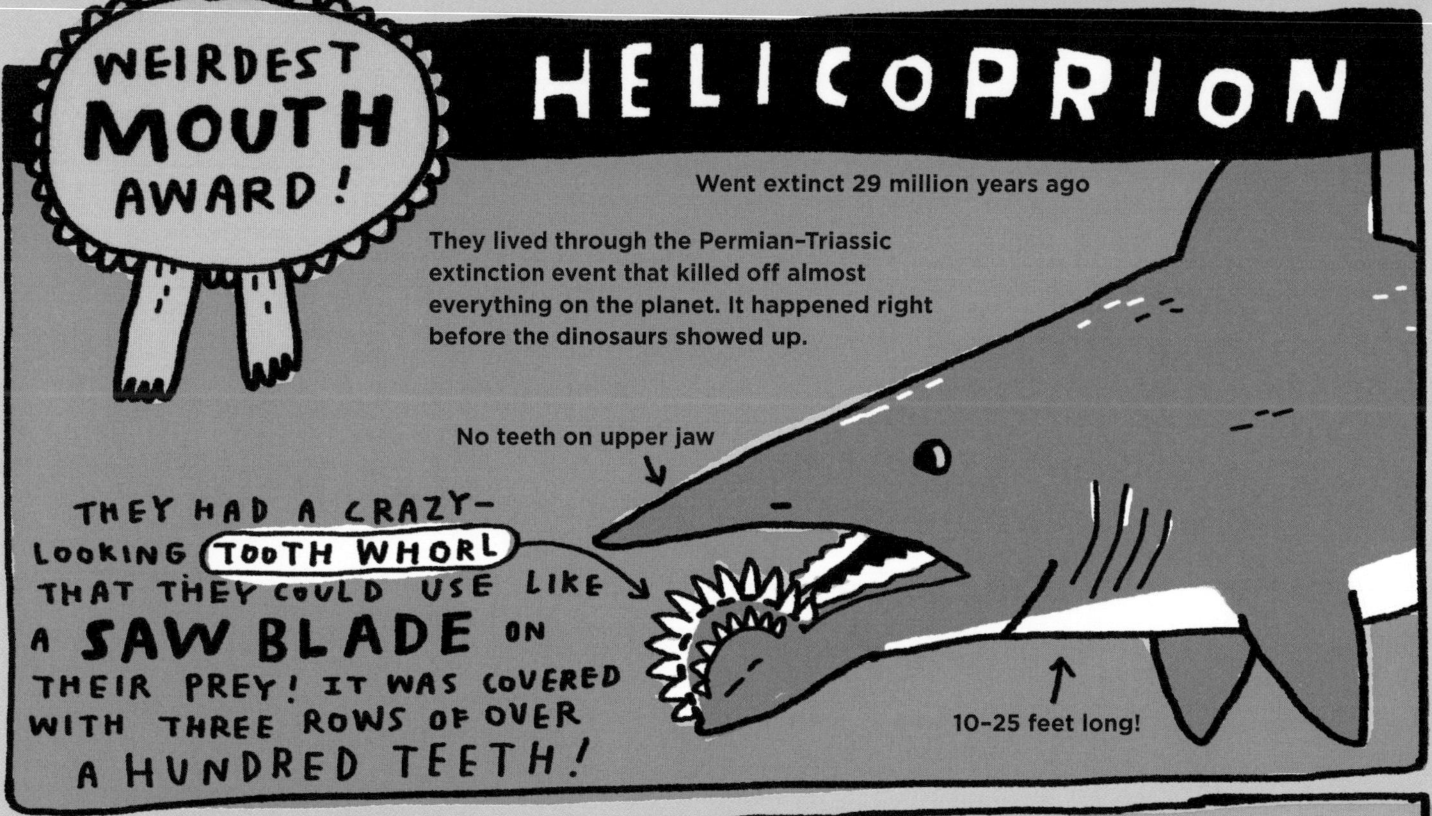
WEIRDEST MOUTH AWARD!
HELICOPRION
Went extinct 29 million years ago
They lived through the Permian–Triassic extinction event that killed off almost everything on the planet. It happened right before the dinosaurs showed up.
No teeth on upper jaw
THEY HAD A CRAZY-LOOKING TOOTH WHORL THAT THEY COULD USE LIKE A SAW BLADE ON THEIR PREY! IT WAS COVERED WITH THREE ROWS OF OVER A HUNDRED TEETH!
10–25 feet long!

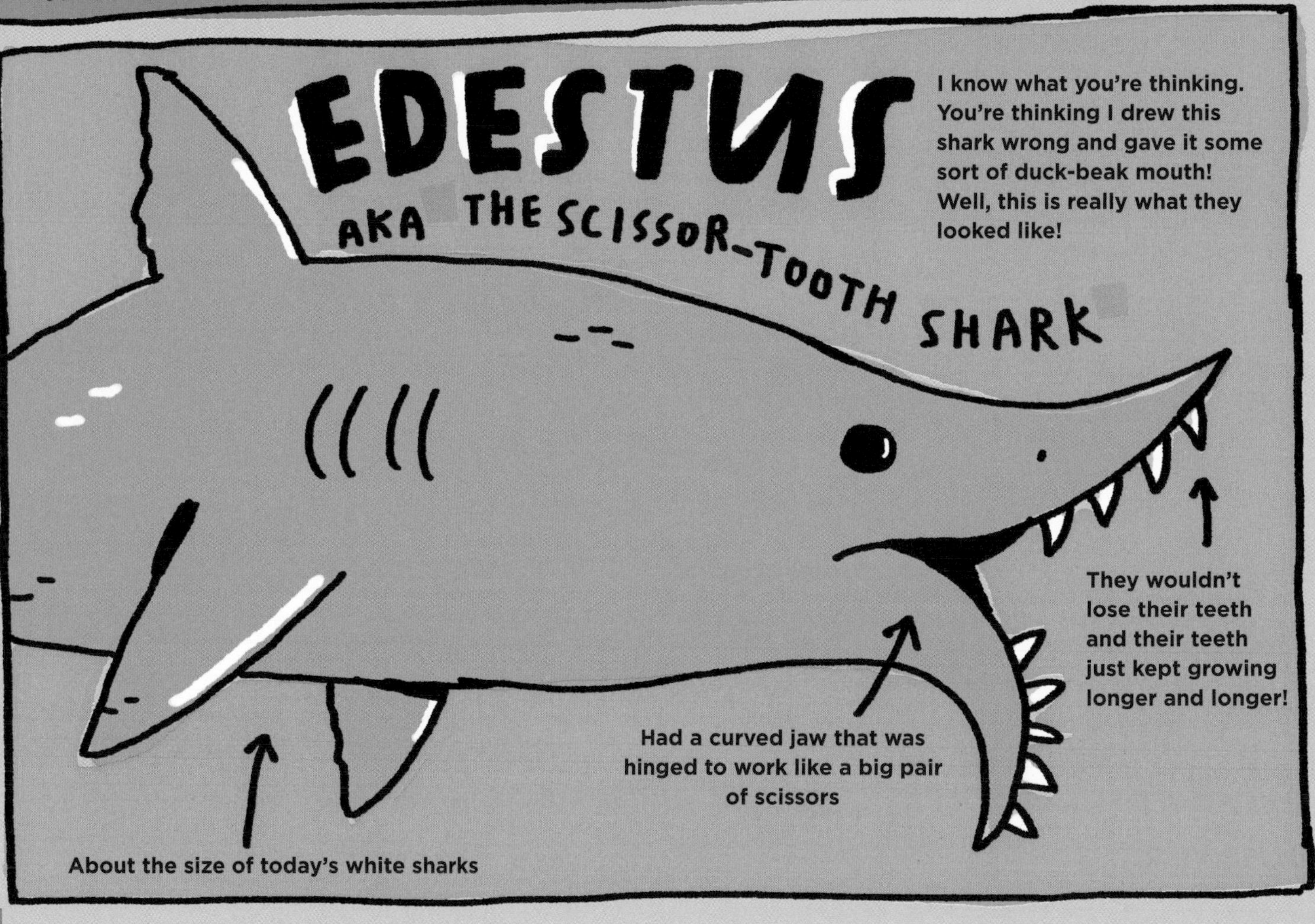
EDESTUS
AKA THE SCISSOR-TOOTH SHARK
I know what you're thinking. You're thinking I drew this shark wrong and gave it some sort of duck-beak mouth! Well, this is really what they looked like!
They wouldn't lose their teeth and their teeth just kept growing longer and longer!
Had a curved jaw that was hinged to work like a big pair of scissors
About the size of today's white sharks

# SHARK SQUADS

Sharks today are divided into 8 large groups called orders.

**SHARK GROUP 1**

# GROUND SHARKS
### aka Carcharhiniformes

GROUND SHARK CHECKLIST: 1 anal fin, 5 gill slits, 2 dorsal fins, no fin spines, mouth behind the eyes, nictitating eyelids

Some are as small as 2–3 feet, while others can grow up to 10 feet long.

This is the biggest group of sharks. There are more than 270 species of these sharks that we know about today and they live in oceans all over the world.

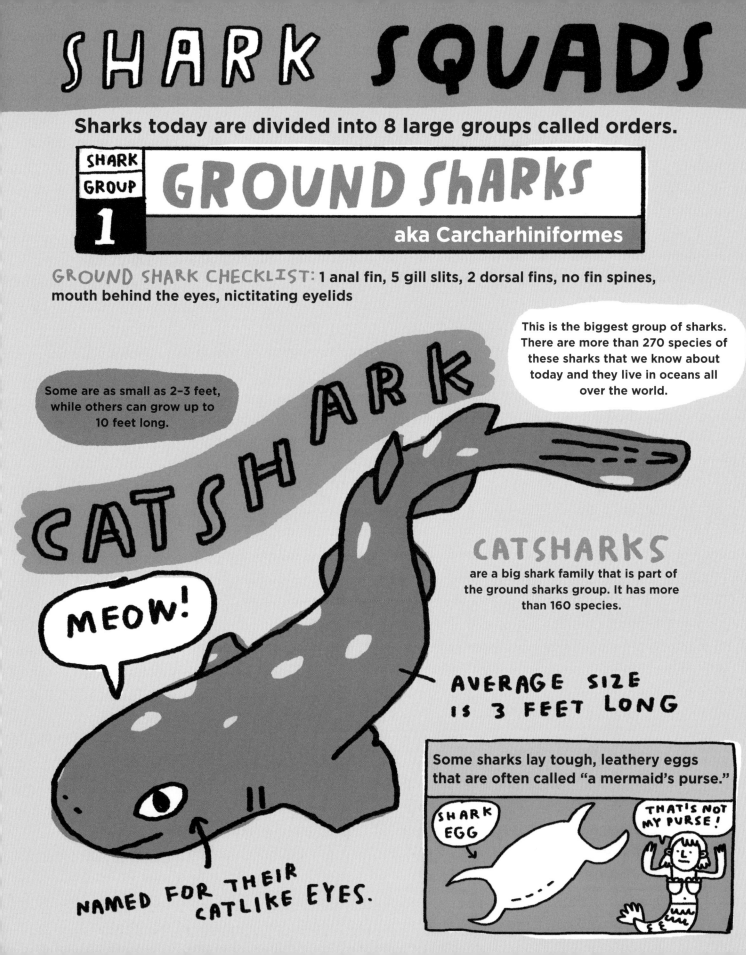

CATSHARK

MEOW!

**CATSHARKS** are a big shark family that is part of the ground sharks group. It has more than 160 species.

AVERAGE SIZE IS 3 FEET LONG

Some sharks lay tough, leathery eggs that are often called "a mermaid's purse."

SHARK EGG

THAT'S NOT MY PURSE!

NAMED FOR THEIR CATLIKE EYES.

# HAMMERHEAD SHARK!

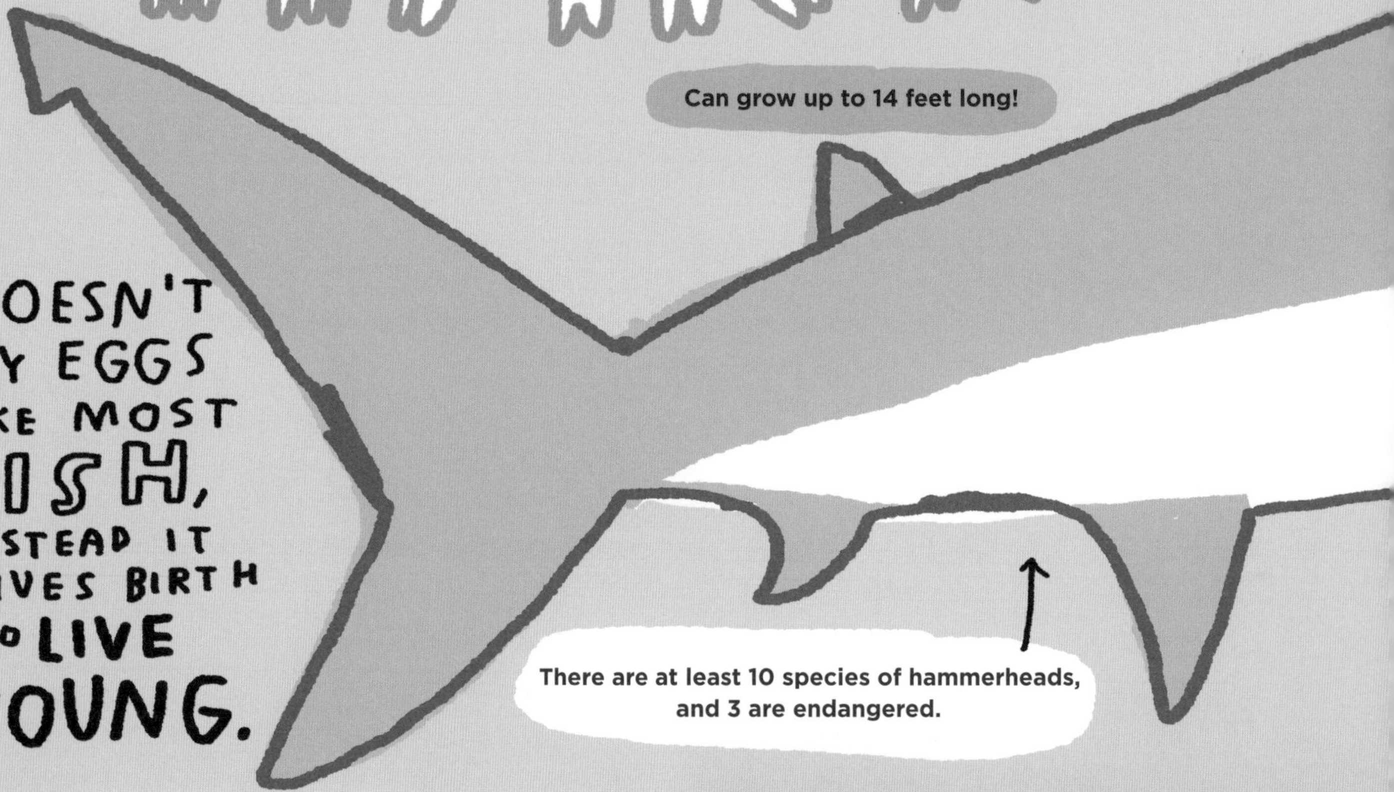

Can grow up to 14 feet long!

DOESN'T LAY EGGS LIKE MOST FISH, INSTEAD IT GIVES BIRTH TO LIVE YOUNG.

There are at least 10 species of hammerheads, and 3 are endangered.

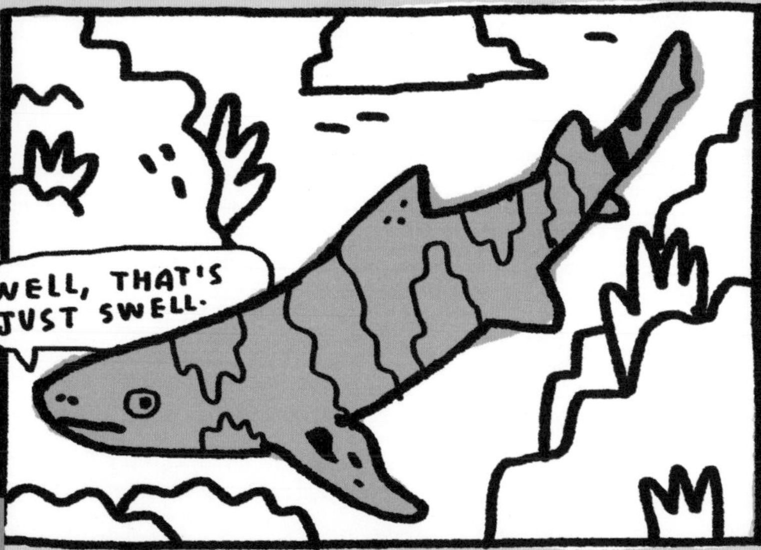
WELL, THAT'S JUST SWELL.

## SWELL SHARKS

To scare off predators, they're able to pump water into their bodies and "swell" up to twice their size! They can also do this with air when they're at the surface of the water, and they even BURP out the air when the danger is gone!

If a swell shark inflates itself between rocks, it makes it tougher for a predator to pull it out.

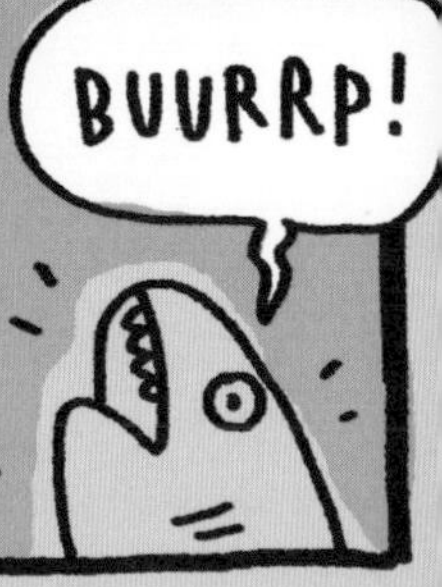
BUURRP!

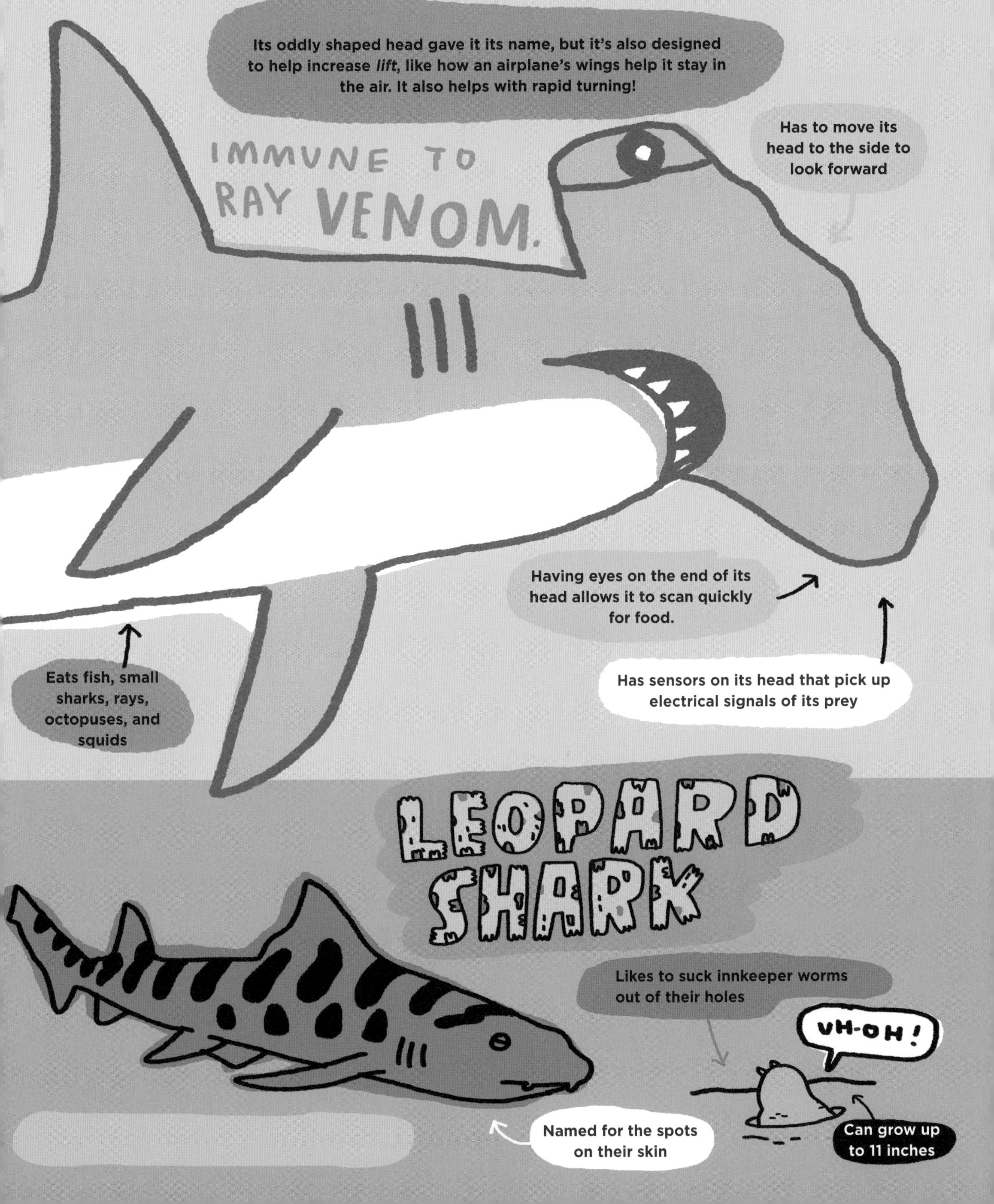

Its oddly shaped head gave it its name, but it's also designed to help increase *lift*, like how an airplane's wings help it stay in the air. It also helps with rapid turning!
IMMUNE TO RAY VENOM.
Has to move its head to the side to look forward
Having eyes on the end of its head allows it to scan quickly for food.
Eats fish, small sharks, rays, octopuses, and squids
Has sensors on its head that pick up electrical signals of its prey
LEOPARD SHARK
Likes to suck innkeeper worms out of their holes
UH-OH!
Named for the spots on their skin
Can grow up to 11 inches

# TIGER SHARK

WATCH OUT!

DANGER!

**Tiger sharks are one of the most dangerous sharks in the world because they eat lots of stuff.**

They're like swimming garbage cans! They eat fish, dolphins, jellyfish, birds, squids, and even crocodiles! They've also been known to take bites out of whales!

Shark attacks are pretty rare, but since these guys like to hang out in shallow, warm water, it's more likely that they would run into humans.

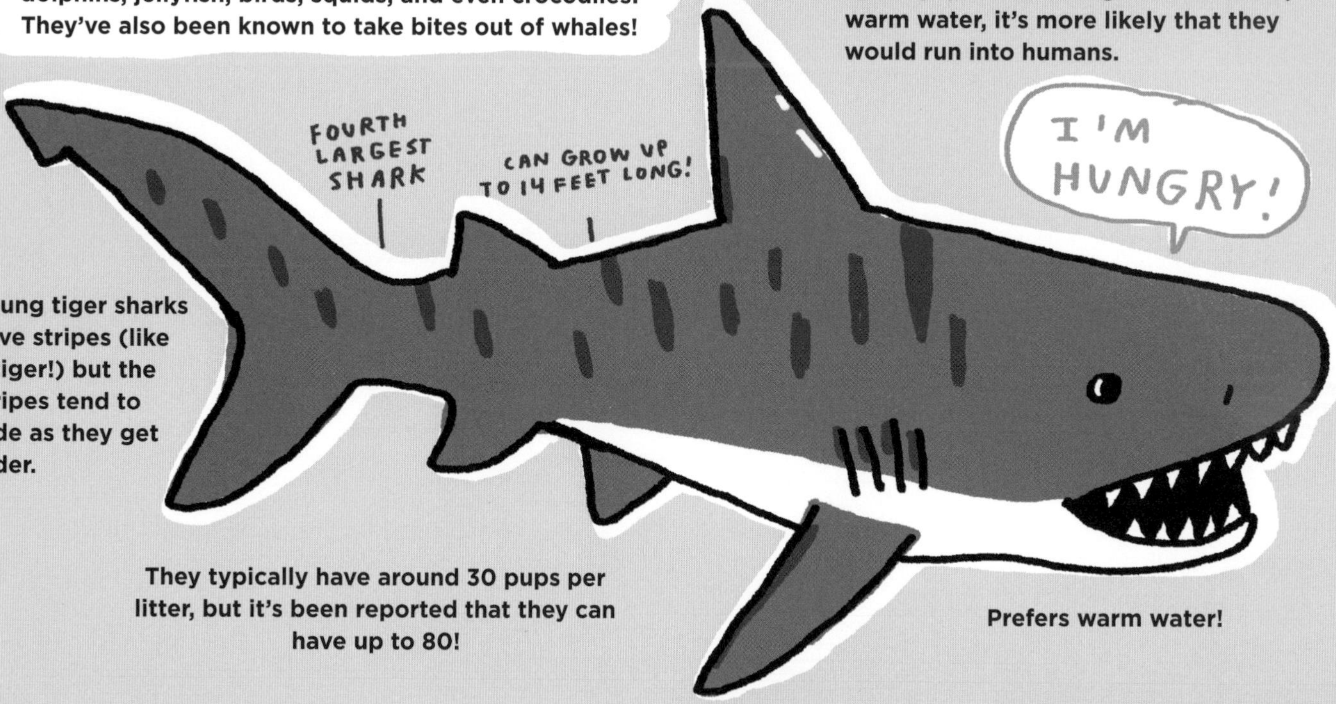

FOURTH LARGEST SHARK
CAN GROW UP TO 14 FEET LONG!
I'M HUNGRY!


Young tiger sharks have stripes (like a tiger!) but the stripes tend to fade as they get older.

They typically have around 30 pups per litter, but it's been reported that they can have up to 80!

Prefers warm water!

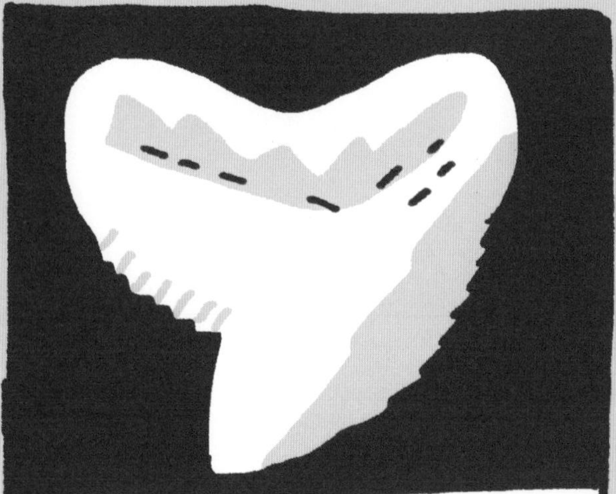

Unlike many other species, the teeth in the upper and lower jaws of a tiger shark are the same! Both rows of teeth are serrated and and have notches.

In the 1930s a tiger shark was caught and put in an aquarium in Australia. A few days later it got sick and threw up some weird stuff, including a rat and . . .

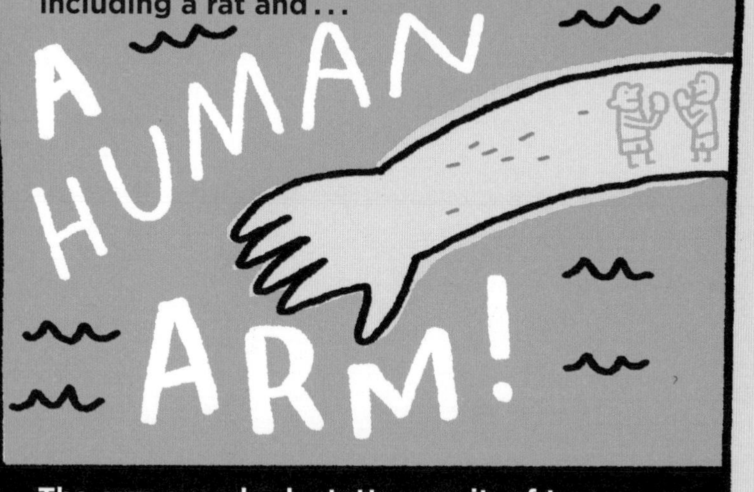

A HUMAN ARM!


The arm even had a tattoo on it, of two boxers. It turned out to be the arm of a man who'd recently gone missing without a trace!

# BLUE SHARKS

YUCK!

They're hunters that like to eat squid, but they're also scavengers that will eat dead whales.

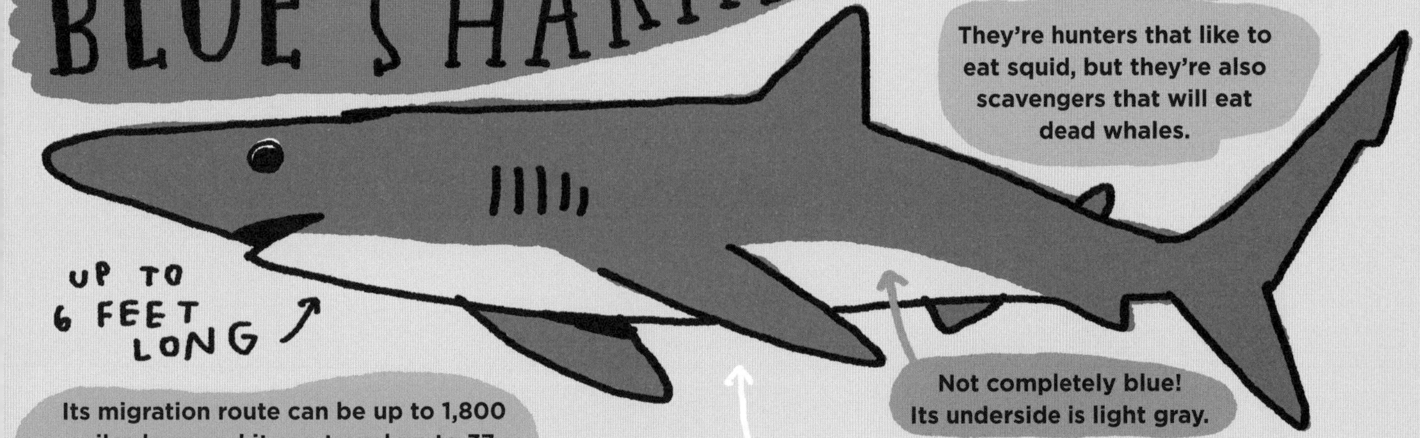

UP TO 6 FEET LONG

Its migration route can be up to 1,800 miles long and it can travel up to 37 miles in one day! (That's almost as long as the Oregon Trail!)

Not completely blue! Its underside is light gray.

They can have more than 130 pups in one litter!

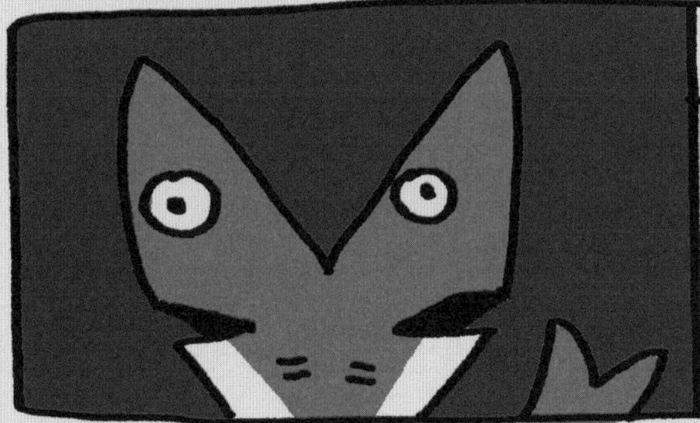

## TWO-HEADED SHARKS!

After a photo of a two-headed blue shark embryo was published, many reports of GIANT two-headed adult sharks started popping up. Turns out they were all fake. It's unlikely that a two-headed pup would survive for very long since it would have trouble swimming, which would make it pretty easy for predators to catch.

# BULL SHARK

This is a shark that likes to swim in areas that are warm and shallow . . . which happens to be where humans like to swim! So sometimes sharks confuse people for prey and attack. Bull sharks actually MIGHT EVEN be the shark that has attacked the most humans, but we aren't sure. Some scientists think that people misidentify them because their color is similar to other kinds of sharks, leading to incorrect counts of attacks.

WATCH OUT! DANGER!

IT GETS ITS NAME BECAUSE IT'S STRONG LIKE A BULL!

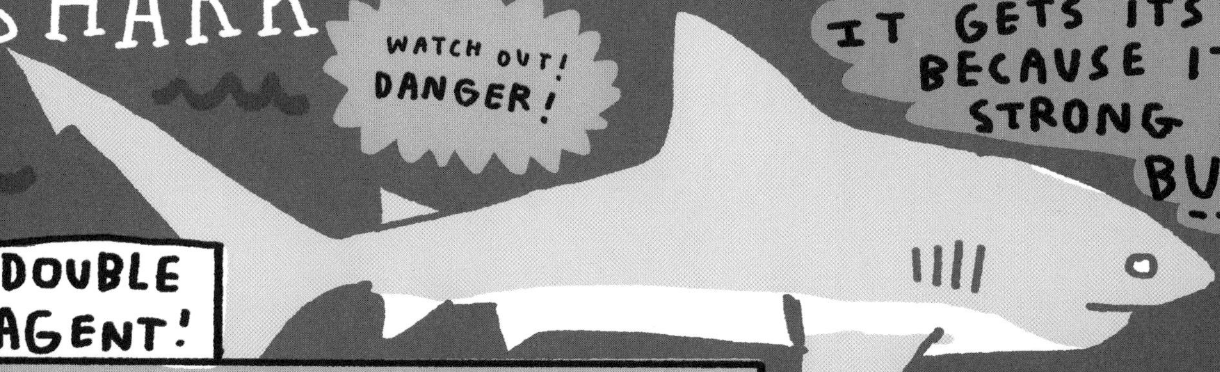

## DOUBLE AGENT!

Most sharks need salt water to survive, but bull sharks have glands near their tails that allow them to store salt when they go into freshwater. They've been spotted hundreds of miles away from the ocean in freshwater rivers.

SHARK GROUP 2

# BULLHEAD SHARKS

aka Heterodontiformes

BULLHEAD SHARK CHECKLIST: **1 anal fin, 5 gill slits, 2 dorsal fins, dorsal fin spines**

**This is a really small group of 9 species of sharks that prefers shallow, tropical water.**

## ZEBRA BULLHEAD SHARK

4 feet long

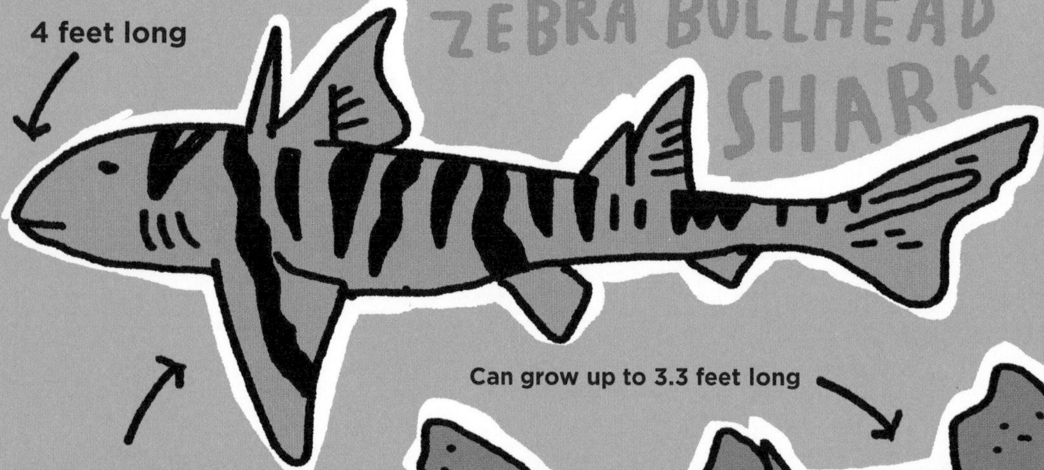

They've got pointy spines on their backs that let predators know that maybe they shouldn't eat them. Babies have the sharpest spines, which helps protect them!

LIKE TO CRAWL ON THE OCEAN FLOOR ON THEIR FRONT FINS.

## HORN SHARK

Can grow up to 3.3 feet long

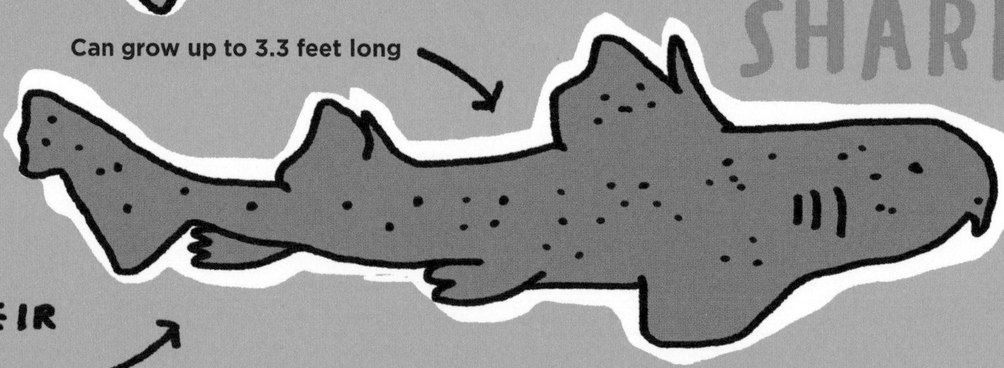

Can lay up to 24 eggs over a two-week period. Afterward, the female will collect all of those eggs in her mouth and put them in small openings of rocks to keep them safe.

## PIG SHARK?!

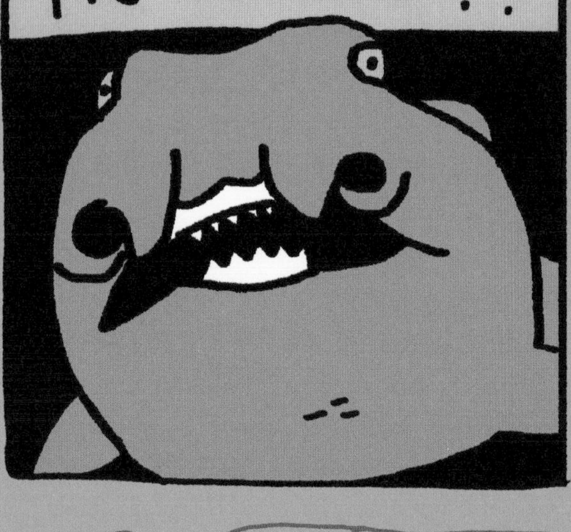

## SCREWY EGGS

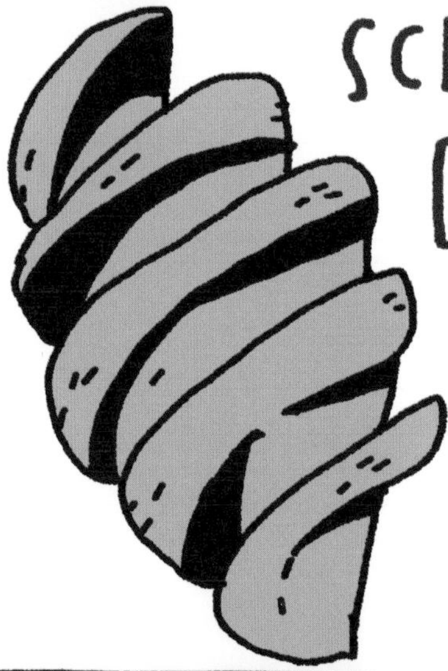

Most shark eggs have a translucent shell, which means you can see through it. Bullhead sharks have SCREW-SHAPED EGGS! It takes the females a few hours to lay each one.

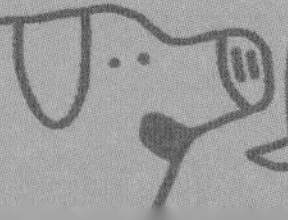

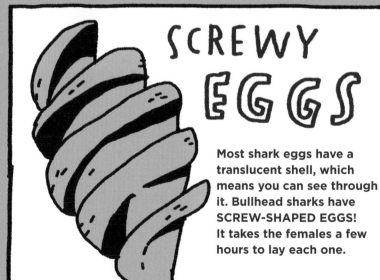

Bullhead sharks have two big nostrils like me!

SHARK GROUP 3

# COW SHARKS

aka Hexanchiformes

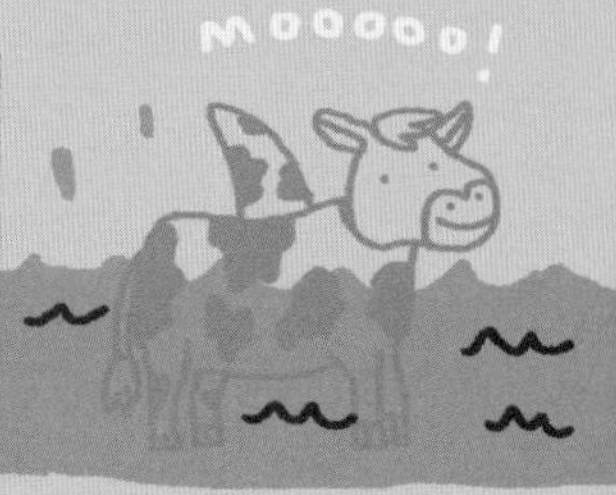
MOOOOOO!

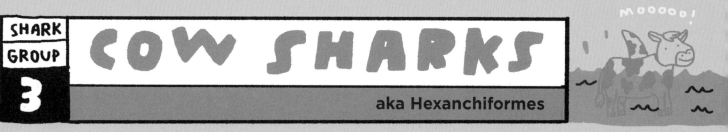

**COW SHARK CHECKLIST:** 1 anal fin, 6–7 gill slits, 1 dorsal fin

They're considered the most primitive of all shark groups because the ones alive today look a lot like the first sharks from this group to have evolved 150 million years ago.

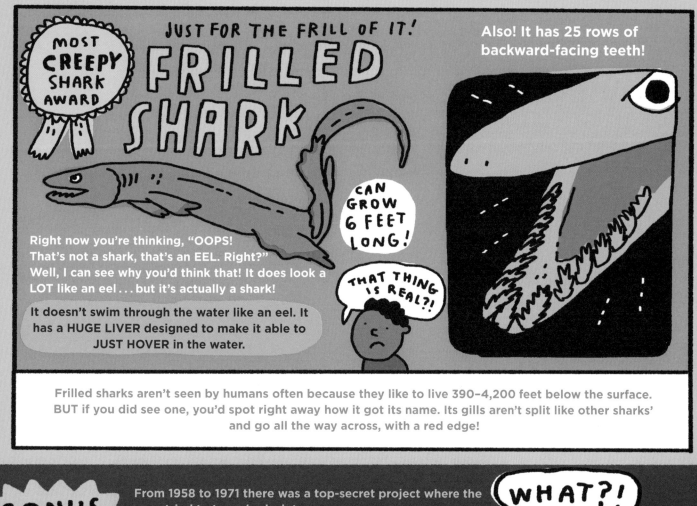

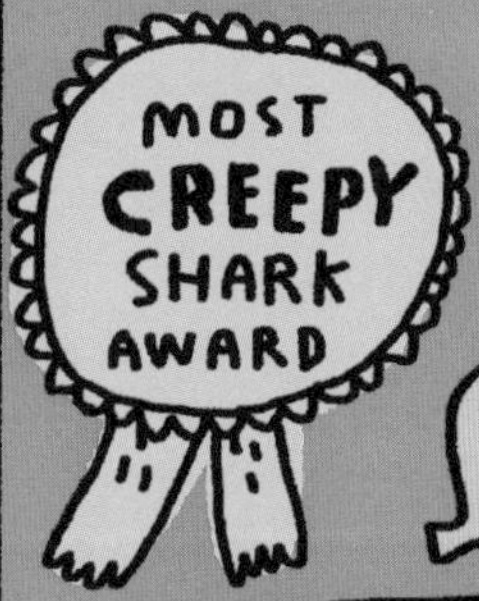
MOST
CREEPY
SHARK
AWARD

JUST FOR THE FRILL OF IT!

## FRILLED SHARK

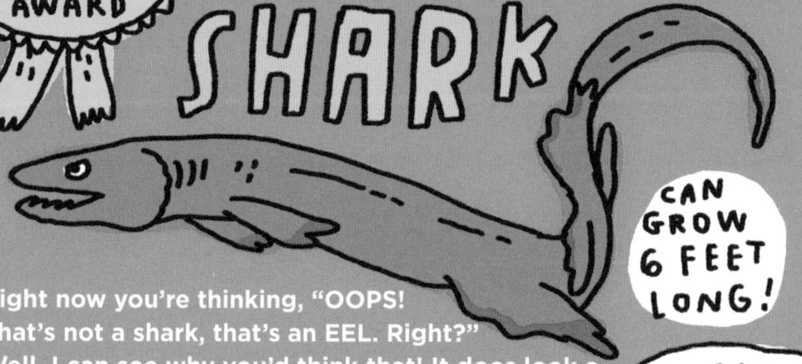

CAN GROW 6 FEET LONG!

Right now you're thinking, "OOPS! That's not a shark, that's an EEL. Right?" Well, I can see why you'd think that! It does look a LOT like an eel . . . but it's actually a shark!

It doesn't swim through the water like an eel. It has a HUGE LIVER designed to make it able to JUST HOVER in the water.

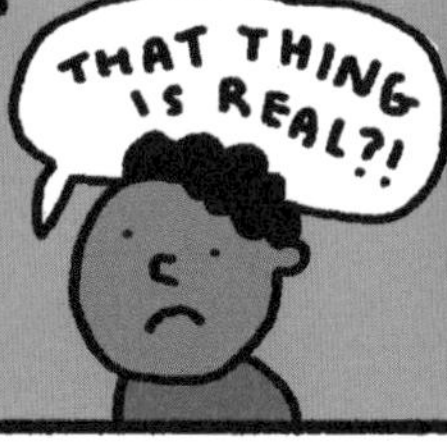
THAT THING IS REAL?!

Also! It has 25 rows of backward-facing teeth!

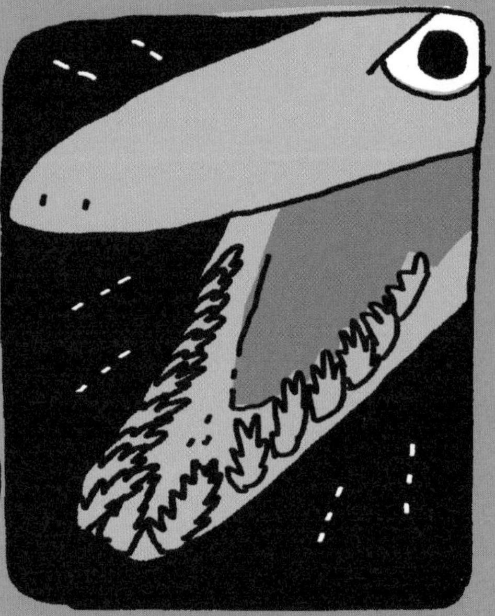

Frilled sharks aren't seen by humans often because they like to live 390–4,200 feet below the surface. BUT if you did see one, you'd spot right away how it got its name. Its gills aren't split like other sharks' and go all the way across, with a red edge!

**BONUS FACT!**

From 1958 to 1971 there was a top-secret project where the navy tried to turn sharks into

**TORPEDOES.**

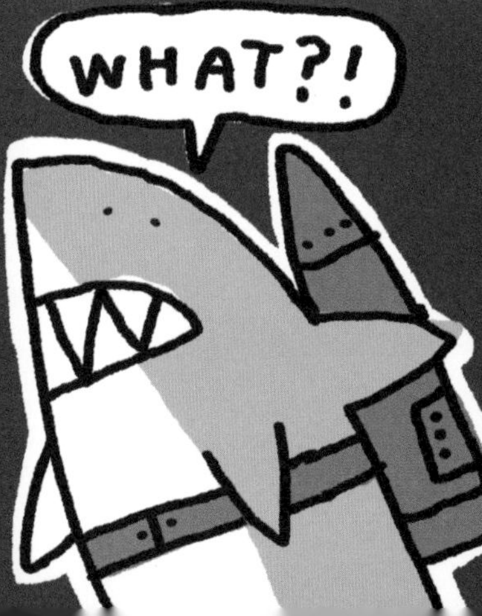
WHAT?!

BOOM!

The idea was that a shark would be strapped down with explosives, and headgear would shock the shark to keep it from going off course until it reached the target.

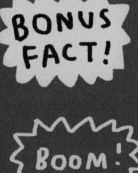

SHARK GROUP 4

# MACKEREL SHARKS

aka Lamniformes

MACKEREL SHARK CHECKLIST: 1 anal fin, 5 gill slits, 2 dorsal fins, no fin spines, mouth behind the eyes, no nictitating eyelids

This group contains a species you might know: THE WHITE SHARK! Early Lamniformes showed up around 120 million years ago, and the Megalodon belonged to this group.

Most mackerel sharks are warm bodied! This is important because this enables them to swim really fast, jump incredibly high, and dive deeper than other sharks.

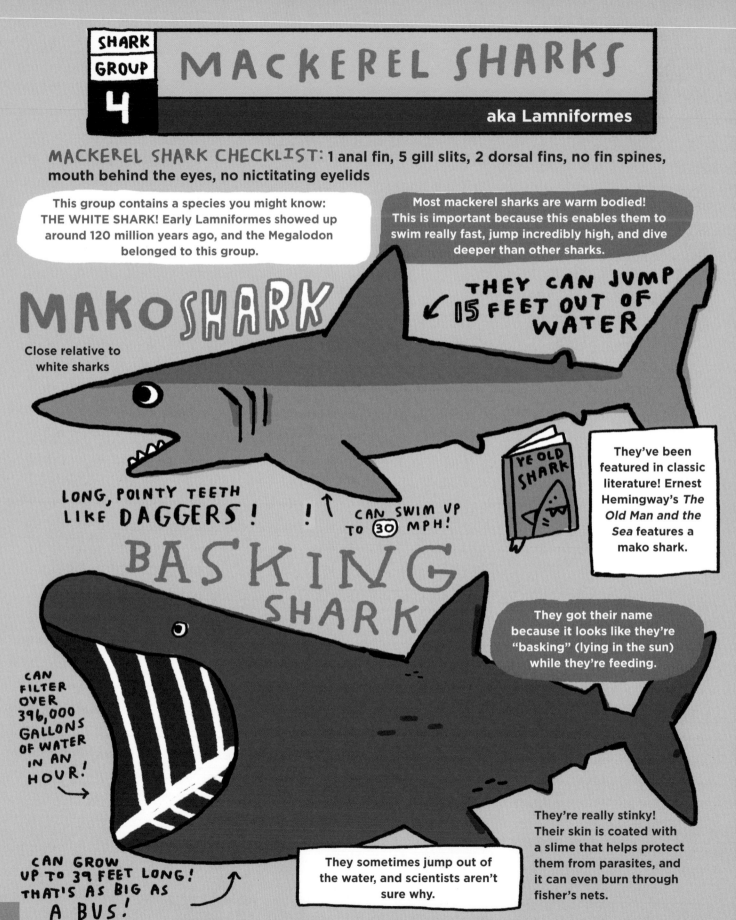

## MAKO SHARK

Close relative to white sharks

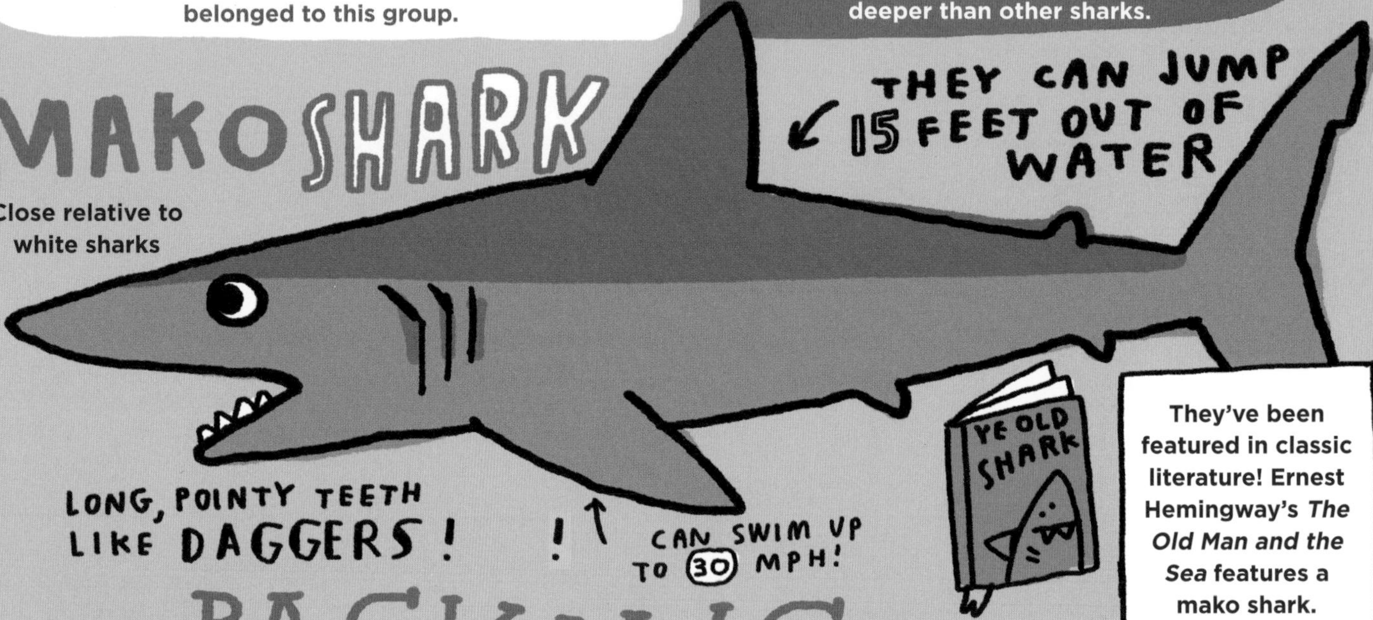

THEY CAN JUMP 15 FEET OUT OF WATER
LONG, POINTY TEETH LIKE DAGGERS!
CAN SWIM UP TO 30 MPH!
YE OLD SHARK


They've been featured in classic literature! Ernest Hemingway's *The Old Man and the Sea* features a mako shark.

## BASKING SHARK

They got their name because it looks like they're "basking" (lying in the sun) while they're feeding.

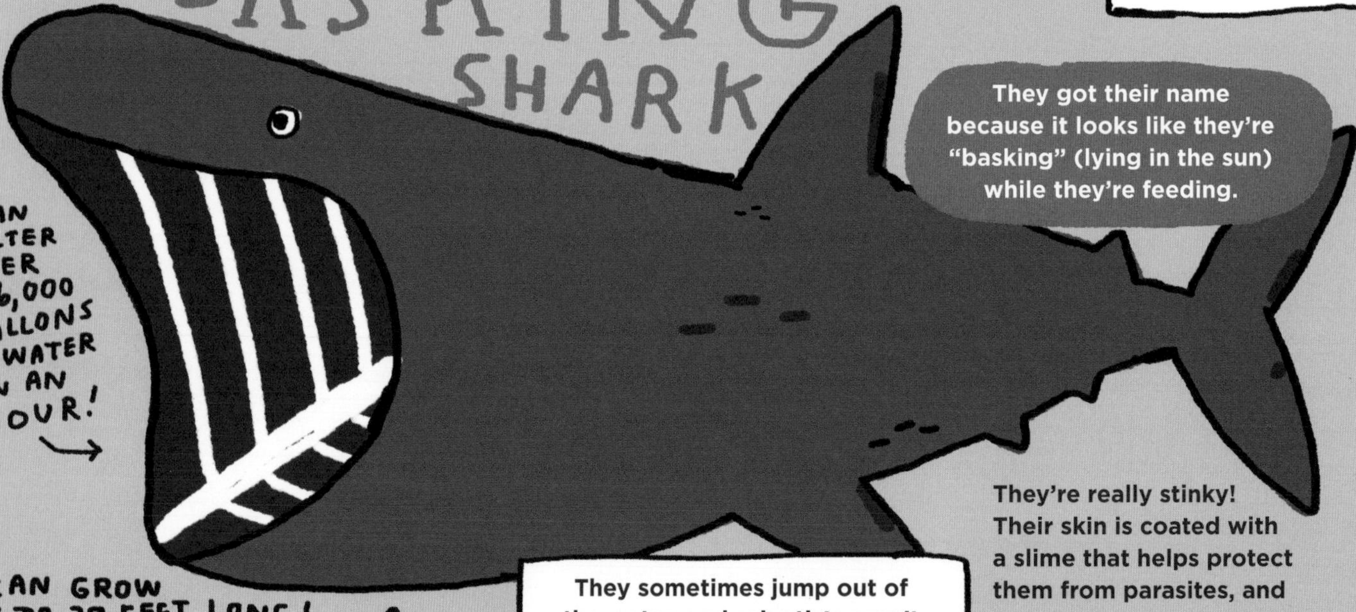

CAN FILTER OVER 396,000 GALLONS OF WATER IN AN HOUR!
CAN GROW UP TO 39 FEET LONG! THAT'S AS BIG AS A BUS!


They sometimes jump out of the water, and scientists aren't sure why.

They're really stinky! Their skin is coated with a slime that helps protect them from parasites, and it can even burn through fisher's nets.

# THRESHER SHARK

LONGEST TAIL AWARD!

You'll notice pretty quickly what makes the thresher shark so unique. The upper part of its tail is usually as long as the rest of its body! Including this incredibly long tail, these sharks can grow up to 20 feet long.

# GOBLIN SHARK

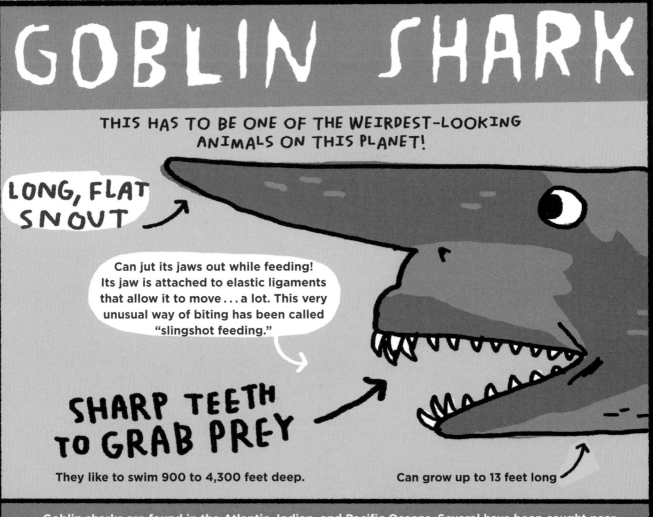

THIS HAS TO BE ONE OF THE WEIRDEST-LOOKING ANIMALS ON THIS PLANET!

LONG, FLAT SNOUT

Can jut its jaws out while feeding! Its jaw is attached to elastic ligaments that allow it to move...a lot. This very unusual way of biting has been called "slingshot feeding."

SHARP TEETH TO GRAB PREY

They like to swim 900 to 4,300 feet deep.

Can grow up to 13 feet long

Goblin sharks are found in the Atlantic, Indian, and Pacific Oceans. Several have been caught near Japan, where some early fishermen who saw them thought they looked like a Japanese demon called Tengu that has a long, pointed nose. So they called them *tengu-zame* ("zame" means "shark"). Later it was translated to "goblin shark."

WATCH OUT!

# WHITE SHARK

DANGER!

Its real name is just white shark, but it's more commonly called great white shark.

Some travel over 4,500 miles a year. One route is from California all the way to Hawaii.

(Though they're still not really that deadly to humans!)

Their contracting muscles warm up and allow them to stay warm in cold water.

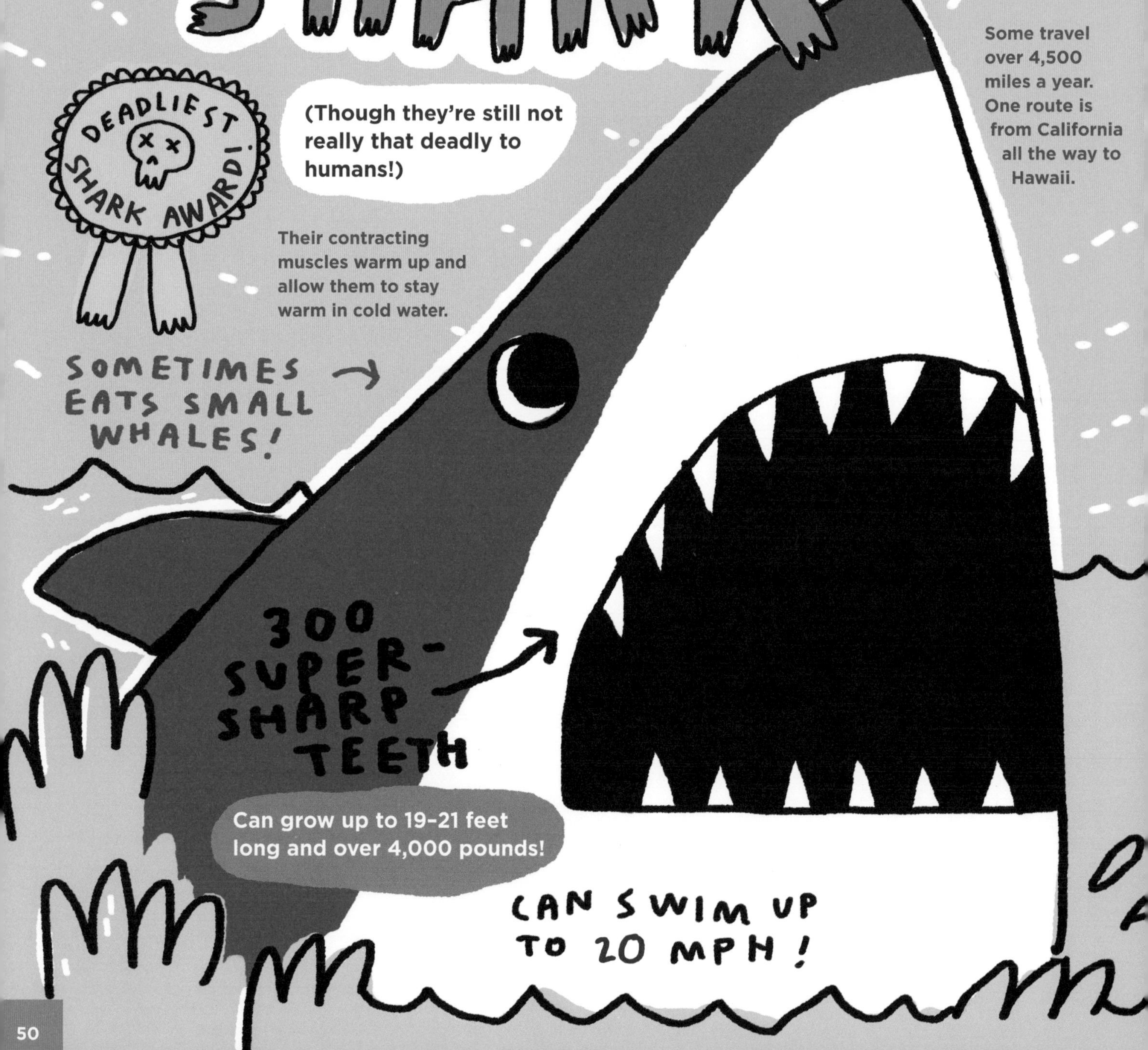
DEADLIEST SHARK AWARD!
SOMETIMES EATS SMALL WHALES!
300 SUPER-SHARP TEETH
CAN SWIM UP TO 20 MPH!

Can grow up to 19–21 feet long and over 4,000 pounds!

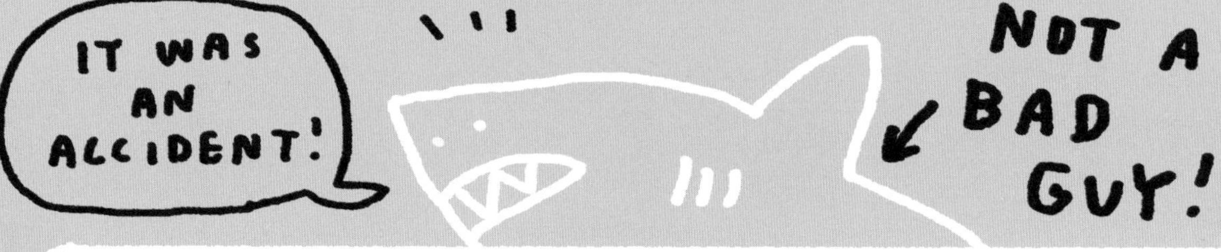

IT WAS AN ACCIDENT!
NOT A BAD GUY!


**Though the white shark is one of the sharks most responsible for human injury, and even death, they're still not very dangerous to humans. Sharks aren't interested in eating us, and a bite is usually just because the shark is curious or a little confused. To a shark, a swimmer in the ocean might look like a strange object or a tasty seal. A shark doesn't have hands like we do; it may examine an unfamiliar object with its mouth, which could result in injury to a human. Divers have also been bitten while harassing sharks, which means the shark was simply defending itself.**

**In 2018, there were only five deaths as the result of shark attacks.**

## STUFF MORE LIKELY TO KILL YOU THAN SHARKS! (TOTALLY TRUE!)

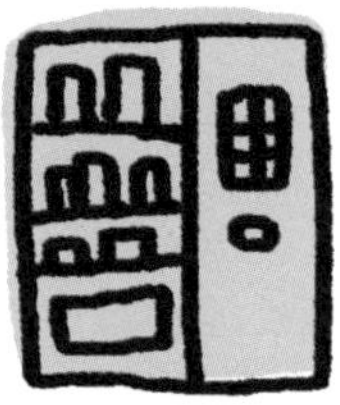

### VENDING MACHINES!

**13 people a year (on average)**

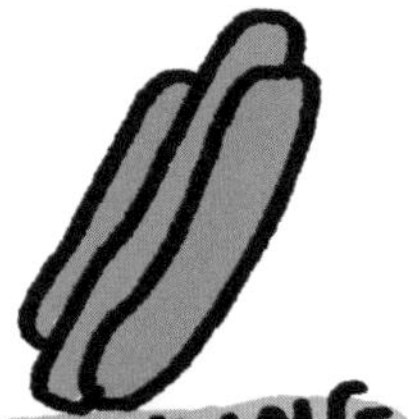

### CHOKING ON A HOT DOG!

**77 people a year (on average)**

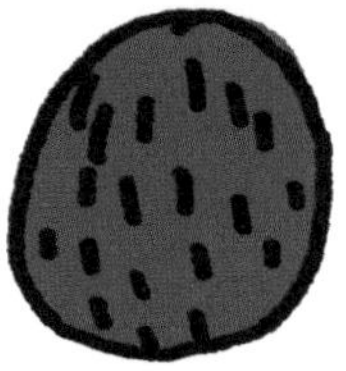

### FALLING COCONUTS!

**150 people a year (on average)**

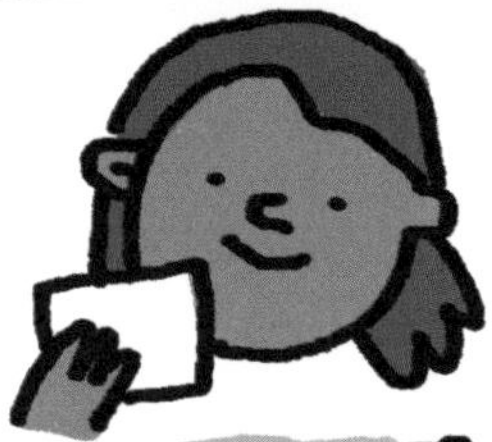

### TAKING A SELFIE!

**In 2015, 12 people died while taking a picture of themselves.**

## THEY CAN ROLL THEIR EYES!

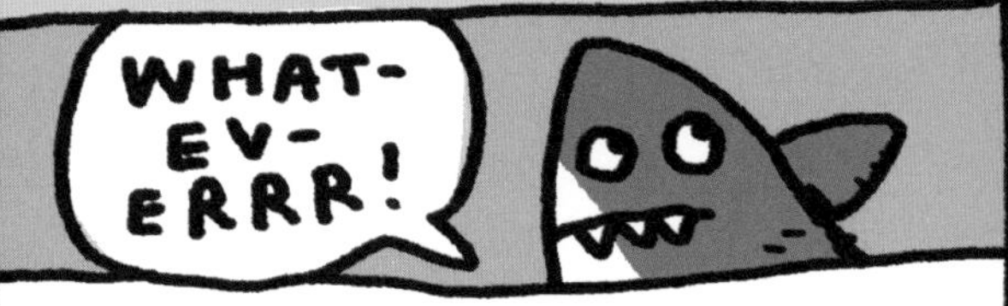

WHAT-EV-ERRR!


White sharks don't have nictitating membranes (those protective extra eyelids) like some sharks do, so they have another way of protecting their eyes. If they sense danger, they can roll their eyes back into their skull.

## SHARK VACATION!

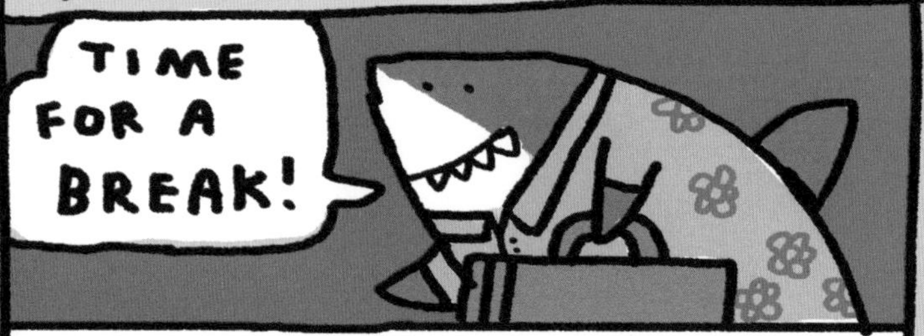

TIME FOR A BREAK!


From April to July, white sharks meet in a spot in the middle of the ocean between Hawaii and Mexico. For years scientists weren't sure why they chose this location, but recently they noticed some males were diving . . . to catch animals that live deep in the ocean. This is why it's often called "The White Shark Cafe."

SHARK GROUP 5

# CARPET SHARKS

aka Orectolobiformes

CARPET SHARK CHECKLIST: **1 anal fin, 5 gill slits, 2 dorsal fins, no fin spines, mouth in front of the eyes, patterned skin**

**This is a really diverse group of sharks. They live in the Indian, Atlantic, and Pacific Oceans. Some of them have barbels that they use for tasting and sensing food.**

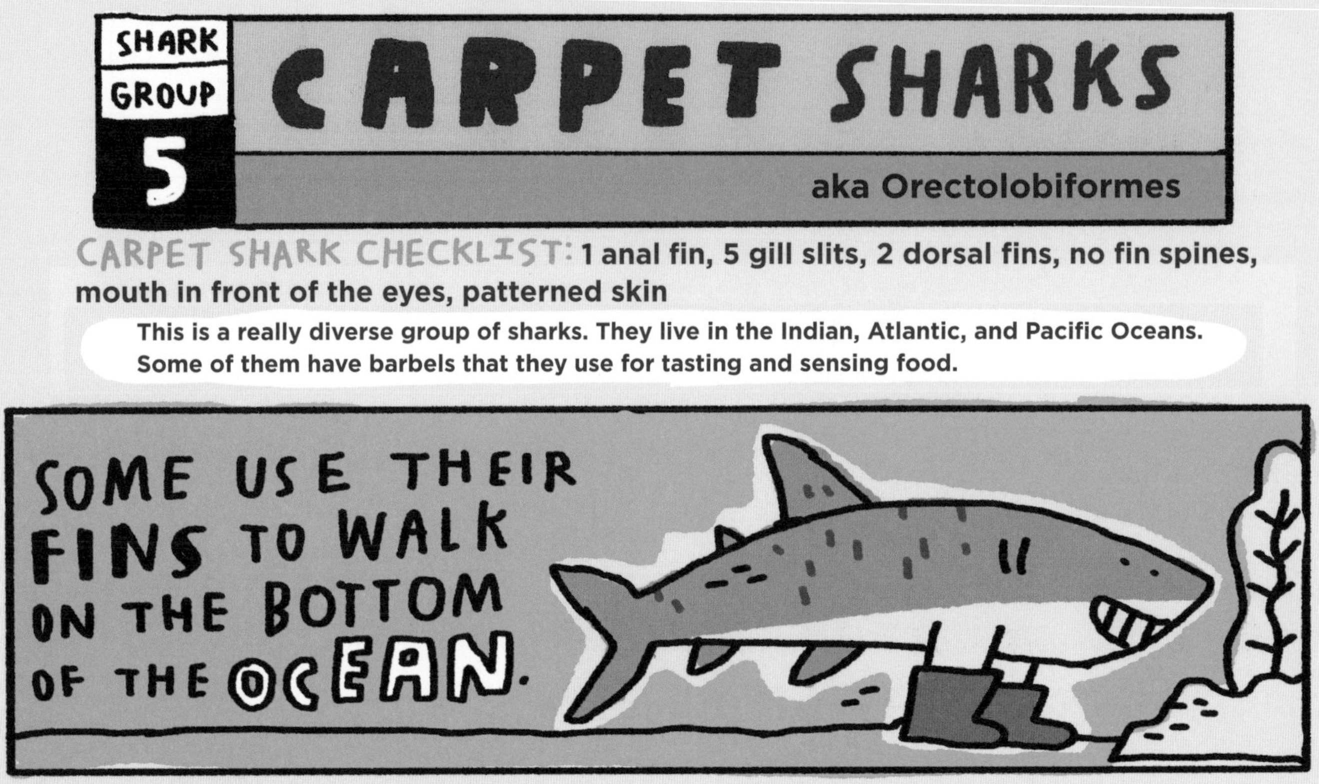
SOME USE THEIR FINS TO WALK ON THE BOTTOM OF THE OCEAN.

## NURSE SHARK

**No one is really sure how they got their name. It might be because when they're hunting for prey, they look like a nursing baby!**

THEY SUCK UP THEIR FOOD LIKE A VACUUM!

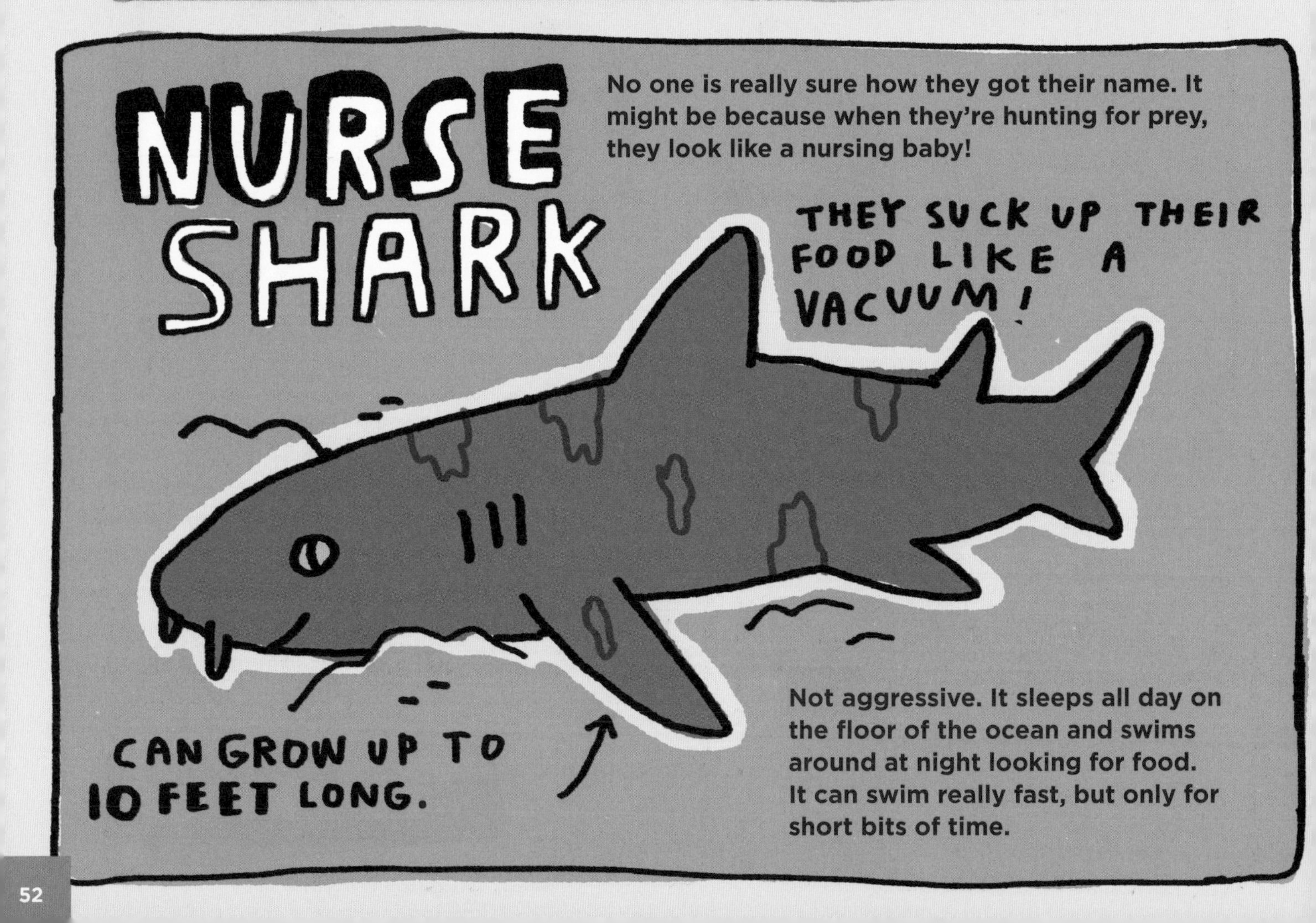

CAN GROW UP TO 10 FEET LONG.

**Not aggressive. It sleeps all day on the floor of the ocean and swims around at night looking for food. It can swim really fast, but only for short bits of time.**

# TASSELED WOBBEGONG SHARK

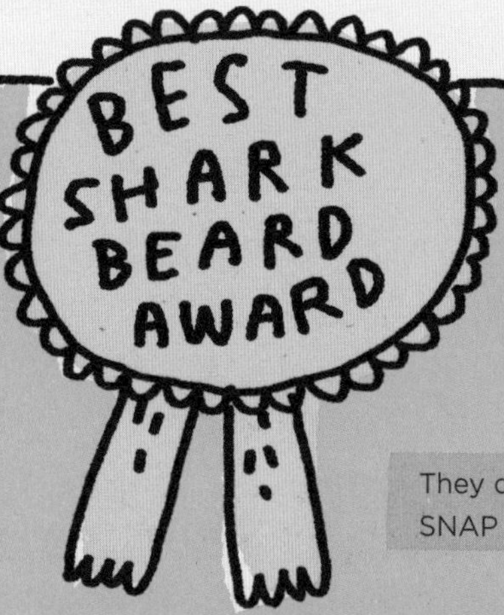
BEST SHARK BEARD AWARD

They don't actively hunt. They lie in wait for prey to get close enough, and then they SNAP really quickly to catch them with their strong jaws and sharp teeth.

**Those things sticking out that look like tree branches are actually barbels! These sharks have bad eyesight and use their barbels to help feel around for prey.**

**Wobbegong sharks aren't dangerous to humans, unless a human accidentally steps on them!**

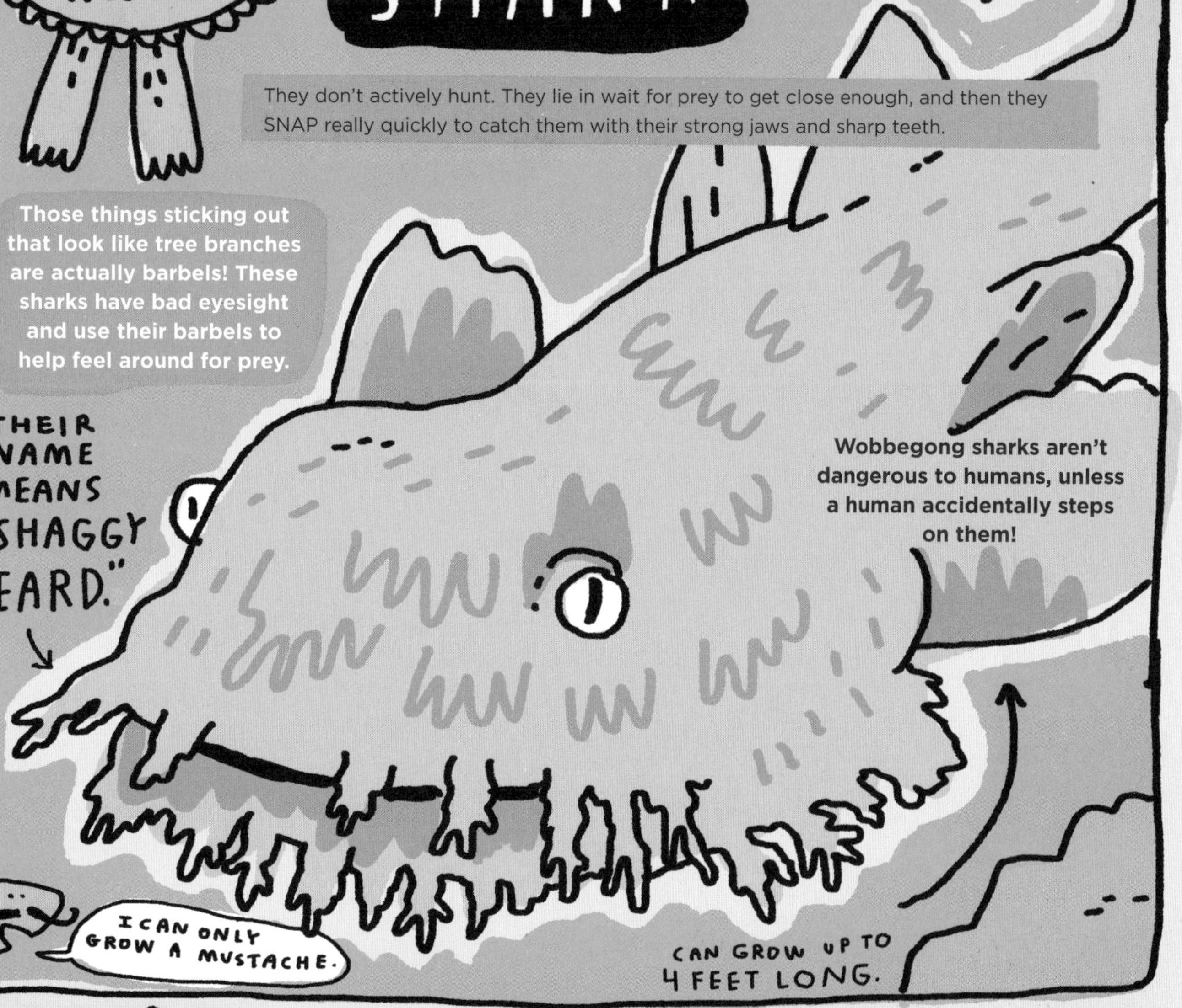
THEIR NAME MEANS "SHAGGY BEARD."
I CAN ONLY GROW A MUSTACHE.
CAN GROW UP TO 4 FEET LONG.

**BONUS FACT!** PART OF THE SOUND YOU HEAR WHEN LISTENING TO A SEASHELL IS THE SOUND OF YOUR BLOOD FLOWING!

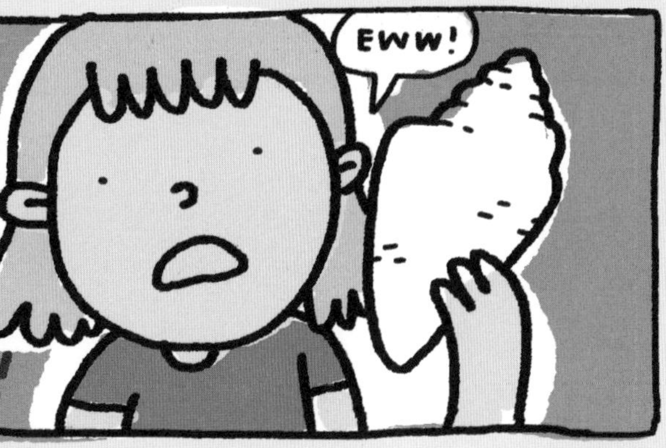
EWW!

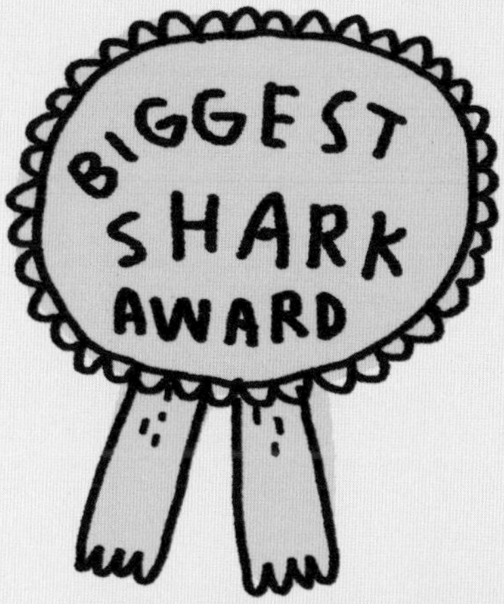
BIGGEST
SHARK
AWARD

# THE LARGEST LIVING SHARK (AND THE BIGGEST FISH) IN THE WORLD!

# WHALE SHARK

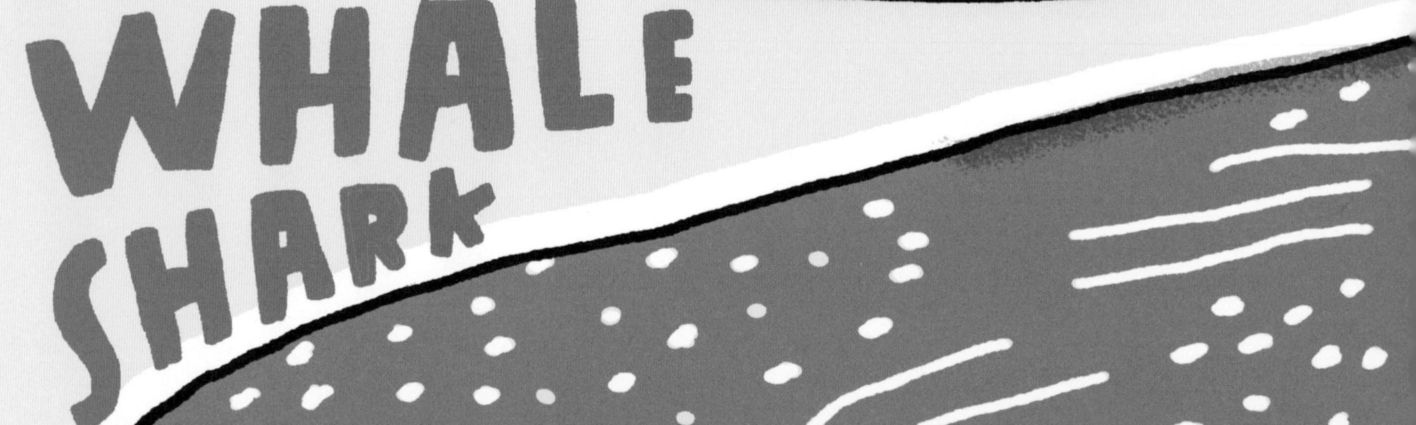

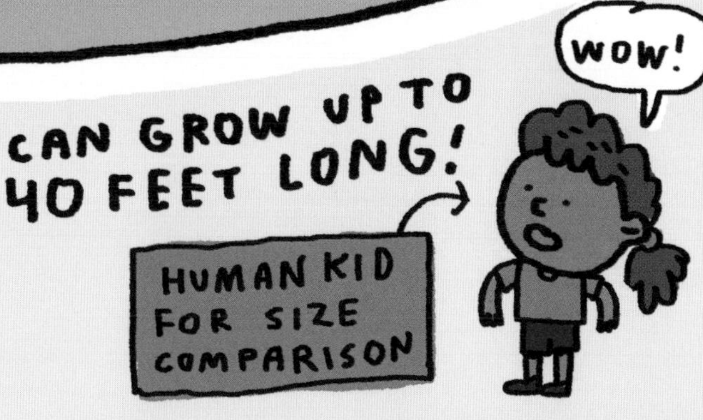
WOW!
CAN GROW UP TO 40 FEET LONG!
HUMAN KID FOR SIZE COMPARISON

**They've got more than 3,000 tiny teeth, but they usually just swallow their food whole.**

They're filter feeders! They open their mouths really wide and gulp down a bunch of water, keep the plankton and little fish, and then spit out the rest.

# TOTALLY UNIQUE!

The pattern of spots on their bodies is as unique as our fingerprints. No two whale sharks have the same pattern.

Scientists aren't totally sure how long they can live. Some guess around 60 years, while others estimate that it could be up to 150 years.

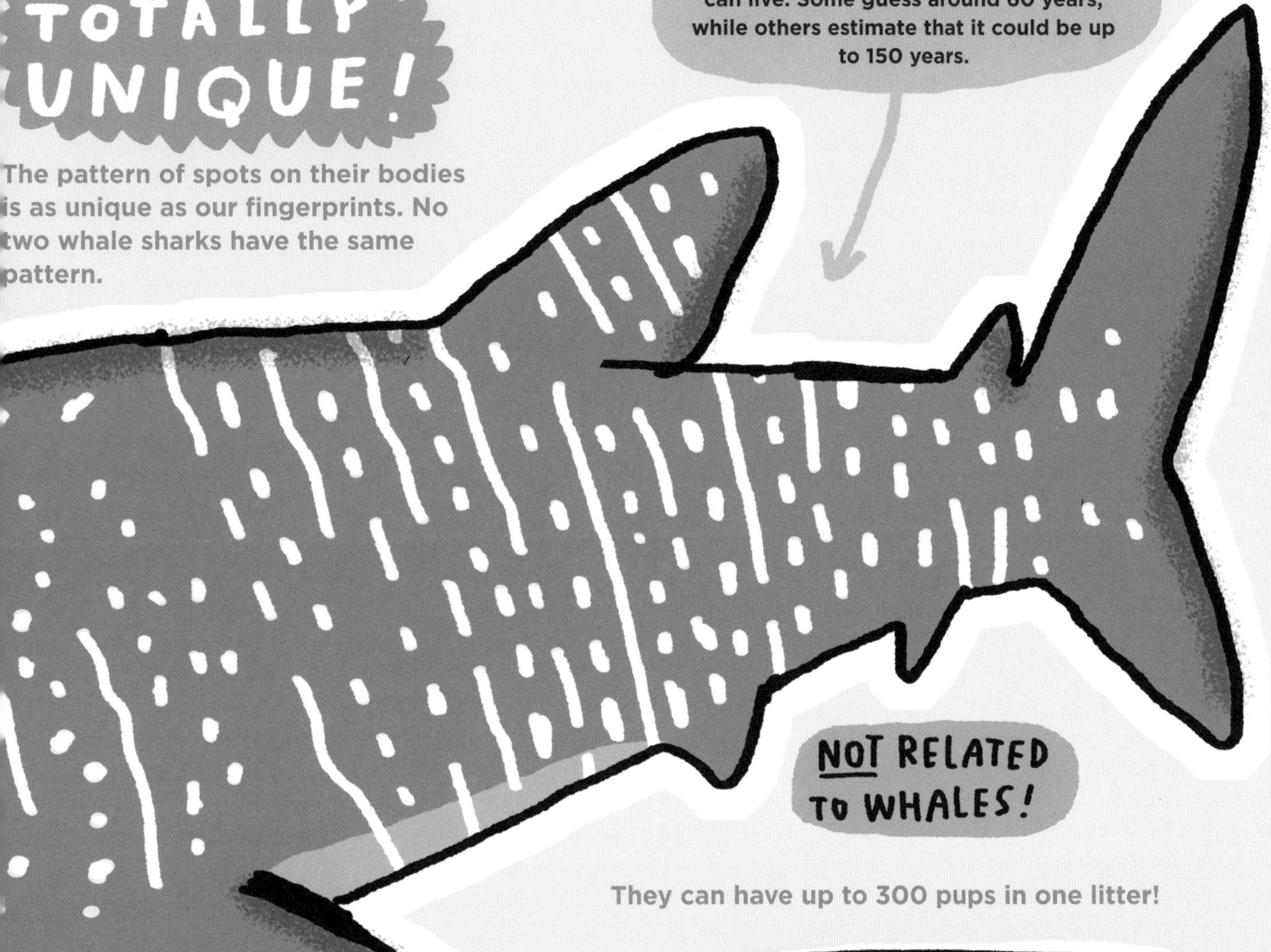

NOT RELATED TO WHALES!

They can have up to 300 pups in one litter!

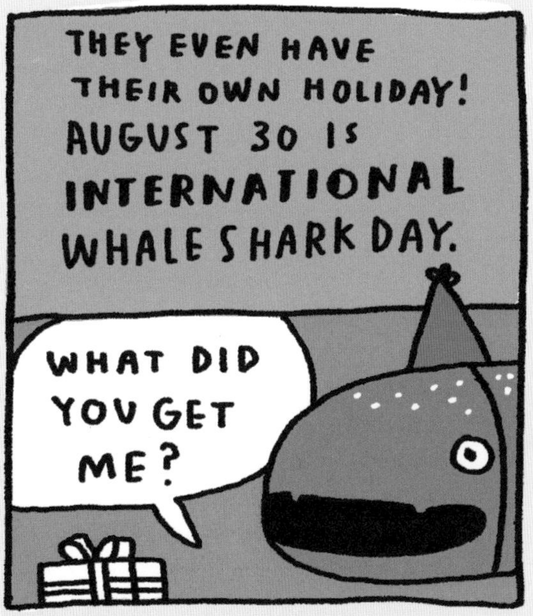
THEY EVEN HAVE THEIR OWN HOLIDAY! AUGUST 30 IS INTERNATIONAL WHALE SHARK DAY.
WHAT DID YOU GET ME?

They usually stay close to the surface of the water but are known to dive as deep as 3,200 feet!

# SAWSHARKS

aka Pristiophoriformes

SAWSHARK CHECKLIST: long snout, mouth on underside of head, no anal fin

## SAWSHARK

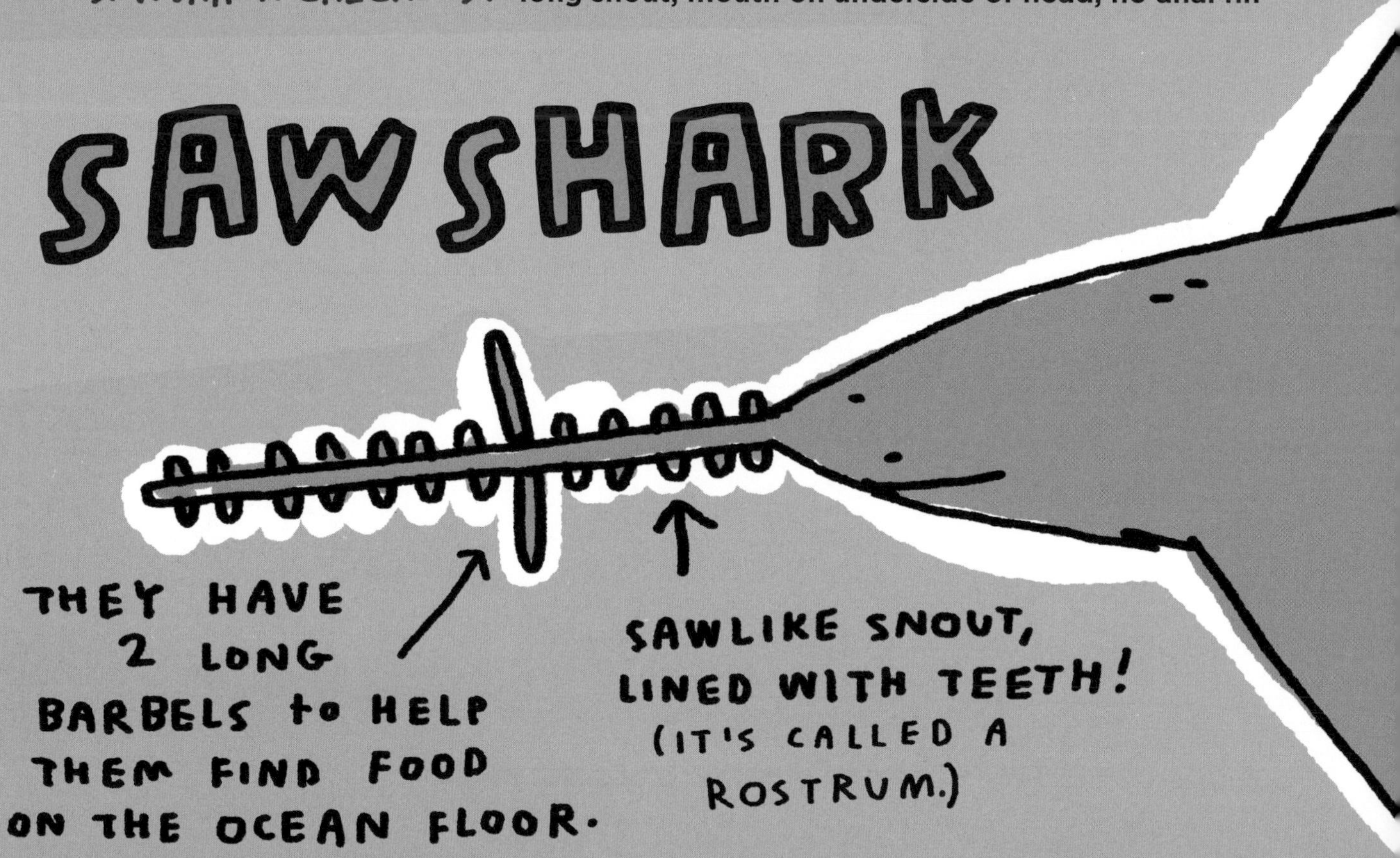
THEY HAVE 2 LONG BARBELS to HELP THEM FIND FOOD ON THE OCEAN FLOOR.
SAWLIKE SNOUT, LINED WITH TEETH! (IT'S CALLED A ROSTRUM.)

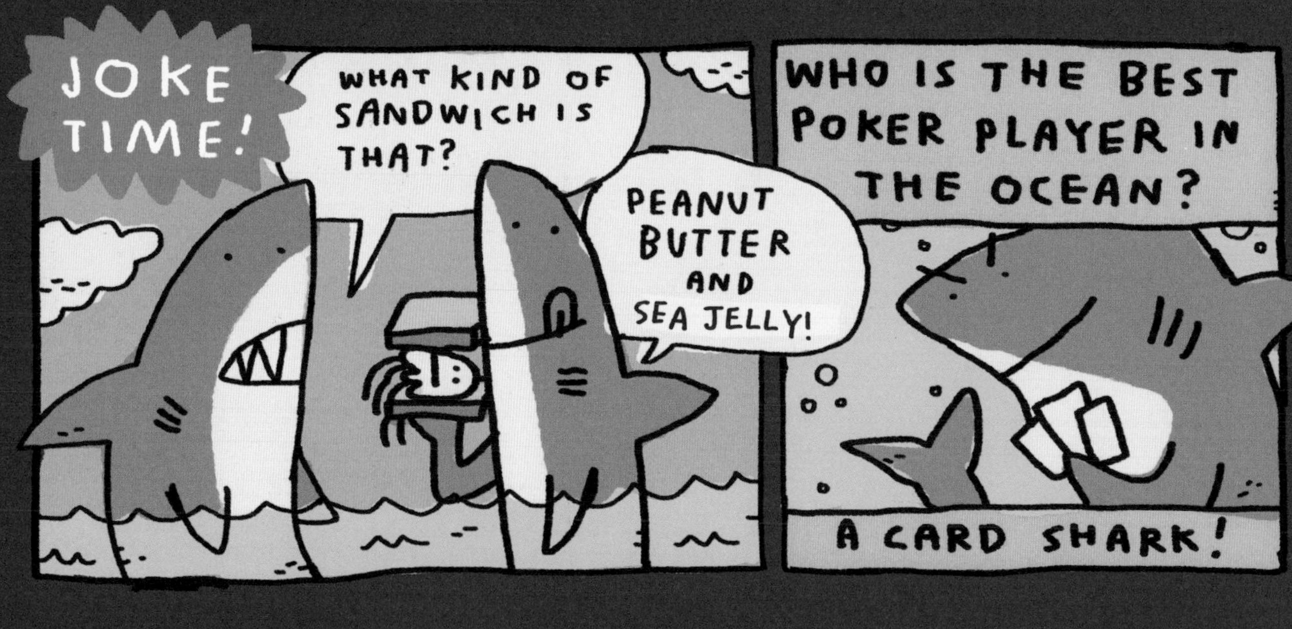
JOKE TIME!
WHAT KIND OF SANDWICH IS THAT?
PEANUT BUTTER AND SEA JELLY!
WHO IS THE BEST POKER PLAYER IN THE OCEAN?
A CARD SHARK!

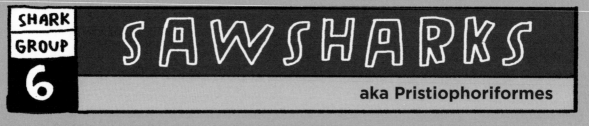

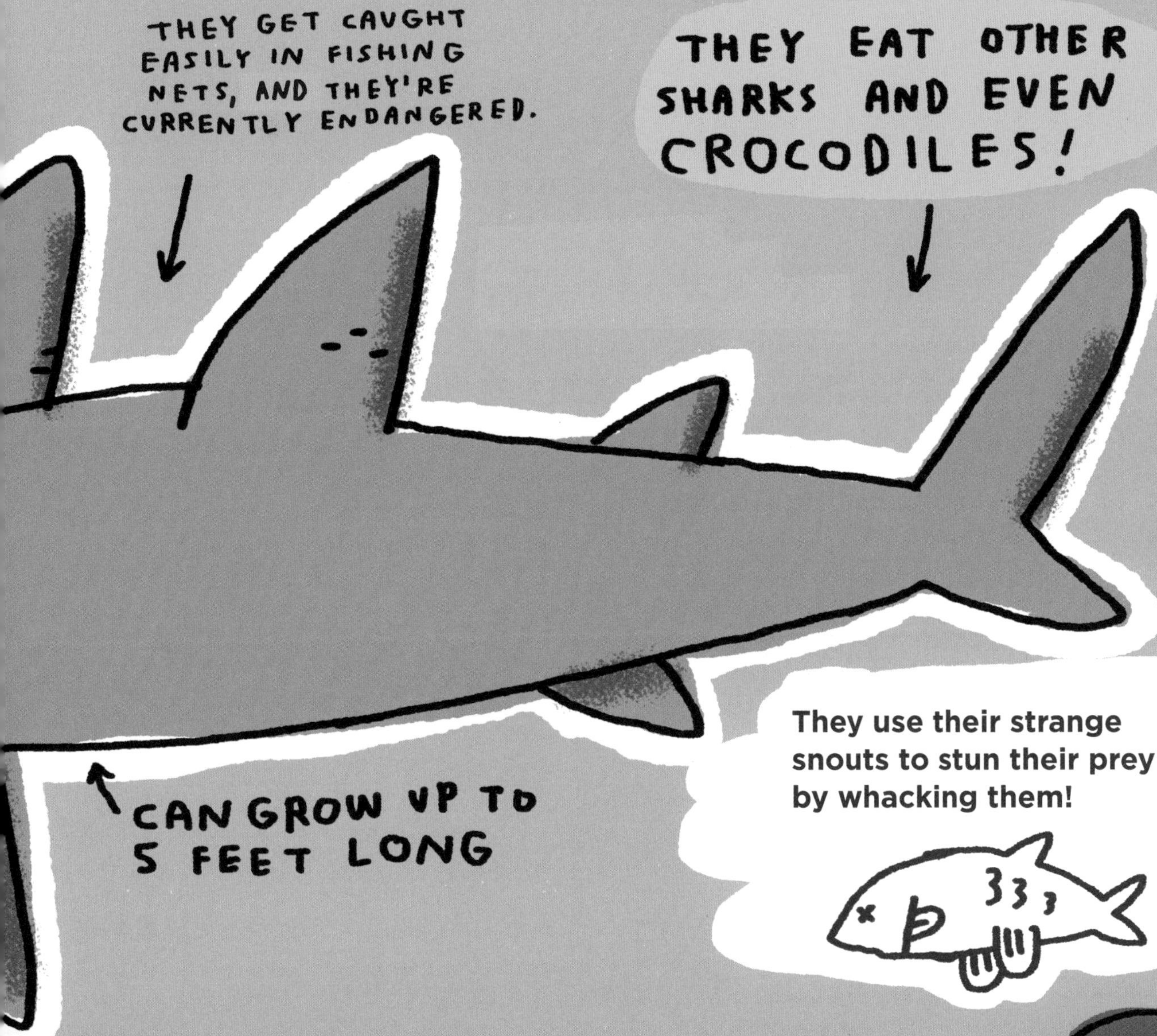

THEY GET CAUGHT EASILY IN FISHING NETS, AND THEY'RE CURRENTLY ENDANGERED.
THEY EAT OTHER SHARKS AND EVEN CROCODILES!
CAN GROW UP TO 5 FEET LONG


They use their strange snouts to stun their prey by whacking them!

# BONUS FACT!

# EASTER ISLAND MYSTERY!

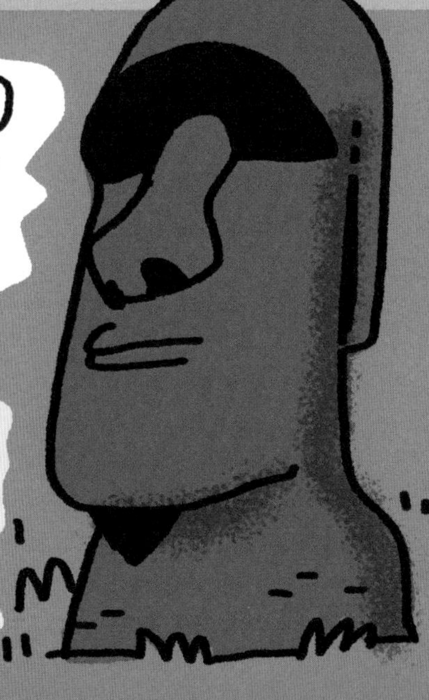

You've probably heard of the giant ancient head statues on Easter Island, but under the waters near the island there's another mystery. There's a modern replica of one of these Moai figures and get this...no one is really sure how it got there. Some think that the locals made it as a tourist attraction, but some think it's actually a prop from a 1994 movie.

SHARK GROUP 7

# DOGFISH SHARKS

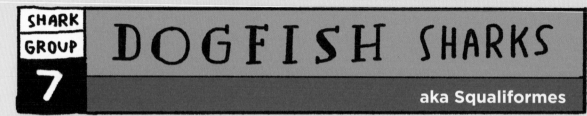

aka Squaliformes

DOGFISH SHARK CHECKLIST: **short snout, mouth on underside of head, no anal fin**

There's a wide variety of Squaliformes that can range from tiny to huge! The world's smallest known shark, the dwarf lantern shark, belongs to this group. They only grow up to about 7 inches long. But this group also includes the Greenland shark, which can grow up to 21 feet long. Squaliformes have long, narrow bodies and a short snout.

## GREENLAND SHARK

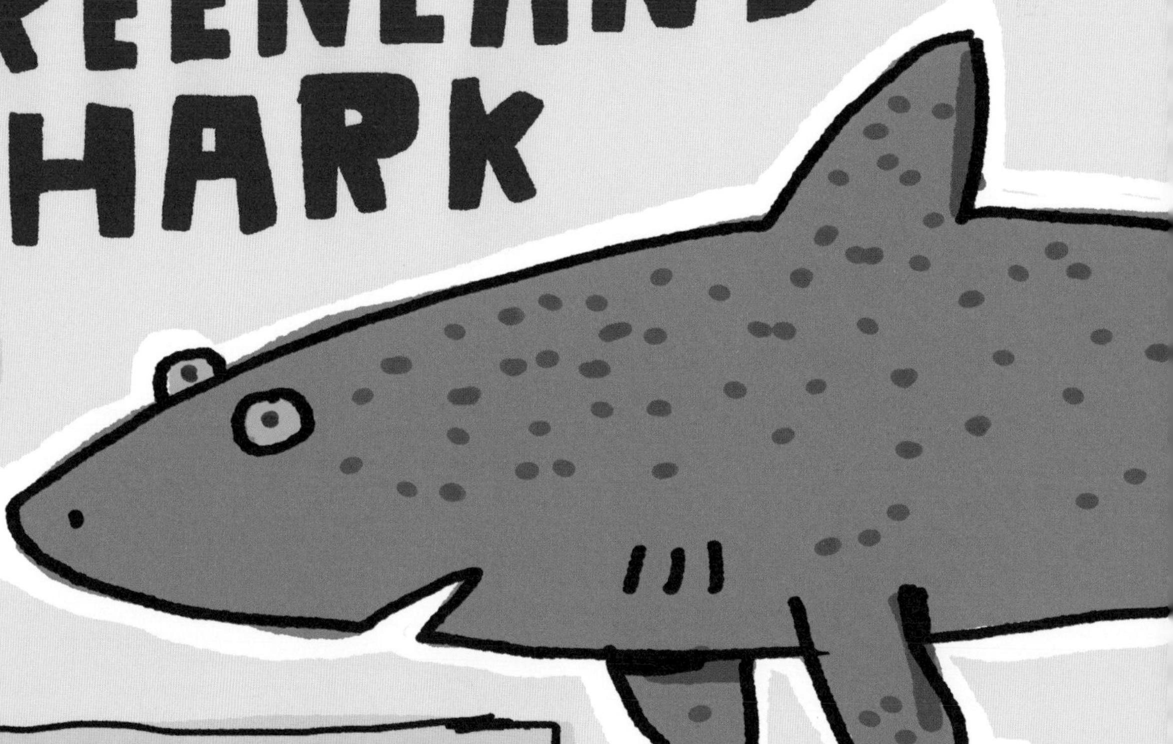

First filmed swimming in 1995, and it was 18 years before anyone got them on video again.

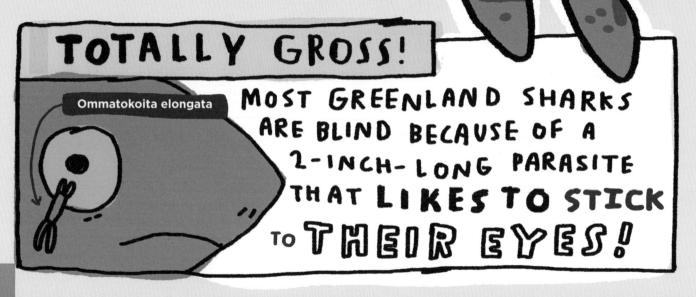

### TOTALLY GROSS!

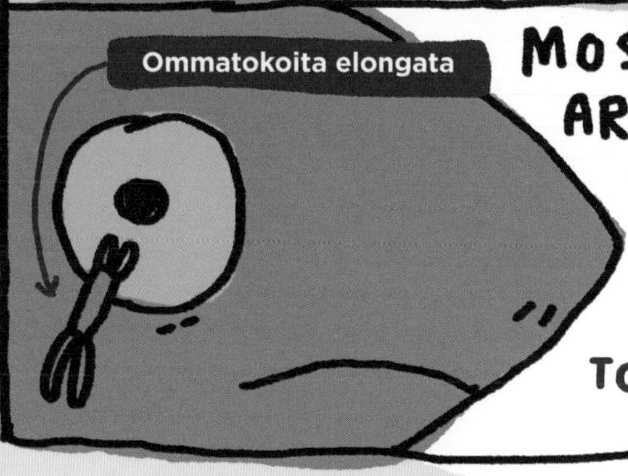
Ommatokoita elongata

MOST GREENLAND SHARKS ARE BLIND BECAUSE OF A 2-INCH-LONG PARASITE THAT LIKES TO STICK TO THEIR EYES!

Some scientists think they can live to be up to

**400 YEARS OLD**

or even longer.

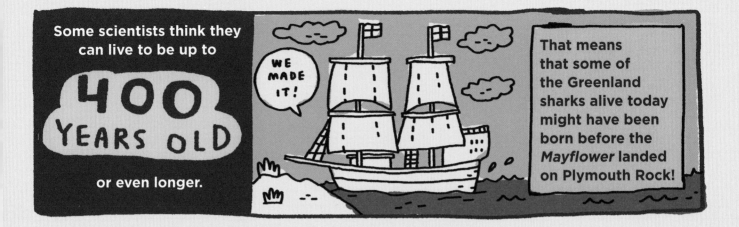

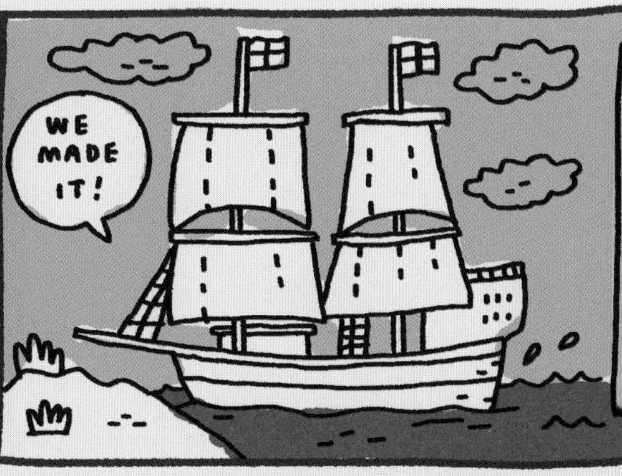
WE MADE IT!

That means that some of the Greenland sharks alive today might have been born before the *Mayflower* landed on Plymouth Rock!

One of the largest sharks in the world, it grows up to 21 feet long and can weigh 2,100 pounds.

WEIGHS AS MUCH AS TWO GRAND PIANOS!

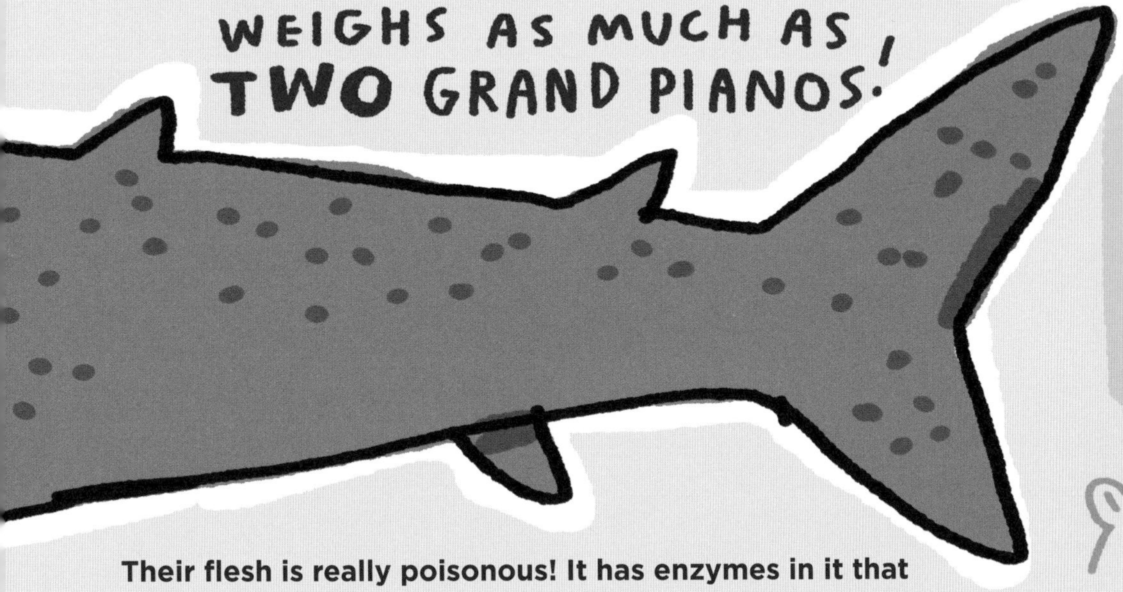

Greenland sharks are scavengers! They've been known to eat live seals as well as dead animals, like reindeer and even polar bears!

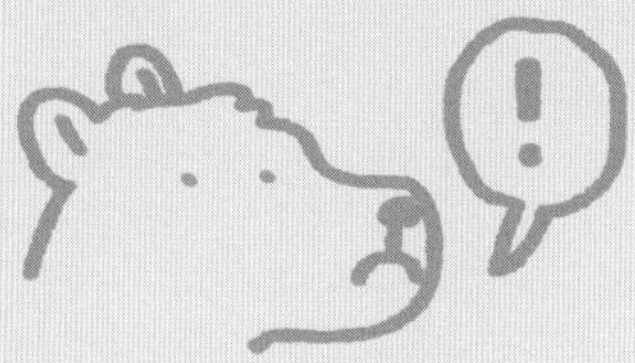
!

Their flesh is really poisonous! It has enzymes in it that protect the sharks against cold water and high pressure, but would make humans pretty sick if we ate it.

## THEY SWIM REAAAAAALLY SLOWWLLY.

**They typically swim less than 1 mile an hour…but that's still faster than slugs!**

(Slugs only go around .19 miles per hour!)

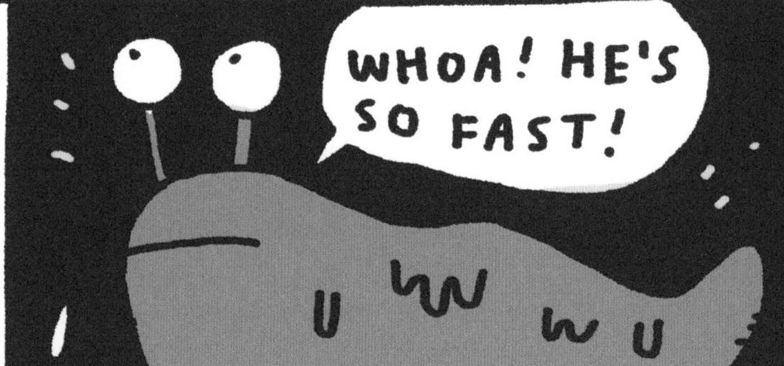
WHOA! HE'S SO FAST!

# COOKIECUTTER SHARK

**SUPER WEIRD!**

aka cigar shark

Up to 22 inches long

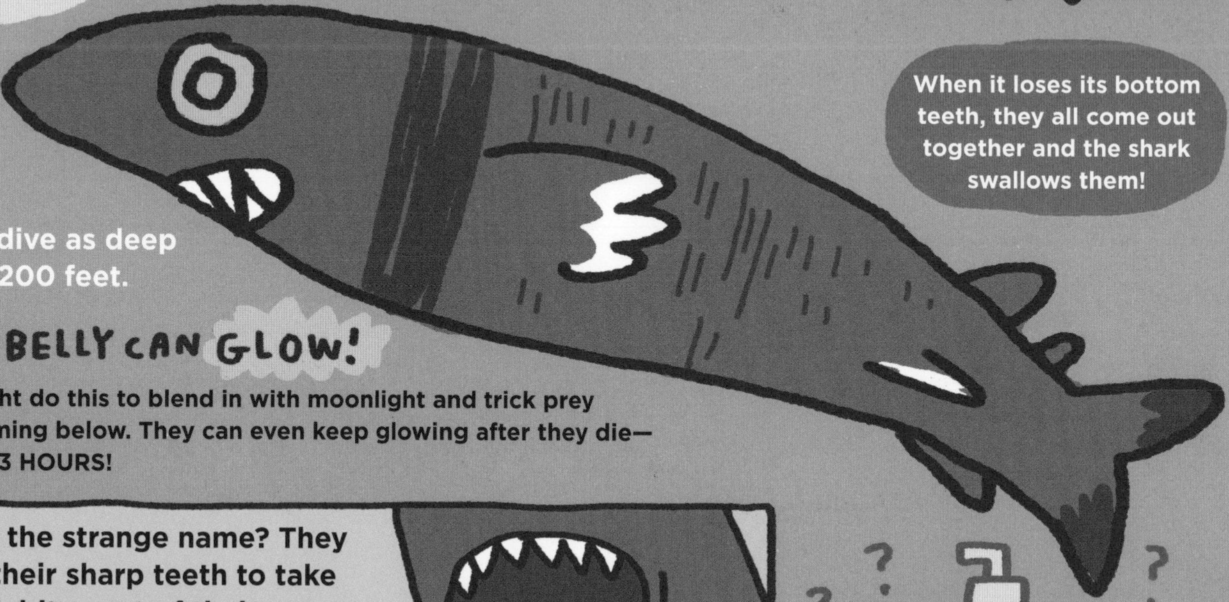

When it loses its bottom teeth, they all come out together and the shark swallows them!

Can dive as deep as 3,200 feet.

## ITS BELLY CAN GLOW!

It might do this to blend in with moonlight and trick prey swimming below. They can even keep glowing after they die—up to 3 HOURS!

**Why the strange name? They use their sharp teeth to take quick bites out of their prey before they swim off.**

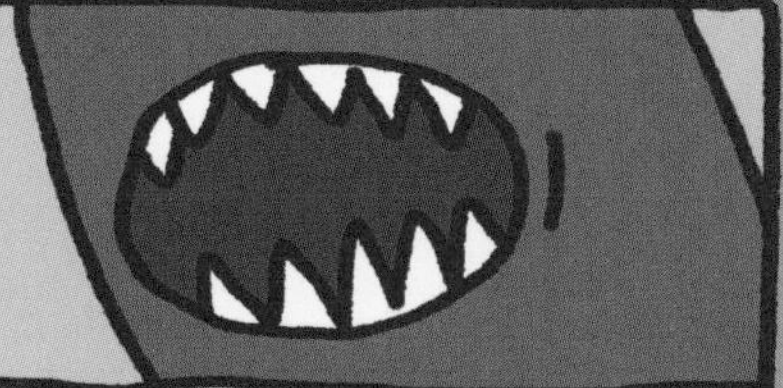

First it uses its lips to stick to prey like a suction cup, then it spins its body and uses its teeth to carve out a chunk 2 inches across and 2.5 inches deep! They like to bite animals that are a lot bigger than them, like whales, dolphins, seals, tuna, swordfish, marlin, even white sharks!

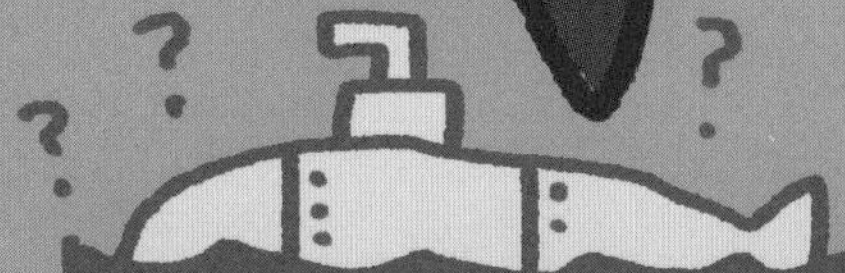

They've even caused trouble for submarines! A cookiecutter shark took bites out of some rubber that was on a sub's sonar device . . . and it made the crew unable to see where they were going!

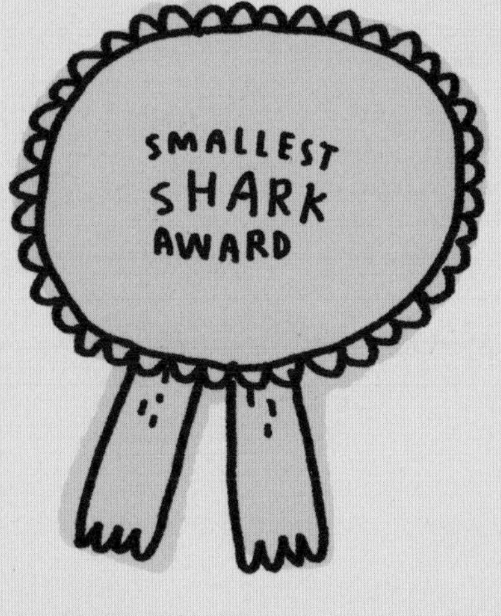
SMALLEST SHARK AWARD

## DWARF LANTERN SHARK!

This little shark grows up to about 8 inches.

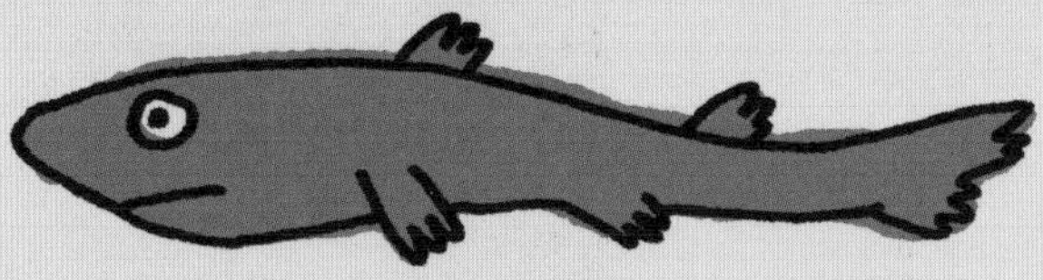

It's the smallest species of shark we know about today.

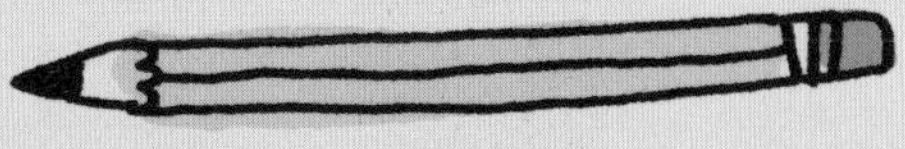

That's about the length of a pencil!

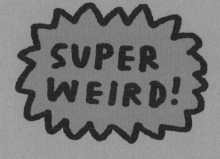

SHARK GROUP 8

# ANGELSHARKS

aka Squatiniformes

**ANGELSHARK CHECKLIST:** mouth at front, no anal fin, flat body

They've got flat bodies, with their mouths in the front like a ray. Their eyes are on the tops of their heads and so is a spiracle, which they use like a snorkel to suck in clean water when they're lying in mud. They're usually about 5 feet long, and they've got simple barbels.

## PACIFIC ANGELSHARK

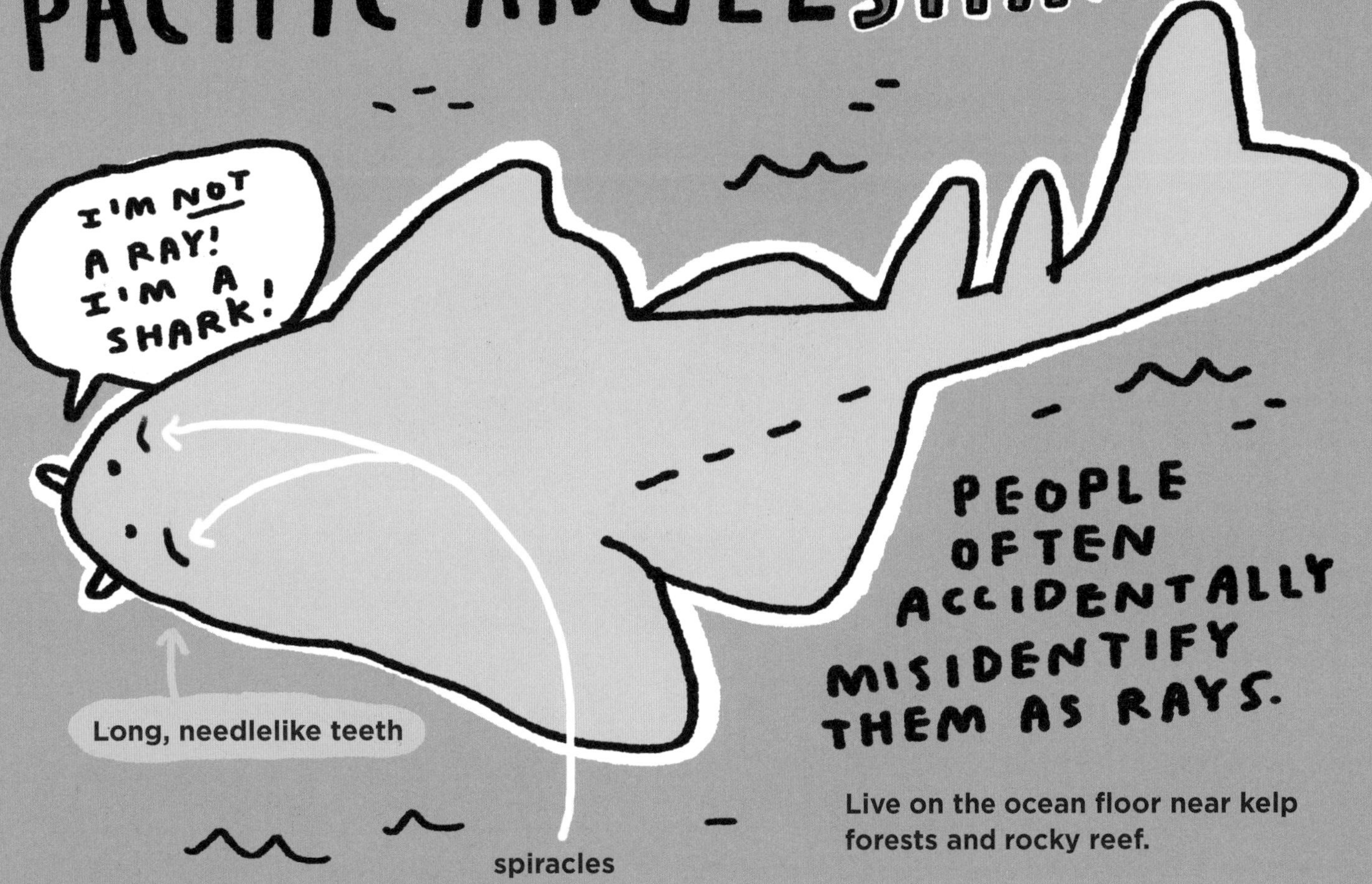
I'M NOT A RAY! I'M A SHARK!
Long, needlelike teeth
spiracles

PEOPLE OFTEN ACCIDENTALLY MISIDENTIFY THEM AS RAYS.

Live on the ocean floor near kelp forests and rocky reef.

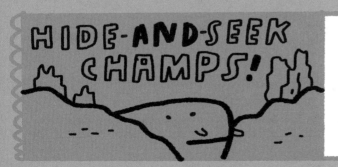

## HIDE-AND-SEEK CHAMPS!

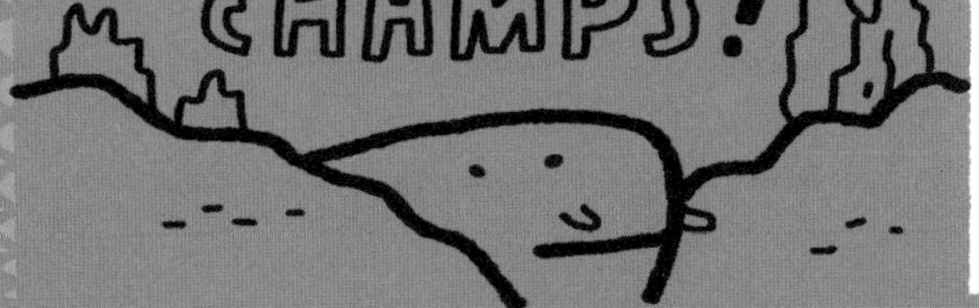

They're an ambush predator...which means they like to hide and wait for prey to swim by. They have special muscles that pump water over their gills so they don't need to keep swimming like other sharks to get oxygen.

# BONUS FACT!

## WEIRD STUFF THAT HAS BEEN FOUND IN SHARKS' STOMACHS.

A BULLDOG HEAD

A FULL SUIT OF ARMOR

A PORCUPINE

CATS

BAGS OF MONEY

A CANNON-BALL

TIRES

PIGS

A HORSE HEAD

NAILS

BOTTLES

A CHICKEN COOP

# PART THREE

# EXTREME MARINE HABITATS

Now that we've talked about the awesomest animals in the ocean, SHARKS, let's talk about the most amazing spots that some aquatic animals call home!

# CORAL REEF

**Often called the "rain forests of the ocean" because they are so biodiverse. They only cover less than 1% of the ocean's surface but it's estimated that around 25% of life in the ocean makes its home here.**

## Thousands of species live here. WHY?

**Little fish can find food and little places to hide . . . and all those little fish make yummy snacks for bigger fish, like SHARKS!**

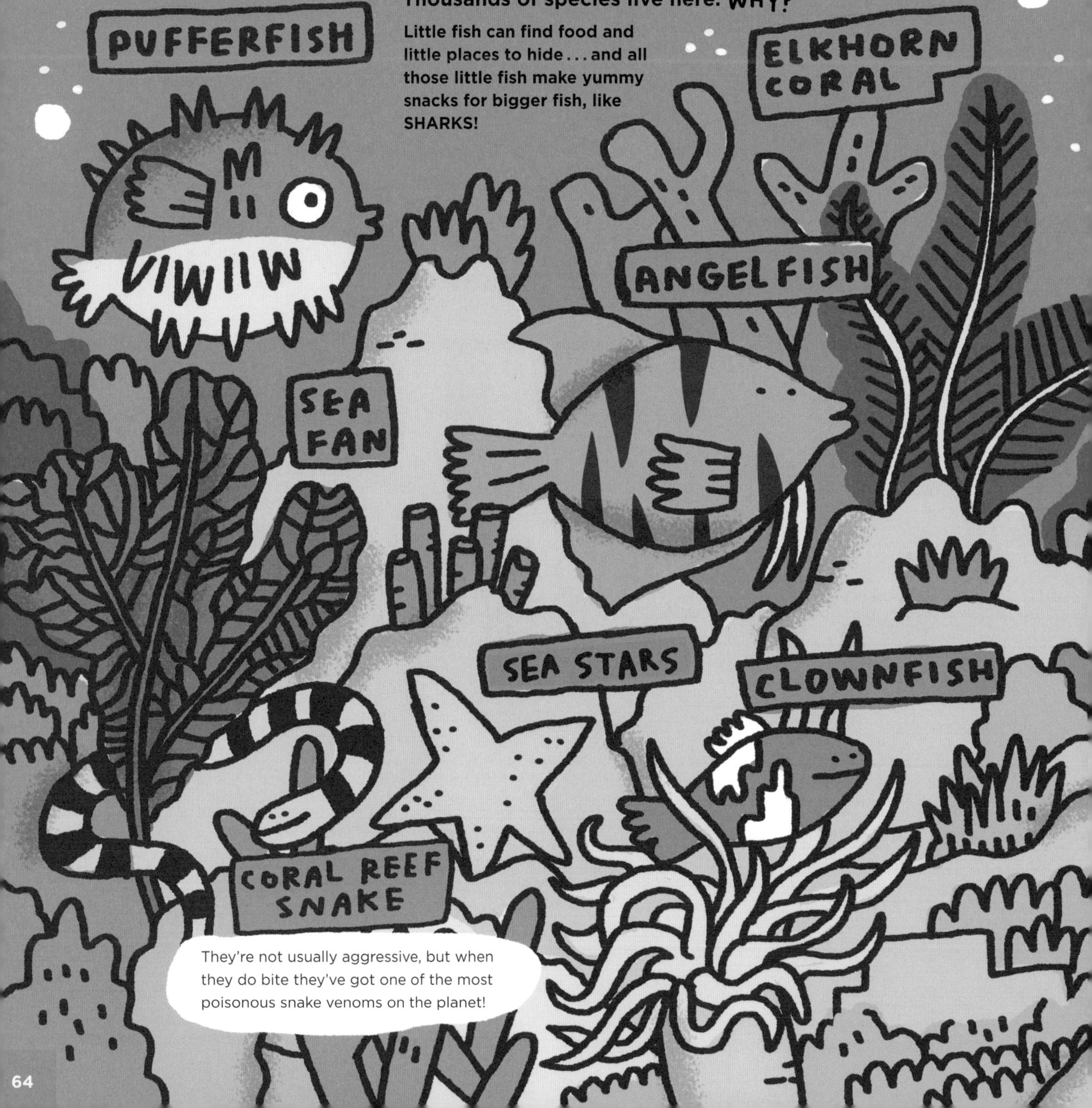
PUFFERFISH
ELKHORN CORAL
ANGELFISH
SEA FAN
SEA STARS
CLOWNFISH
CORAL REEF SNAKE

They're not usually aggressive, but when they do bite they've got one of the most poisonous snake venoms on the planet!

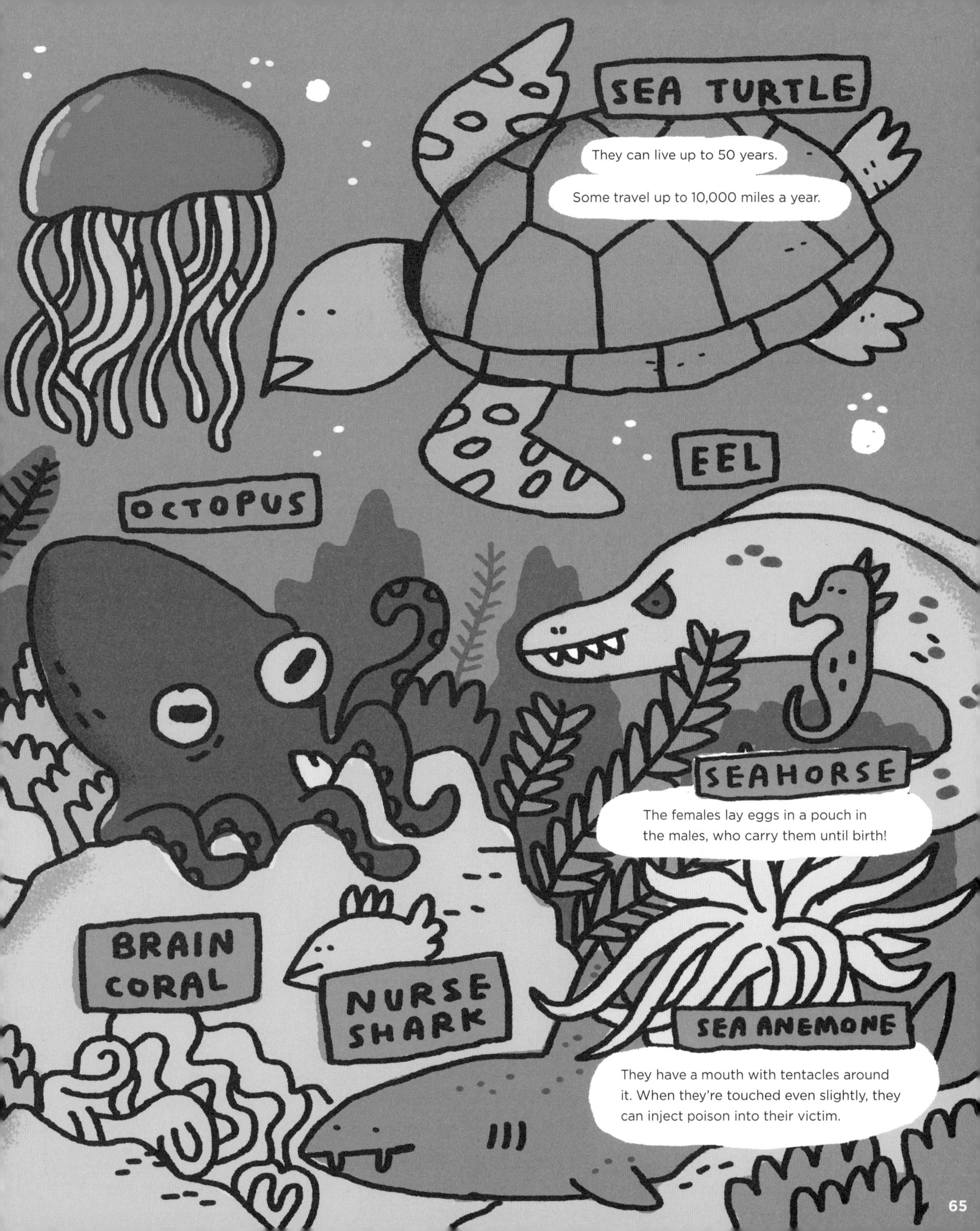
SEA TURTLE
They can live up to 50 years.
Some travel up to 10,000 miles a year.
EEL
OCTOPUS
SEAHORSE
The females lay eggs in a pouch in the males, who carry them until birth!
BRAIN CORAL
NURSE SHARK
SEA ANEMONE
They have a mouth with tentacles around it. When they're touched even slightly, they can inject poison into their victim.

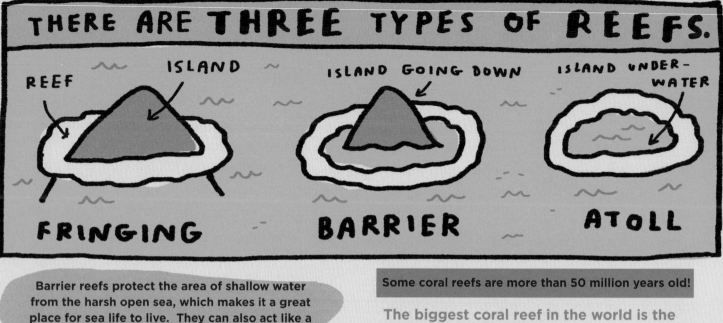

# THERE ARE THREE TYPES OF REEFS.

REEF
ISLAND
FRINGING
ISLAND GOING DOWN
BARRIER
ISLAND UNDER-WATER
ATOLL

Barrier reefs protect the area of shallow water from the harsh open sea, which makes it a great place for sea life to live. They can also act like a filter to clean the water.

AUSTRALIA

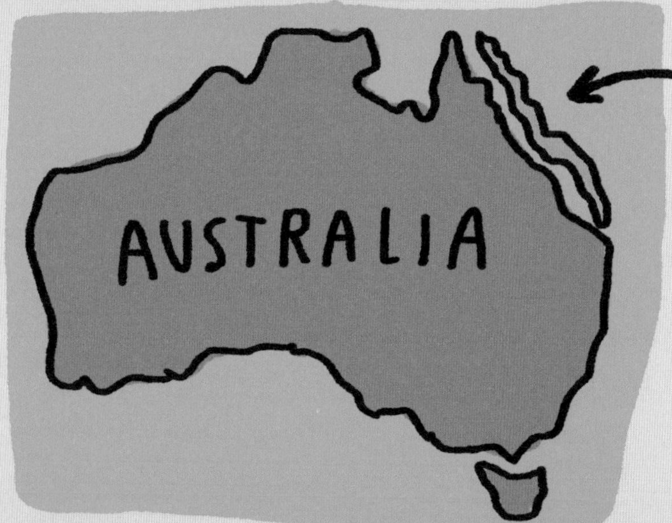

Some coral reefs are more than 50 million years old!

The biggest coral reef in the world is the

## GREAT BARRIER REEF.

It's 1,430 miles long, making it the largest living structure on our planet!

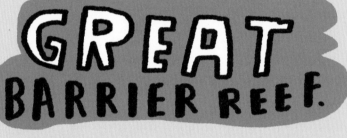

**CORAL HAS BEEN ON THIS PLANET FOR MORE THAN 400 MILLION YEARS!**

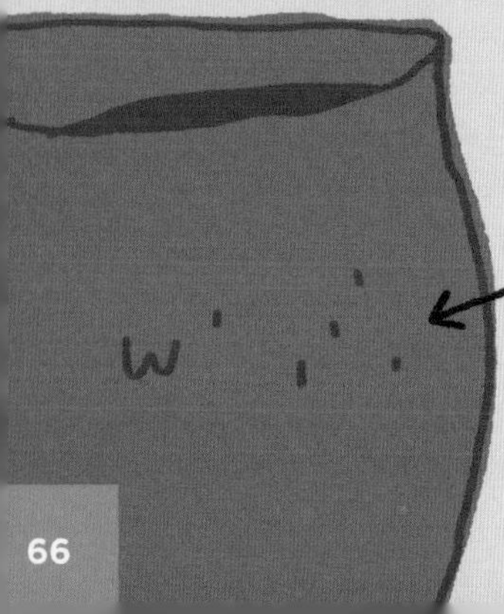

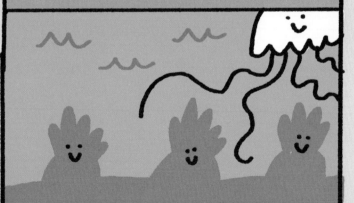

Coral reefs are made up of tiny invertebrate animals called polyps that are related to sea jellies.

But, unlike jellyfish, coral polyps don't float around and prefer to stay in one spot. They grow together in groups called colonies. A coral reef is made up of a bunch of corals growing close together.

Coral grows slowly, only a few inches a year.

GIANT BARREL SPONGE

These massive Caribbean sponges can grow up to 8 feet in diameter and can live for hundreds of years!

# BEACHES ARE MADE OF FISH POOP?!

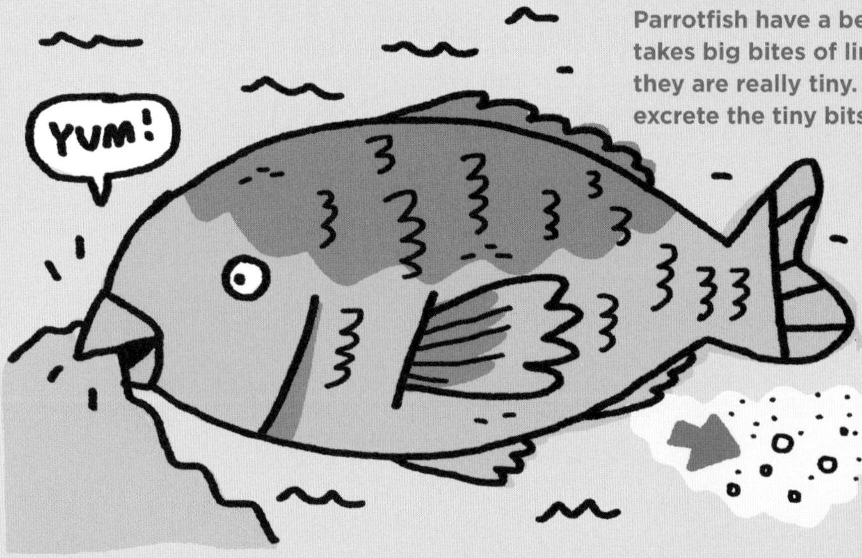
YUM!

Parrotfish have a beak so strong they can bite through rock! It takes big bites of limestone and polyps and crushes them up until they are really tiny. They keep the polyps as food and . . . um . . . excrete the tiny bits of limestone.

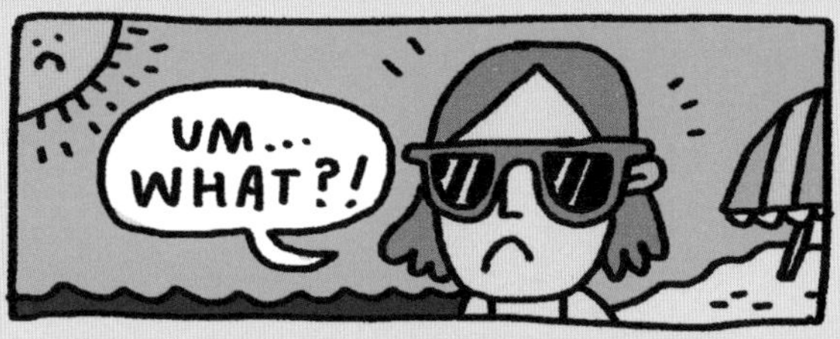
UM... WHAT?!

That means that the beautiful white sand beaches in your aunt's photos . . . were really just parrotfish poop!

In one year a parrotfish can make up to 1,000 pounds of sand! That's about the weight of a grand piano!

# SNOT ARMOR

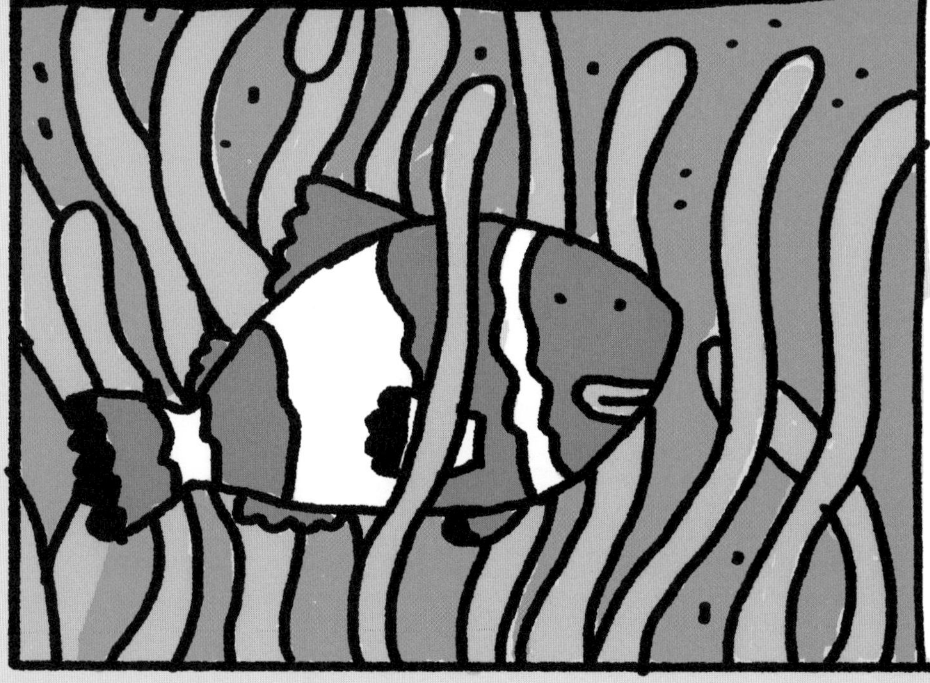

Clownfish have a protective layer of mucus that protects them from the poison of sea anemones. This lets them hide down in their tentacles from predators.

In return, the sea anemone eats little bits of food that the clownfish leaves after its meals. Clownfish also help clean the anemones.

# KELP FORESTS

Do you know what you call really big algae in the sea? Seaweed! Yep, seaweed isn't technically a plant, it's algae. Seaweed must live underwater, and there are areas where seaweed grow incredibly big. There it's called kelp, and it grows so dense that it's like a forest.

The biggest kelp forests are off the coasts of Alaska and California.

Some forms of seaweed can live in water up to 130 feet deep as long as there is sunlight. A frond can be as long as 165 feet, which is about the height of the Arc de Triomphe in Paris!

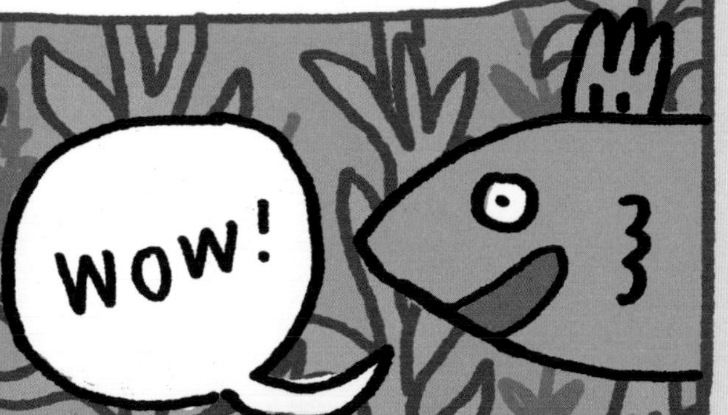
WOW!

Anchored! Kelp is able to hold onto the bottom of the ocean by clinging to rocks with a clawlike base called a holdfast. They look like roots, but don't help to nourish the plant the way that roots do.

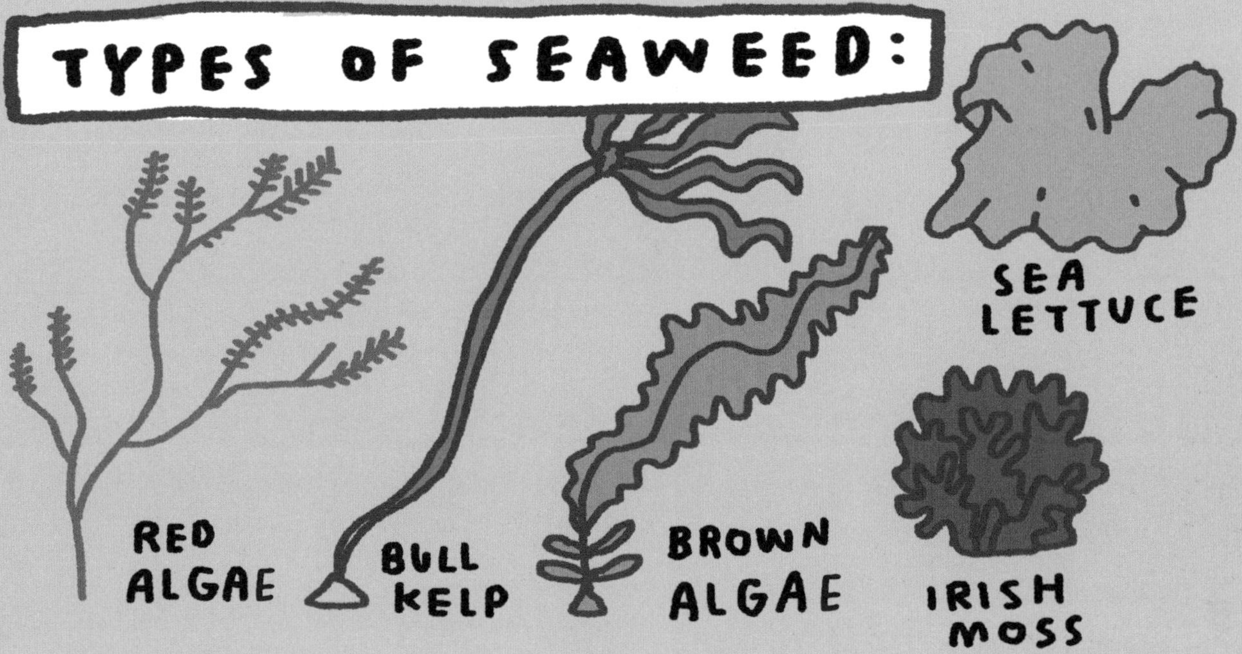
TYPES OF SEAWEED:
RED ALGAE
BULL KELP
BROWN ALGAE
SEA LETTUCE
IRISH MOSS

# SEA URCHIN

This isn't a pincushion! Sea urchins are actually little animals.

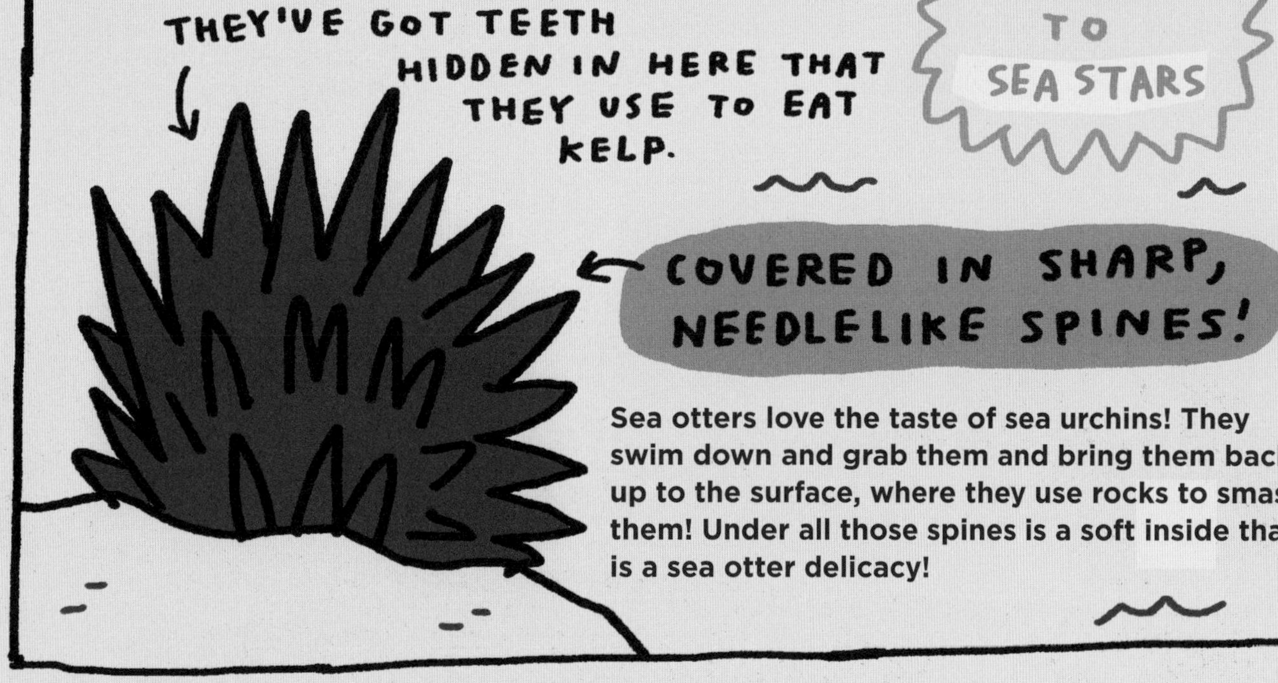
THEY'VE GOT TEETH HIDDEN IN HERE THAT THEY USE TO EAT KELP.
RELATED TO SEA STARS
COVERED IN SHARP, NEEDLELIKE SPINES!

Sea otters love the taste of sea urchins! They swim down and grab them and bring them back up to the surface, where they use rocks to smash them! Under all those spines is a soft inside that is a sea otter delicacy!

# DEEP SEA

**Take a deep breath because way down below the light layers of the ocean, life still manages to exist. And some of the weirdest and awesomest creatures live down there!**

## TWILIGHT ZONE

**650–3,000 feet deep**

### LANTERN FISH

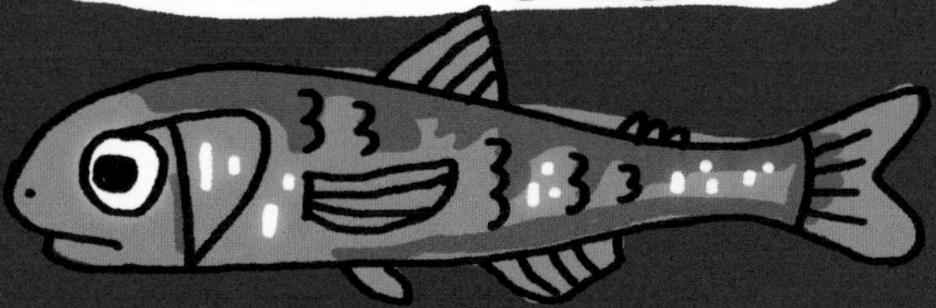

Lantern fish mostly live in the twilight zone, but will swim 1,500 feet up into areas with more light to feed on algae and plankton before returning at night. That's higher than the Empire State Building (and keep in mind the fish is only about 6–12 inches long)! This trip can take up to 3 hours each way. They like to spend their nights in the twilight zone as a way to not be seen by their predators. Since this happens all over the world, every single day, some scientists call it the biggest migration on Earth.

### HATCHETFISH

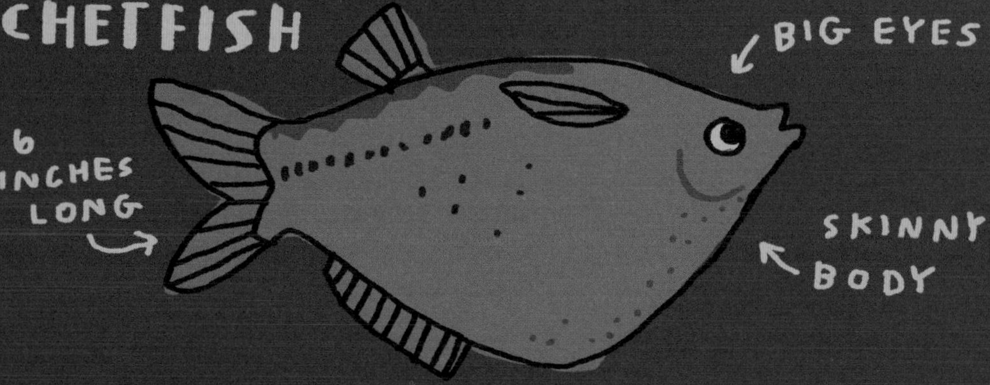
BIG EYES
6 INCHES LONG
SKINNY BODY

CHECK THIS OUT!

### OARFISH

**Doesn't have scales like other fish**

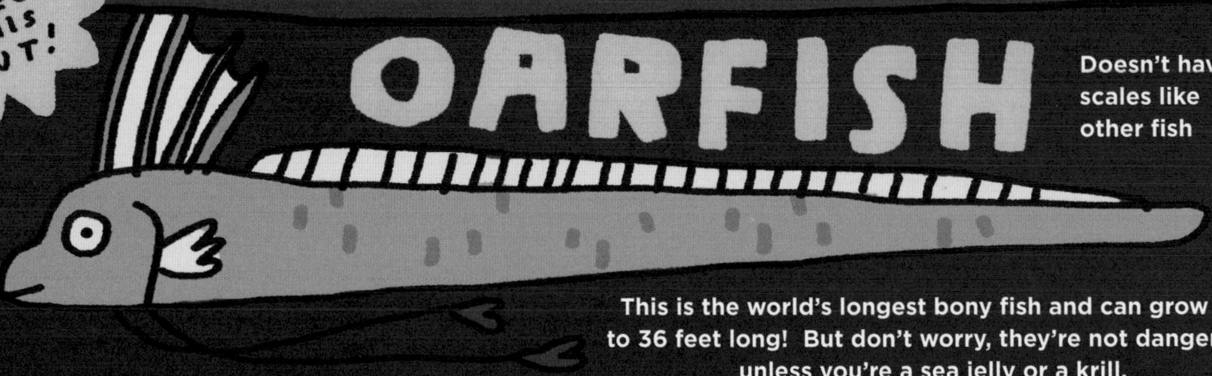

**This is the world's longest bony fish and can grow up to 36 feet long! But don't worry, they're not dangerous unless you're a sea jelly or a krill.**

# GLOWING CREATURES

Many of the animals down here have developed an odd way to attract prey. They have organs called photophores that emit energy as light. This is called

## BIOLUMINESCENCE.

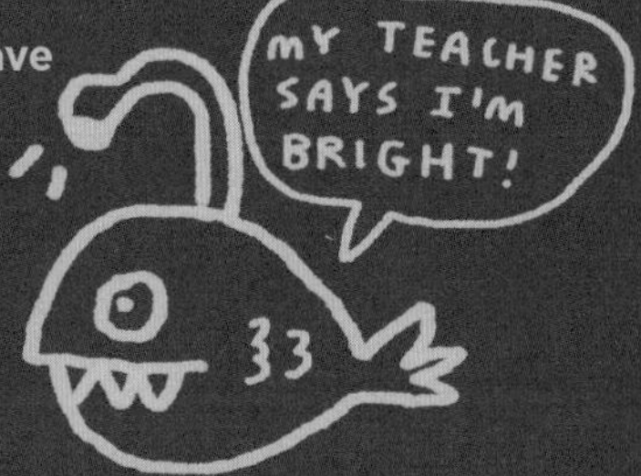
MY TEACHER SAYS I'M BRIGHT!

## FIREFLY SQUID

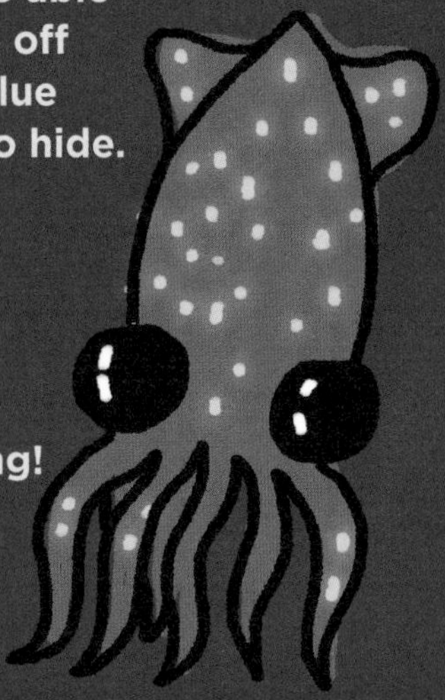

They're able to turn off their blue glow to hide.

Only 3 inches long!

Long tentacles covered in suckers

## VIPERFISH

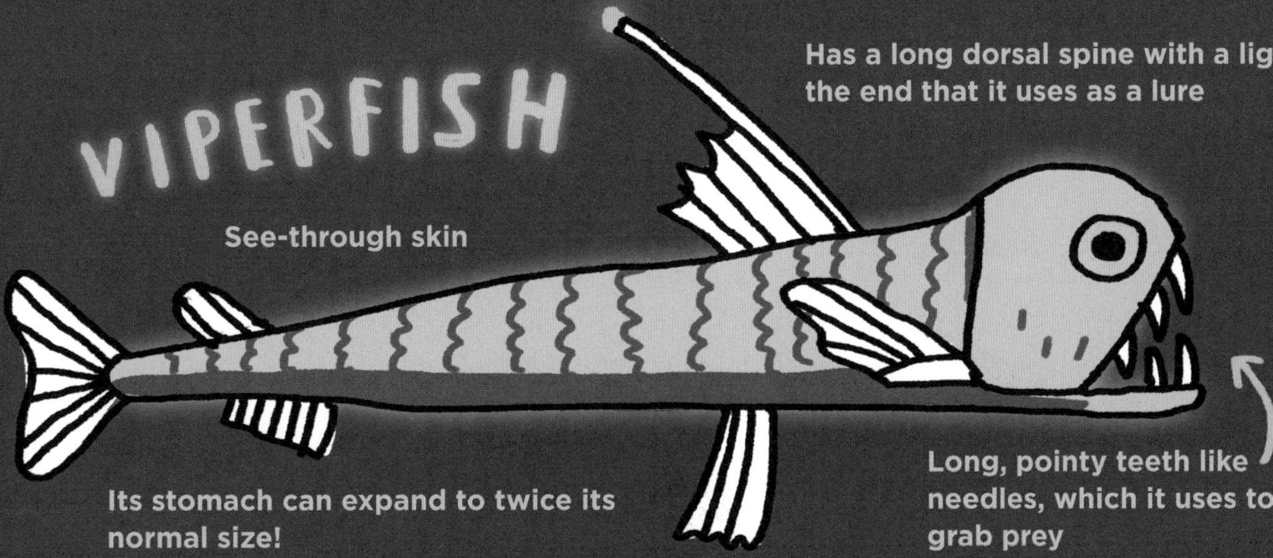

Has a long dorsal spine with a light on the end that it uses as a lure

See-through skin

Its stomach can expand to twice its normal size!

Long, pointy teeth like needles, which it uses to grab prey

# DARK ZONE

## TERRIBLE CLAW LOBSTER!

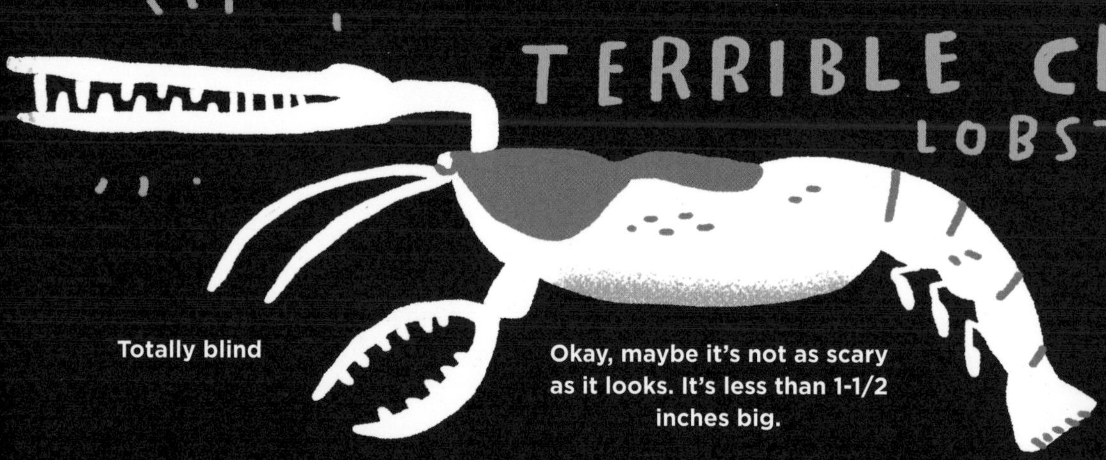

Totally blind

Okay, maybe it's not as scary as it looks. It's less than 1-1/2 inches big.

## ANGLER-FISH

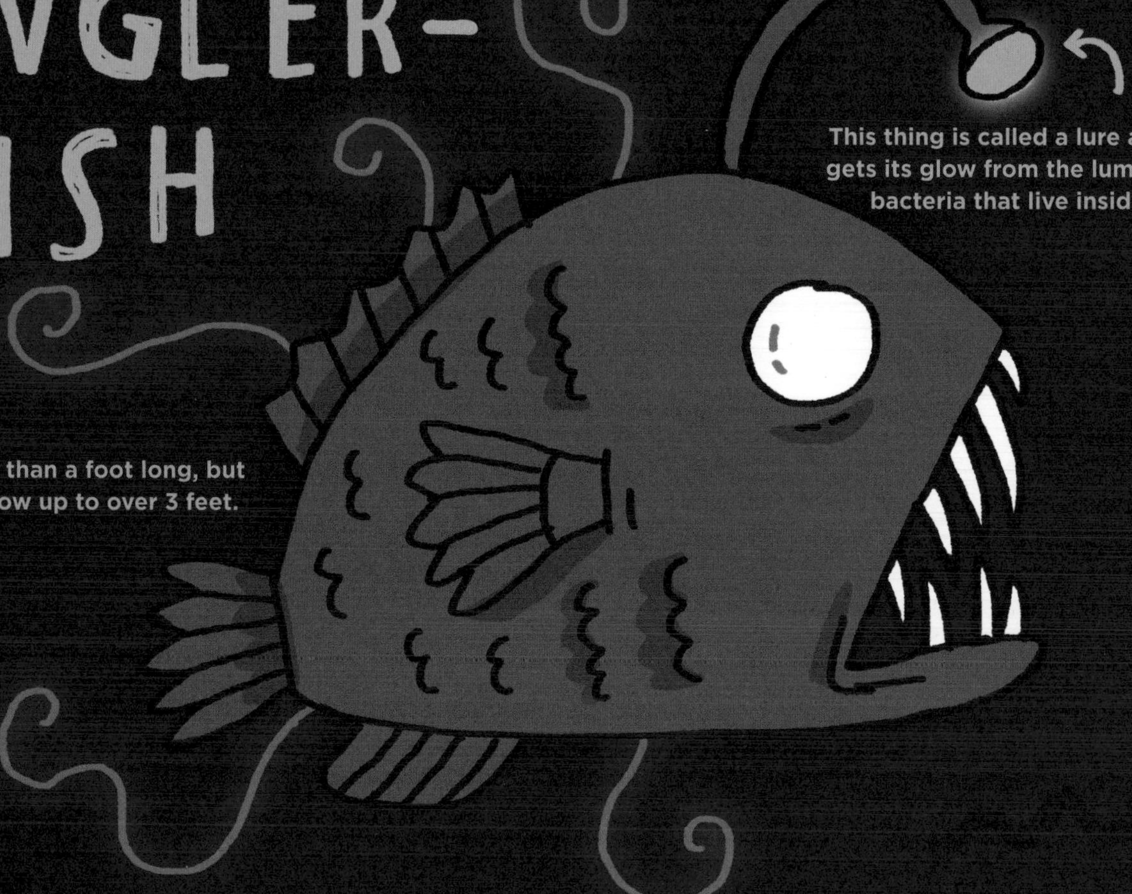

This thing is called a lure and it gets its glow from the luminous bacteria that live inside!

Most are less than a foot long, but some can grow up to over 3 feet.

# VAMPIRE SQUID

Grows up to 1 foot long

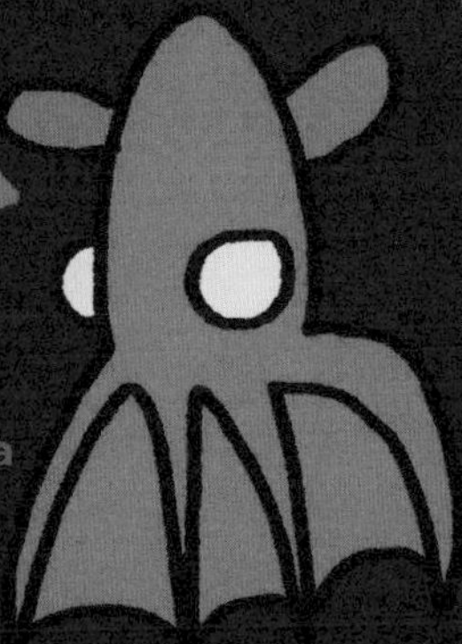

Only has to eat a few times a week

It gets its name from its dark red coloring and its webbing that looks like a cloak a vampire would wear!

Doesn't shoot out ink like most squids, instead it shoots out a kind of mucus when it's startled or threatened. Sometimes they can shoot it out for up to ten minutes, which allows them to get away since they aren't very fast swimmers.

# GULPER EEL

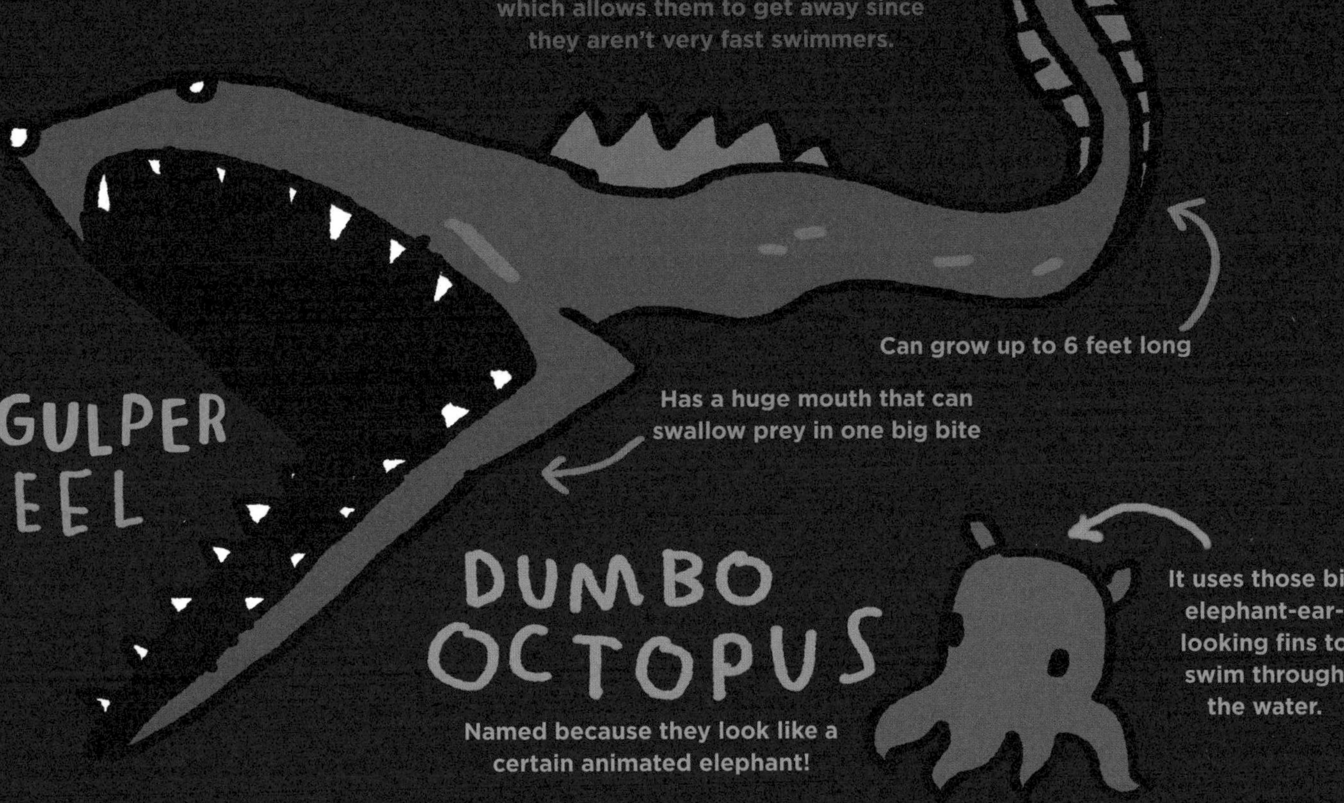

Can grow up to 6 feet long

Has a huge mouth that can swallow prey in one big bite

# DUMBO OCTOPUS

It uses those big elephant-ear-looking fins to swim through the water.

Named because they look like a certain animated elephant!

Most are about 12 inches long, but one was found that was over 5 feet long.

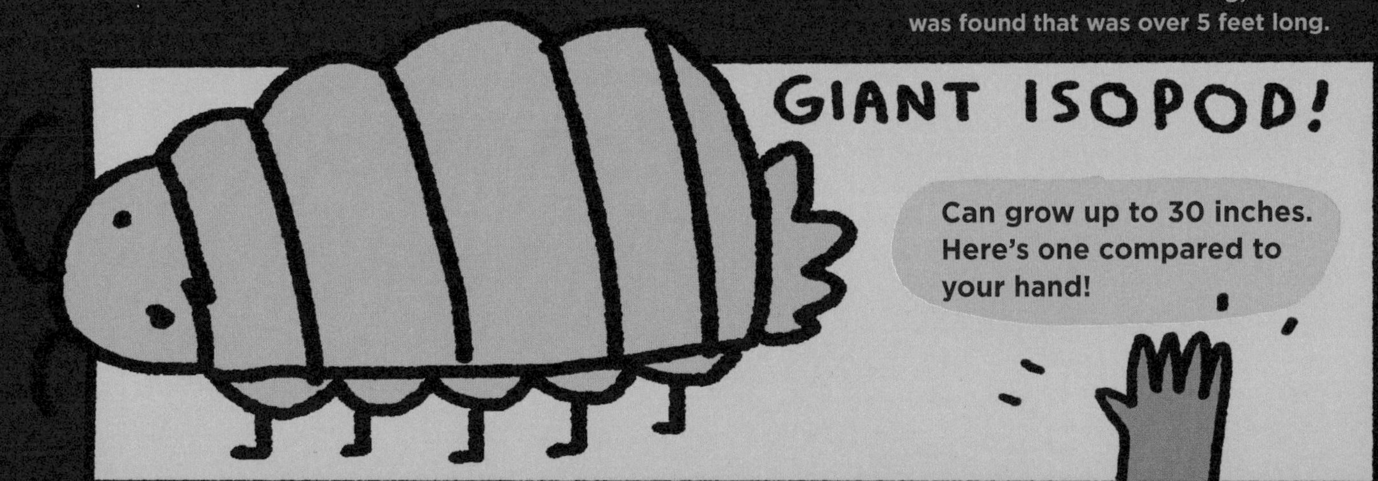
GIANT ISOPOD!
Can grow up to 30 inches. Here's one compared to your hand!

# DEEP SEA BATTLE!

**Lots of the animals down in this spooky dark zone are really small, but there are a few GIANT creatures down here, too.**

## SPERM WHALE

They like to live closer to the surface but can make extreme dives in search of giant squids!

They like to eat all kinds of squid and some can eat up to 800 A DAY!

They produce a waxy substance called spermaceti, which helps them with long-distance communication! It was also used as fuel for candles and lanterns in the 1700s until kerosene lamps were developed!

Can weigh up to 130,000 pounds. That's 9 times heavier than a T. REX!

They can hold their breath for 90 minutes!

They can communicate with other sperm whales with loud clicks!

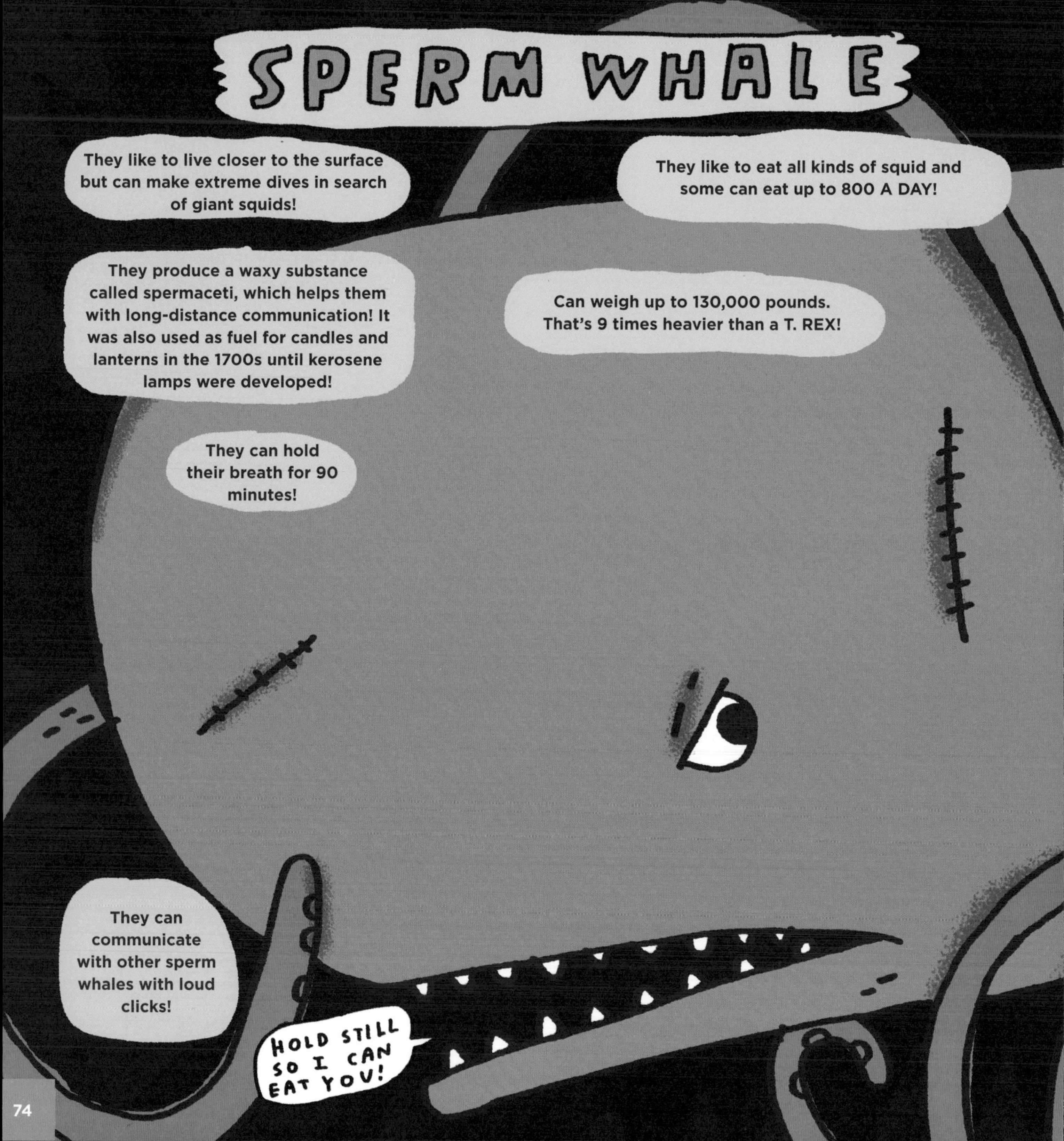
HOLD STILL SO I CAN EAT YOU!

# GIANT SQUID

Has a doughnut-shaped brain!

Some scientists believe that there are MILLIONS of giant squids in the ocean!

HUGE, 11-INCH EYES! That's the size of a dinner plate!

Has three hearts!

Some have been known to grow up to 43 feet long. Which means they're as long as a brachiosaurus is tall! Or more than TWICE as tall as a giraffe!

You'd think something this huge would have it easy way down here, but think again. They're eaten by the even bigger SPERM WHALE. But they don't die without a fight! The squids have strong, sharp beaks and sharp-toothed suckers on their tentacles!

Can regrow tentacles that they lose!

Grab your winter coat! We are headed into...

# POLAR WATER

BRRR!

During winter months, there's very little sunlight in the Arctic and Antarctic. The temperatures drop below freezing and can even go as low as -133.6 degrees in Antarctica. This means the surfaces of the oceans turn into large, dense areas of ice. When the sun comes back in the summer, lots of the ice melts, which causes plankton growth to BOOM! This attracts other marine life that eat the plankton.

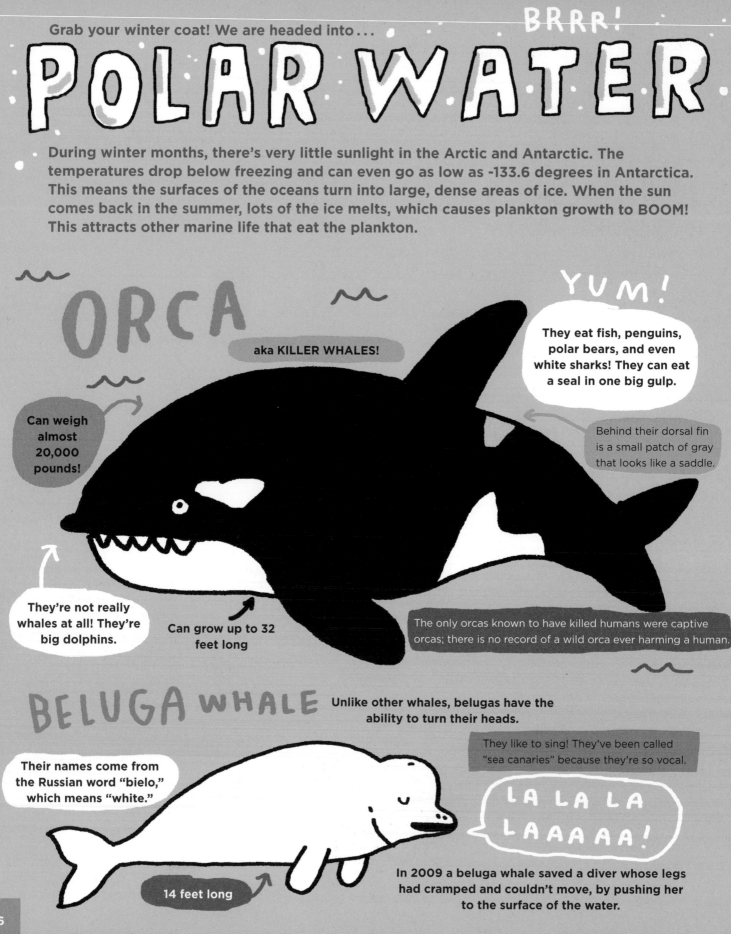

## ORCA

aka KILLER WHALES!

YUM!

They eat fish, penguins, polar bears, and even white sharks! They can eat a seal in one big gulp.

Can weigh almost 20,000 pounds!

Behind their dorsal fin is a small patch of gray that looks like a saddle.

They're not really whales at all! They're big dolphins.

Can grow up to 32 feet long

The only orcas known to have killed humans were captive orcas; there is no record of a wild orca ever harming a human.

## BELUGA WHALE

Unlike other whales, belugas have the ability to turn their heads.

They like to sing! They've been called "sea canaries" because they're so vocal.

Their names come from the Russian word "bielo," which means "white."

LA LA LA LAAAAA!

14 feet long

In 2009 a beluga whale saved a diver whose legs had cramped and couldn't move, by pushing her to the surface of the water.

# NARWHAL

THE SWIMMING UNICORN!

Its tusk can grow 10 feet long!

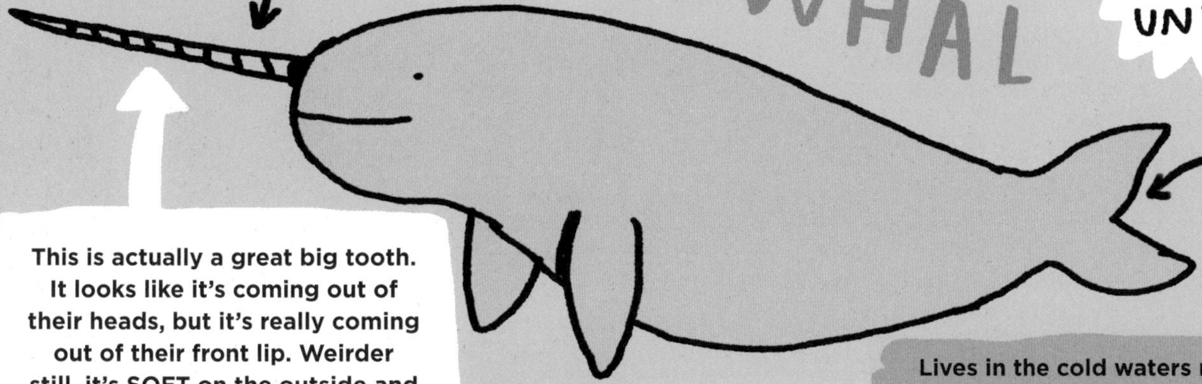

This is actually a great big tooth. It looks like it's coming out of their heads, but it's really coming out of their front lip. Weirder still, it's SOFT on the outside and has a rigid interior.

Eats squid, fish, and shrimp

Lives in the cold waters near Canada, Greenland, Norway, and Russia.

# ONLY 10%

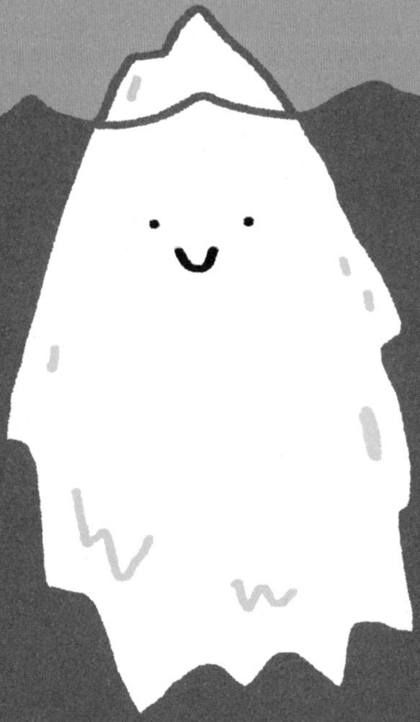

OF AN ICEBERG CAN BE SEEN OVER THE SURFACE OF THE WATER!

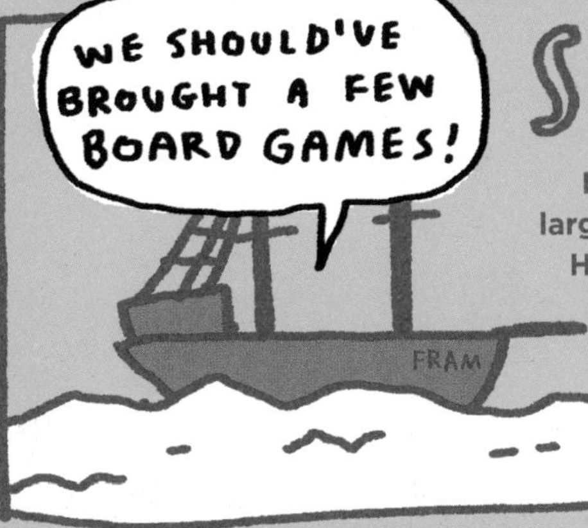
WE SHOULD'VE BROUGHT A FEW BOARD GAMES!
FRAM

# STUCK IN ICE!

In the 1800s an explorer set out to prove that polar ice drifted over large areas. He did so by letting his ship, *Fram*, become frozen in the ice! He stayed stuck there for three years while he floated over the North Pole, until he finally got free near Norway.

# HYDROTHERMAL VENTS

## BLACK SMOKERS

They might look like underwater factory smokestacks, but they are hydrothermal vents that are created when seawater makes its way through cracks at the boundaries of the tectonic plates. The seawater is heated up by molten rock and then it's shot back up into the ocean at up to 650 degrees.

Sounds like pretty terrible living conditions, right? Well, some weird creatures call it home.

## POMPEII WORMS

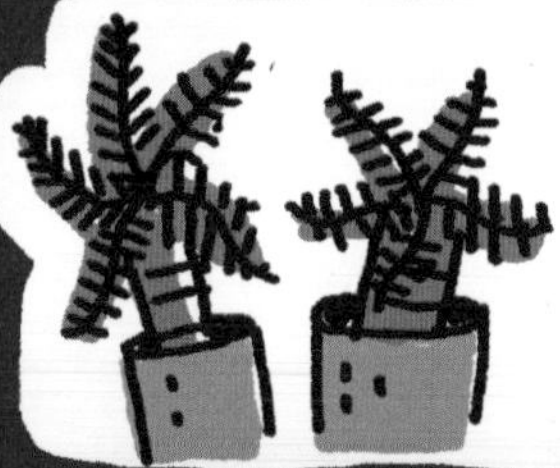

Live in tubes anchored to the sides of the vents

5 inches long

## GIANT TUBE WORMS

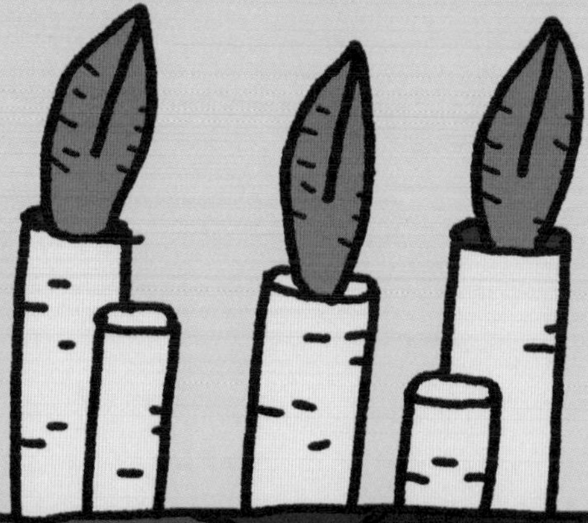

Can grow up to 6-7 feet long

They're not really worms. They're mollusks (like snails and slugs).

The vents can be up to 180 feet tall. That's about as tall as the Leaning Tower of Pisa!

WARNING!!!

# PART FOUR

# THE WEIRDEST AND DEADLIEST SEA CREATURES

CAUTION!

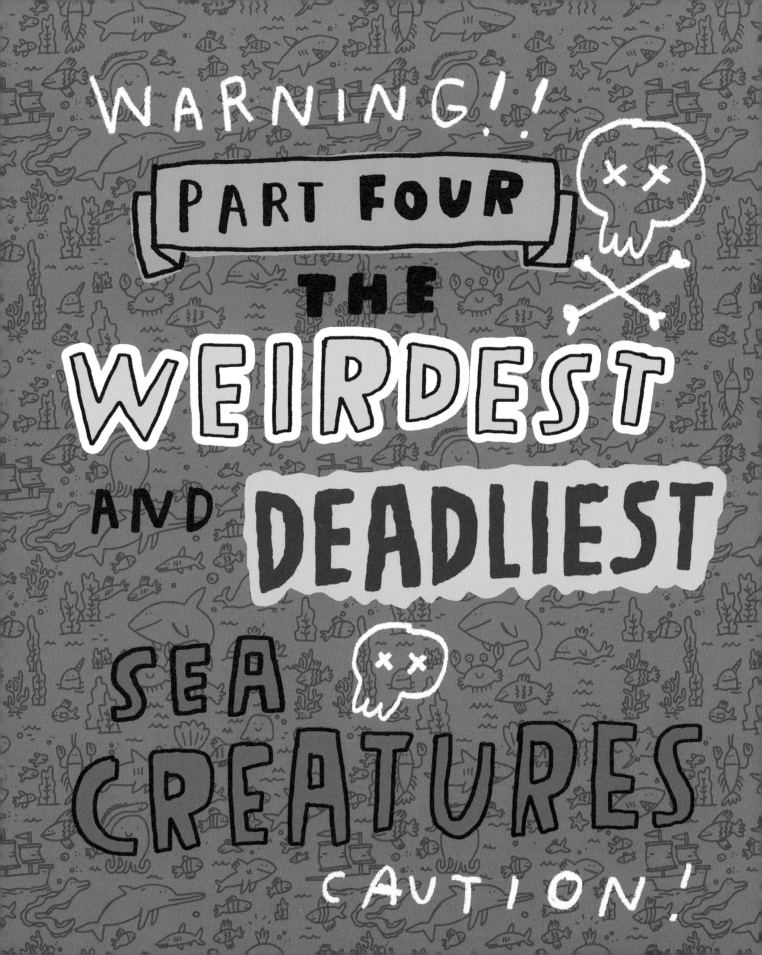

# LIONFISH

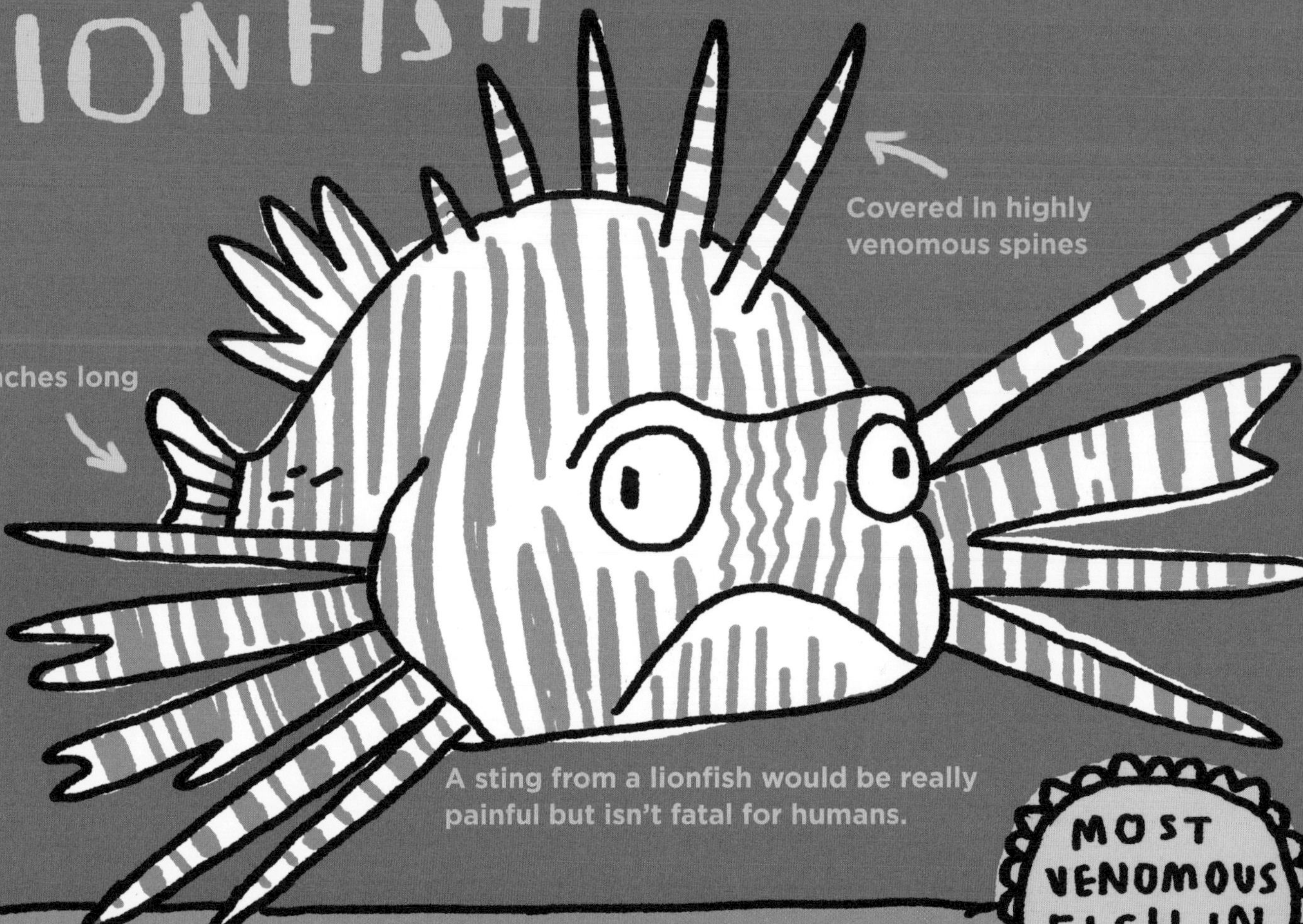

Covered in highly venomous spines

15 inches long

A sting from a lionfish would be really painful but isn't fatal for humans.

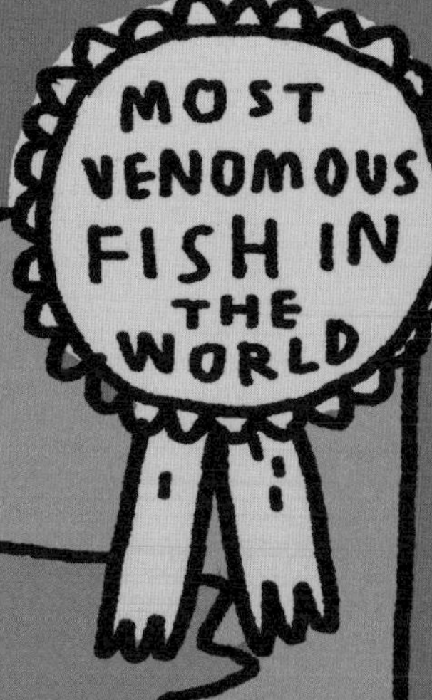
MOST VENOMOUS FISH IN THE WORLD

# STONEFISH

Its poison can paralyze you or even kill you.

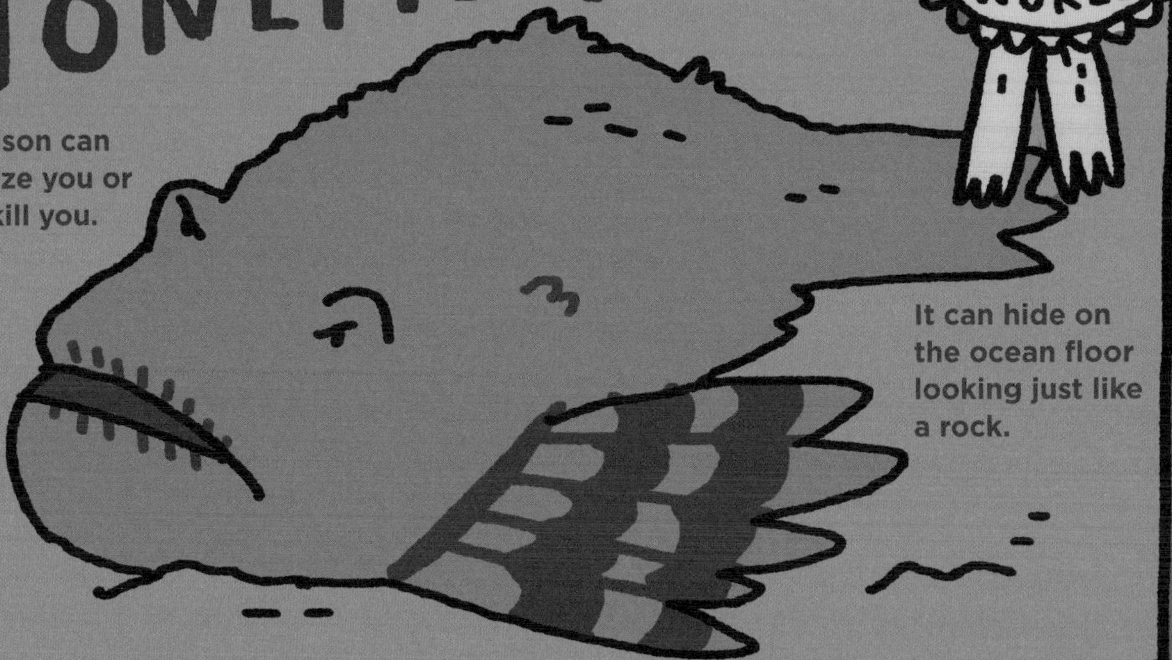

It can hide on the ocean floor looking just like a rock.

# KILLER SNAIL?!

## CONE SNAIL

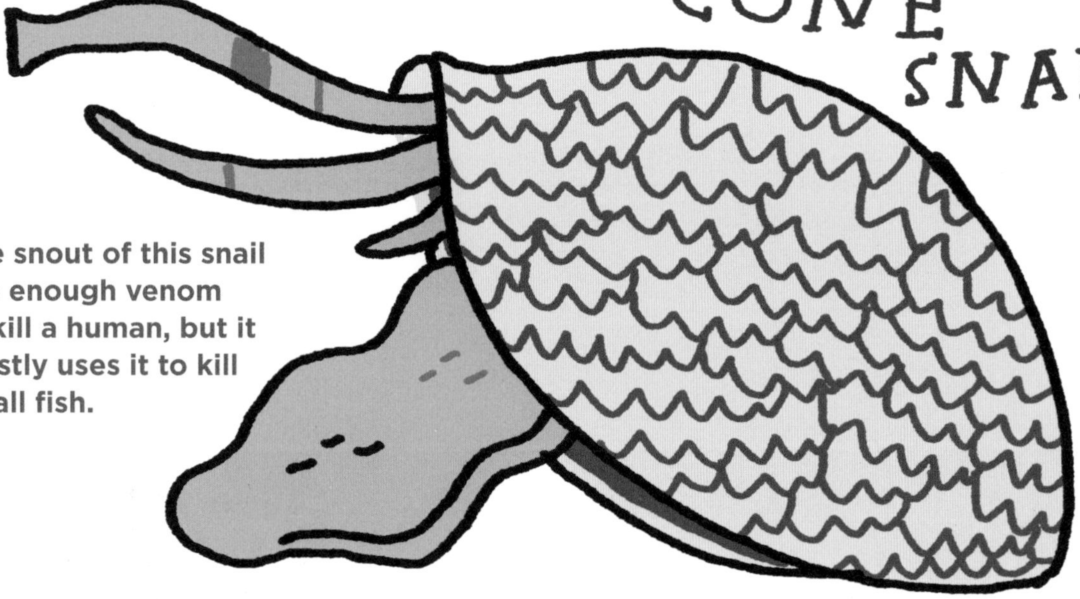

The snout of this snail has enough venom to kill a human, but it mostly uses it to kill small fish.

Mostly found in tropical coral reefs

## OYSTER TOAD FISH

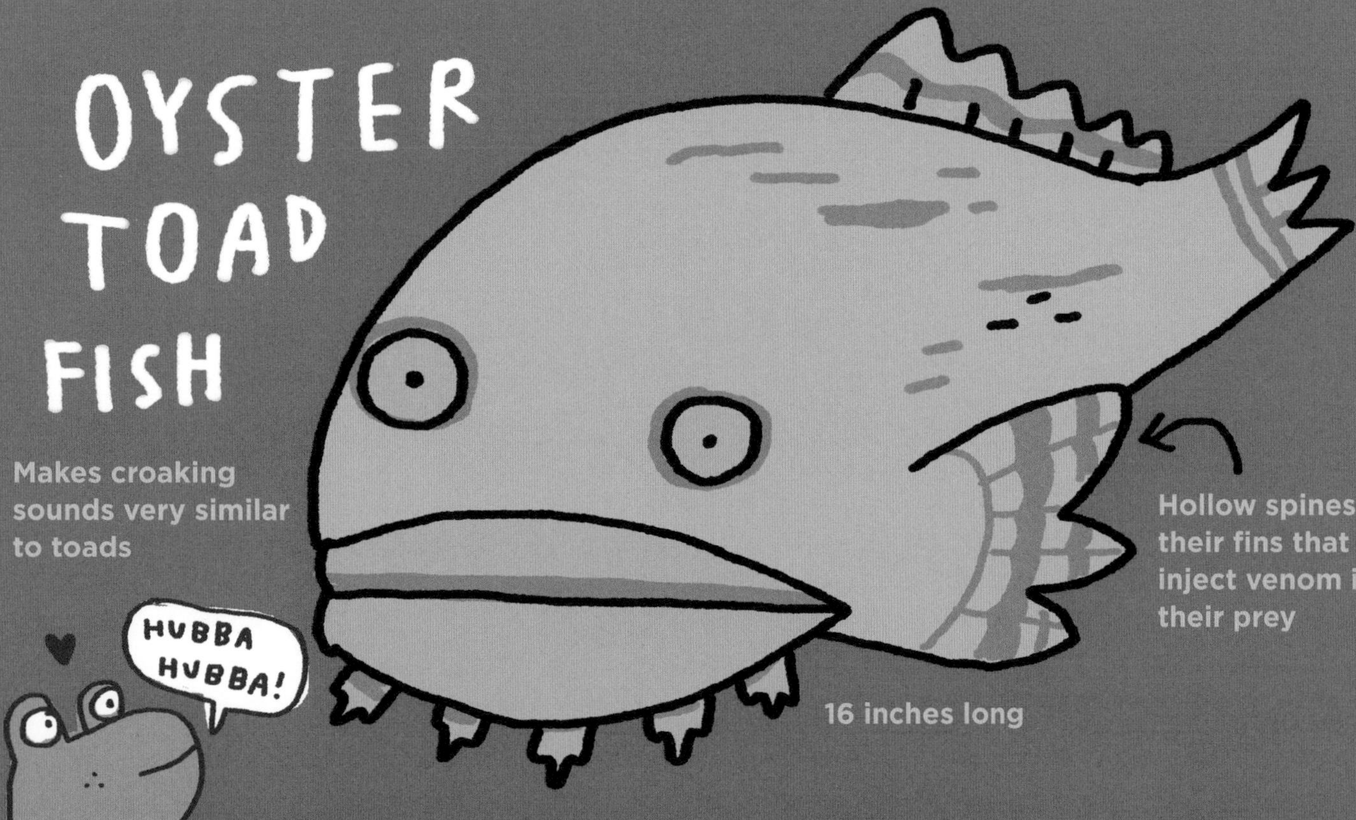

HUBBA HUBBA!


Makes croaking sounds very similar to toads

Hollow spines on their fins that can inject venom into their prey

16 inches long

# INDONESIAN NEEDLEFISH

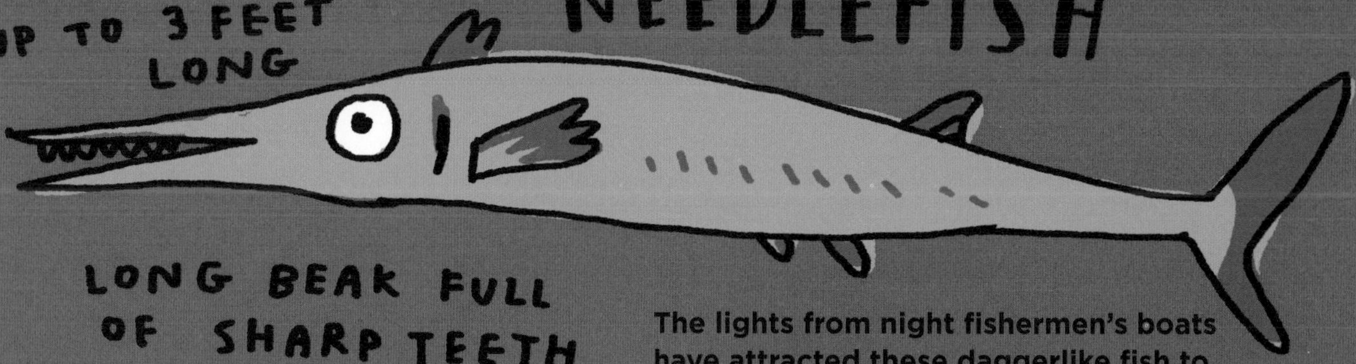
UP TO 3 FEET LONG
LONG BEAK FULL OF SHARP TEETH

The lights from night fishermen's boats have attracted these daggerlike fish to jump out of the water and strike them.

# YELLOW SEA ANEMONE

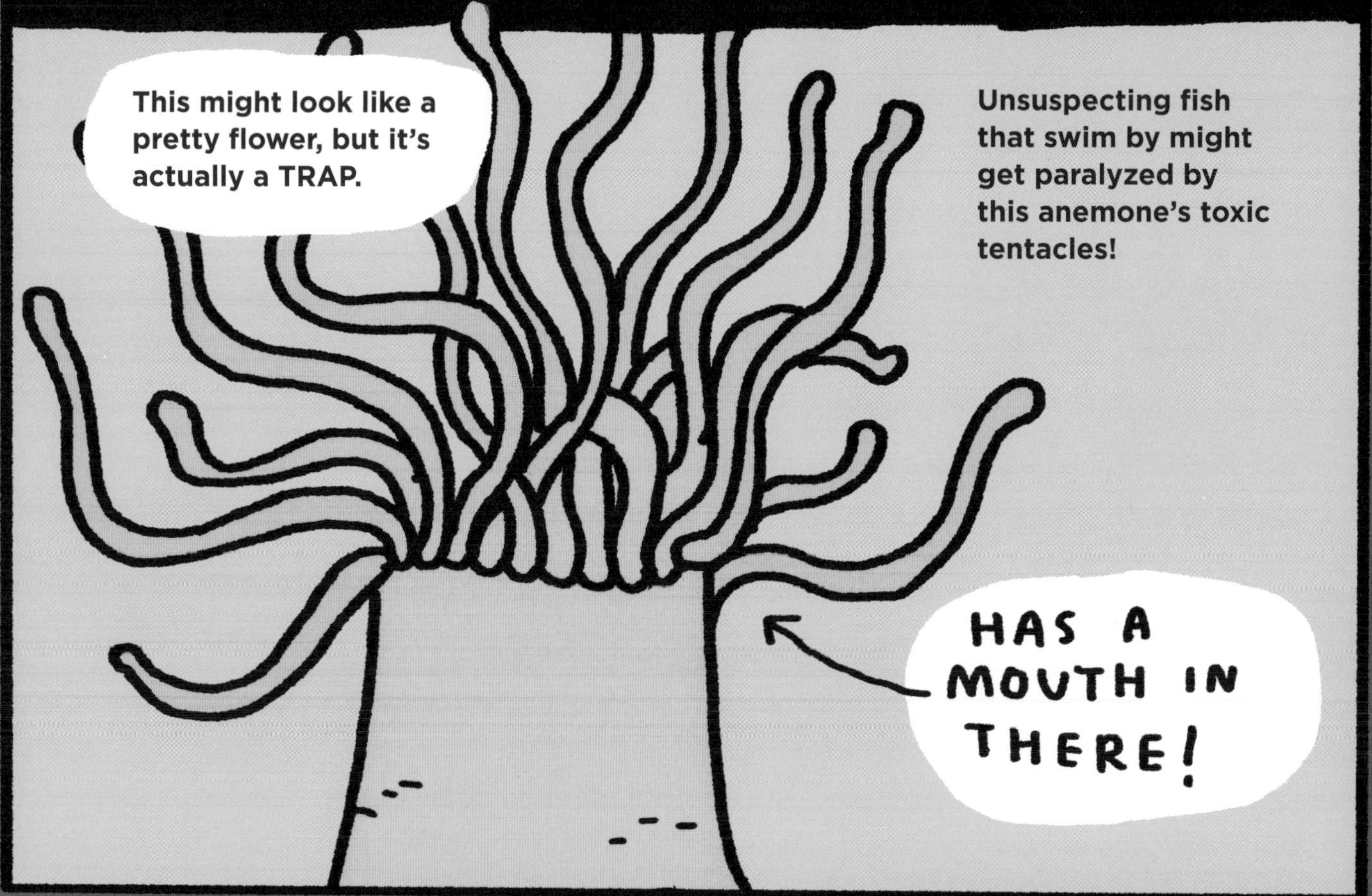
HAS A MOUTH IN THERE!

This might look like a pretty flower, but it's actually a TRAP.

Unsuspecting fish that swim by might get paralyzed by this anemone's toxic tentacles!

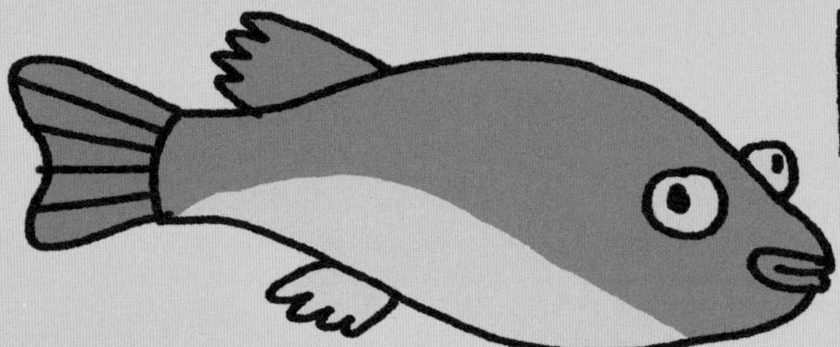

# PUFFER FISH

If they sense danger, they can suck in water and swell up to twice their normal size.

CONTAINS A POISON MORE DEADLY THAN CYANIDE!

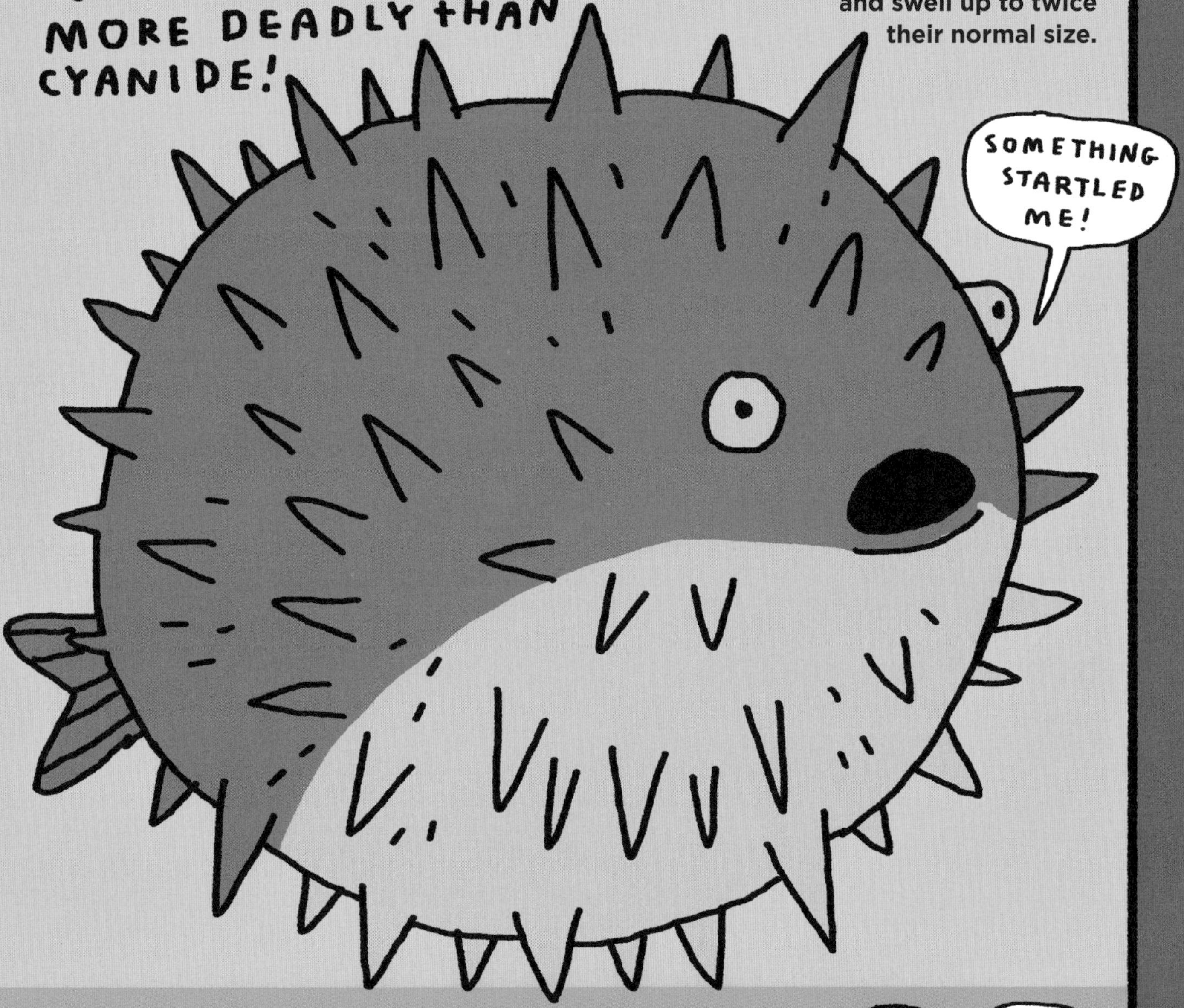
SOMETHING STARTLED ME!

And yet for some reason some people want to eat it. In Japan there are specially trained chefs who cook and serve puffer fish, and if not prepared correctly, the diner could die.

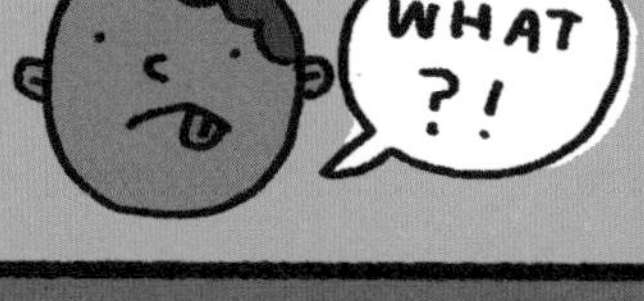
WHAT ?!

# OCTOPUS

The blue-ringed octopus has enough poison to paralyze a human.

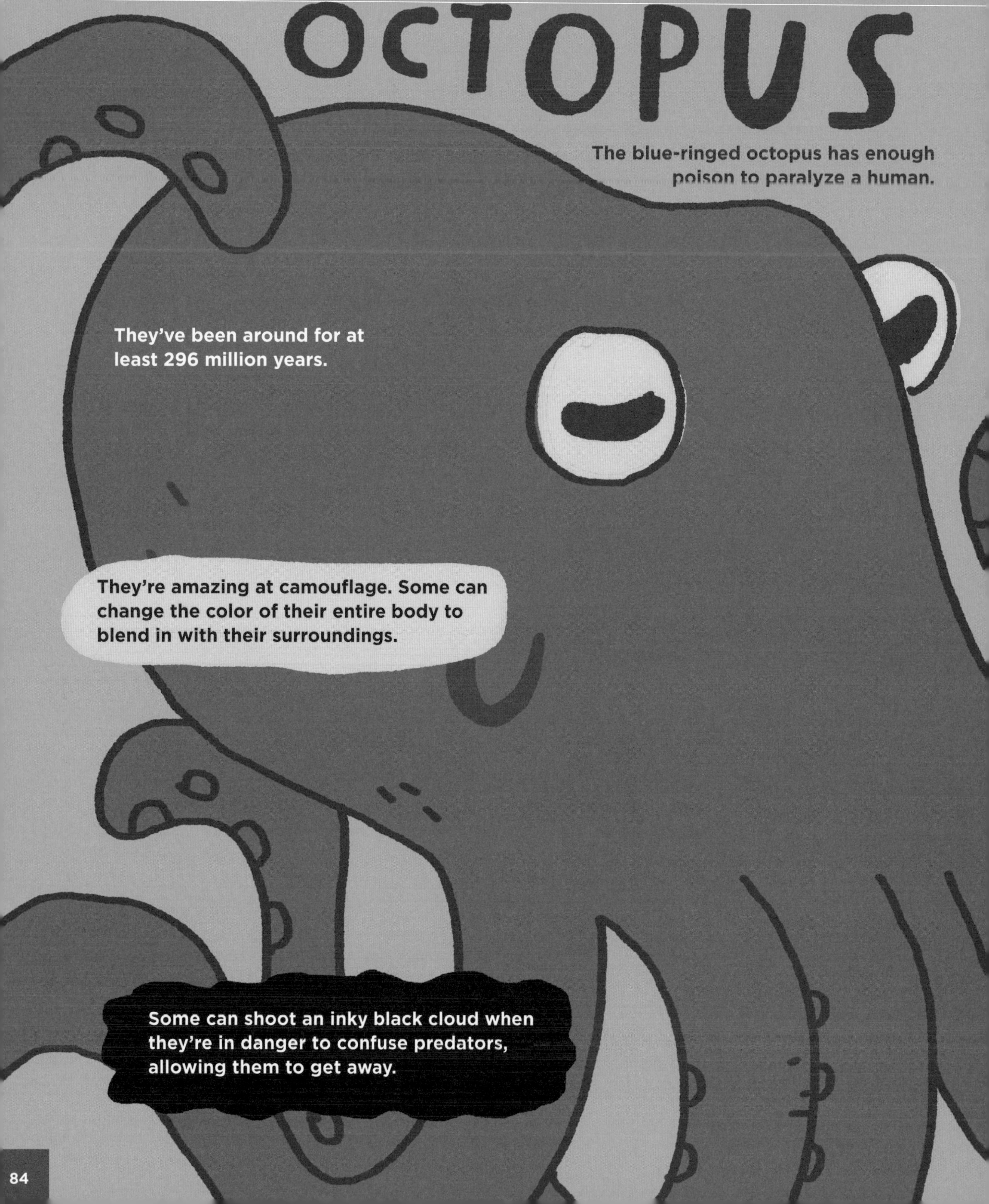

They've been around for at least 296 million years.

They're amazing at camouflage. Some can change the color of their entire body to blend in with their surroundings.

Some can shoot an inky black cloud when they're in danger to confuse predators, allowing them to get away.

# OCTOPUSES, OCTOPI, OR OCTOPODES?

**How do you say more than one octopus?! It's a debate that's been going on for a long time, and to find the answer . . . it's a little complicated. Due to its Greek origin, the word could be pluralized as "octopodes" OR "octopi." But according to Merriam-Webster and the Oxford English Dictionary, the version that is more correct in modern-day English is "octopuses." However, they also mention that "octopi" is an acceptable way to say it as well.**

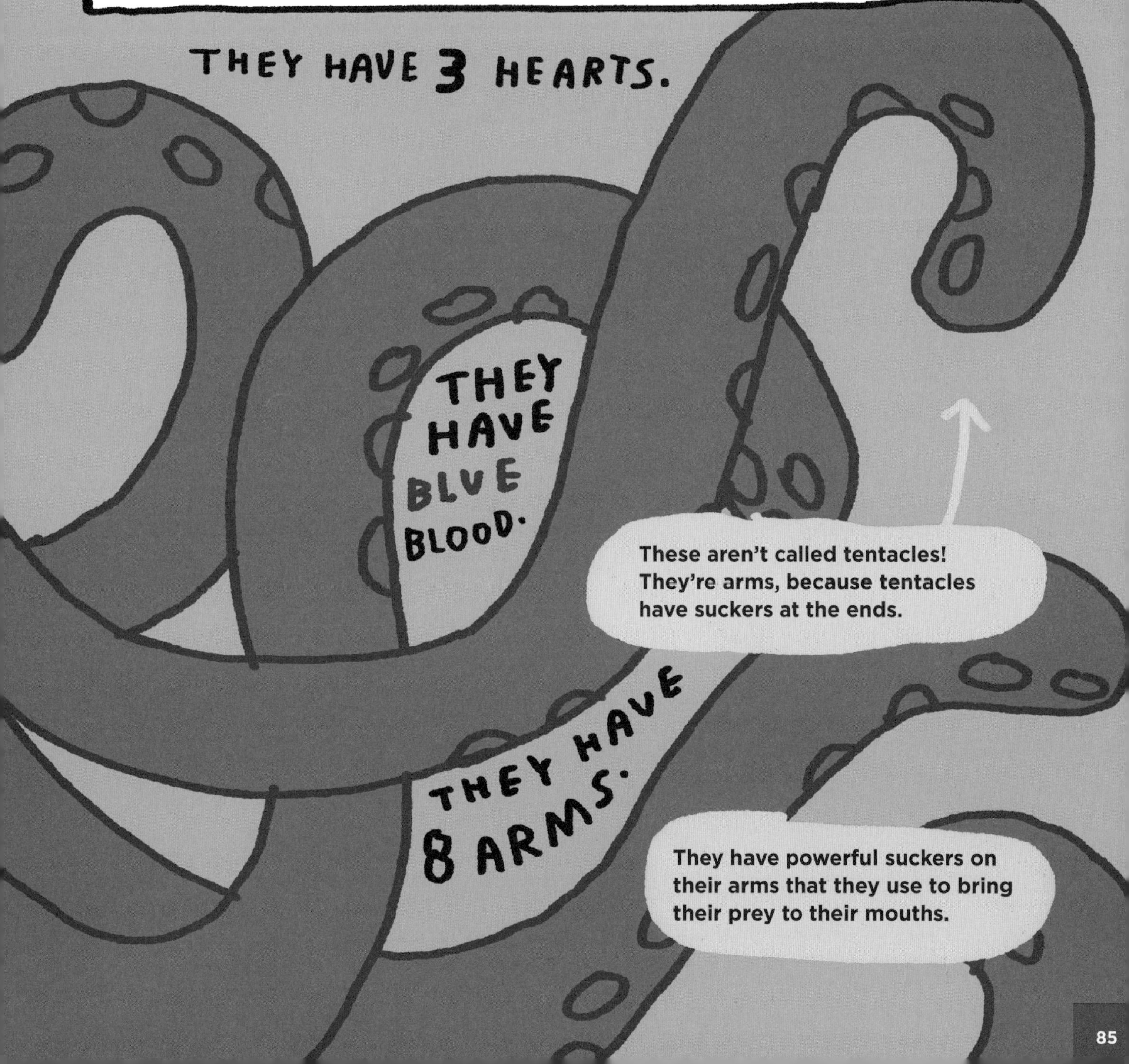
THEY HAVE 3 HEARTS.
THEY HAVE BLUE BLOOD.
These aren't called tentacles! They're arms, because tentacles have suckers at the ends.
THEY HAVE 8 ARMS.
They have powerful suckers on their arms that they use to bring their prey to their mouths.

# MORAY EEL

They're not related to snakes, they're fish.

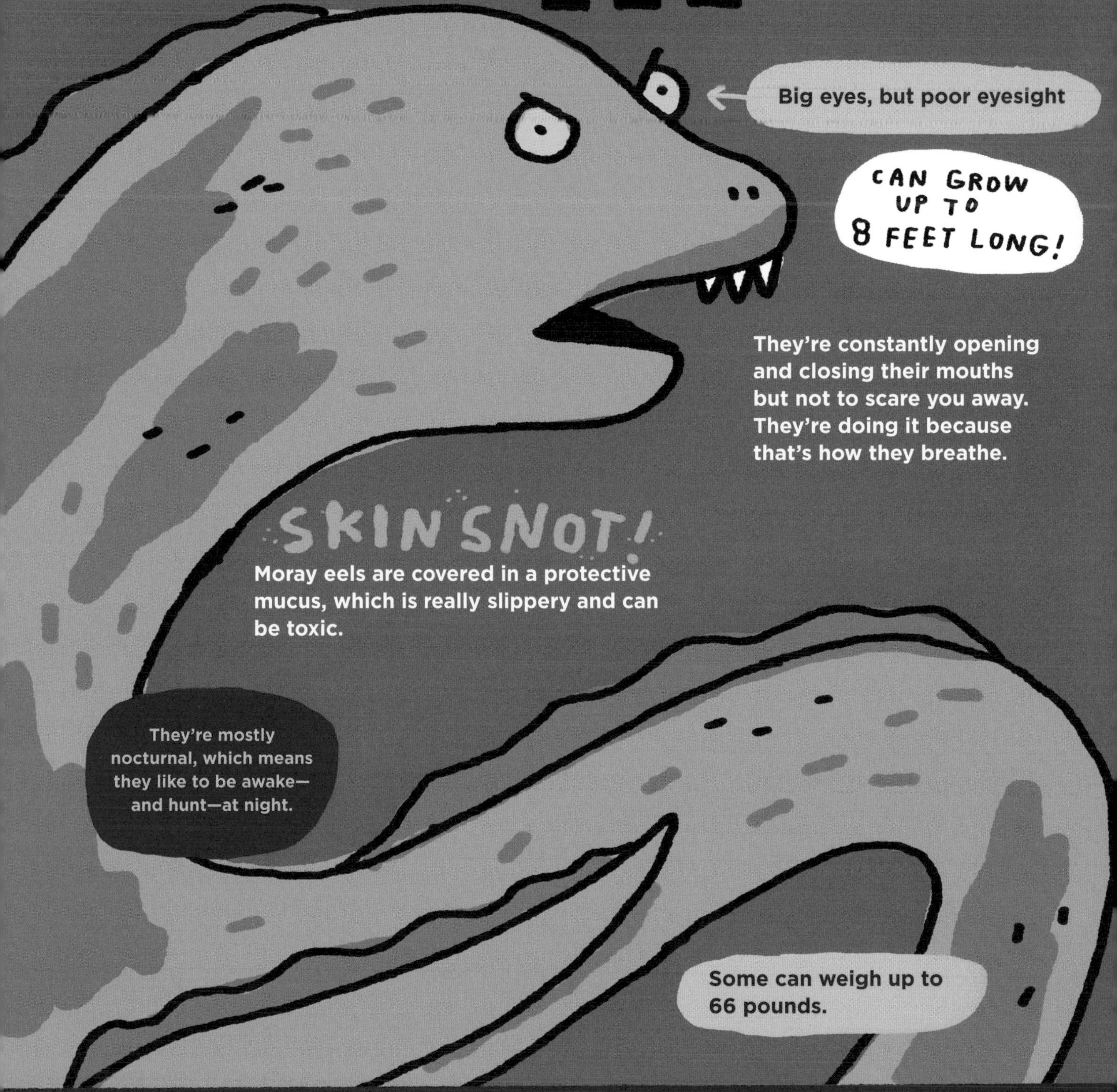

Big eyes, but poor eyesight

CAN GROW UP TO 8 FEET LONG!

They're constantly opening and closing their mouths but not to scare you away. They're doing it because that's how they breathe.

## SKIN SNOT!

Moray eels are covered in a protective mucus, which is really slippery and can be toxic.

They're mostly nocturnal, which means they like to be awake—and hunt—at night.

Some can weigh up to 66 pounds.

THEY HAVE TWO SETS OF JAWS! ONE SET IS HIDDEN AND COMES OUT WHEN THEY ATTACK.

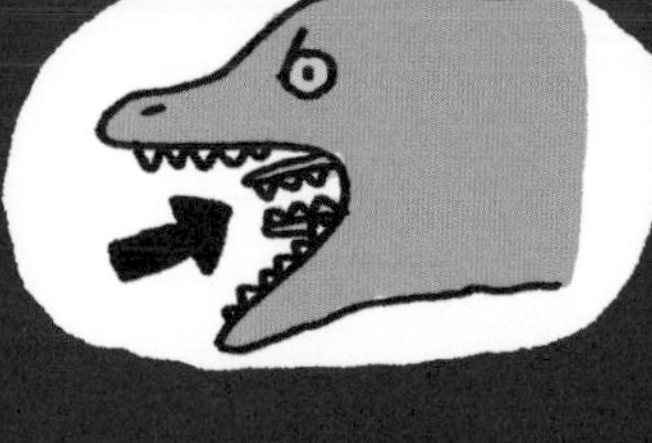

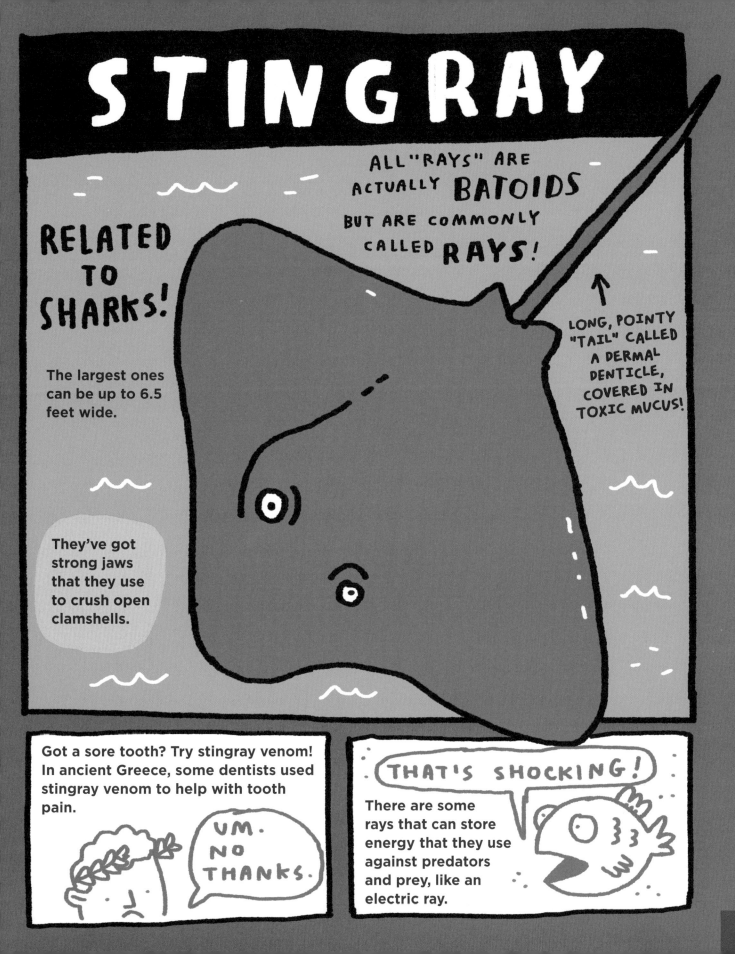

# STINGRAY

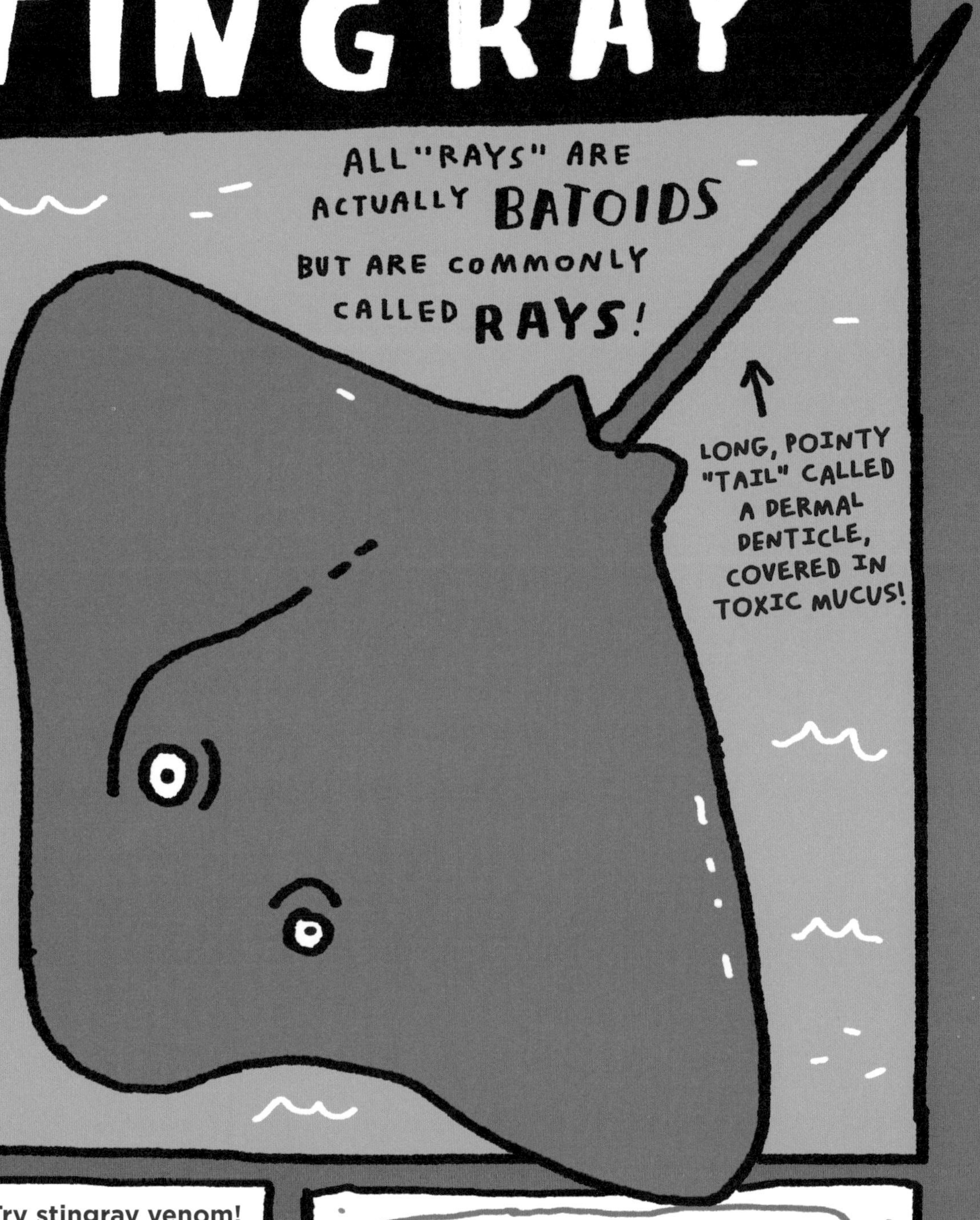
ALL "RAYS" ARE ACTUALLY BATOIDS BUT ARE COMMONLY CALLED RAYS!
RELATED TO SHARKS!
LONG, POINTY "TAIL" CALLED A DERMAL DENTICLE, COVERED IN TOXIC MUCUS!

The largest ones can be up to 6.5 feet wide.

They've got strong jaws that they use to crush open clamshells.

Got a sore tooth? Try stingray venom! In ancient Greece, some dentists used stingray venom to help with tooth pain.

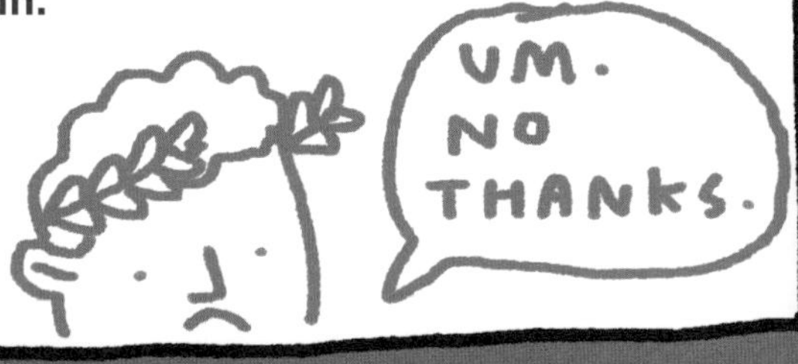
UM. NO THANKS.

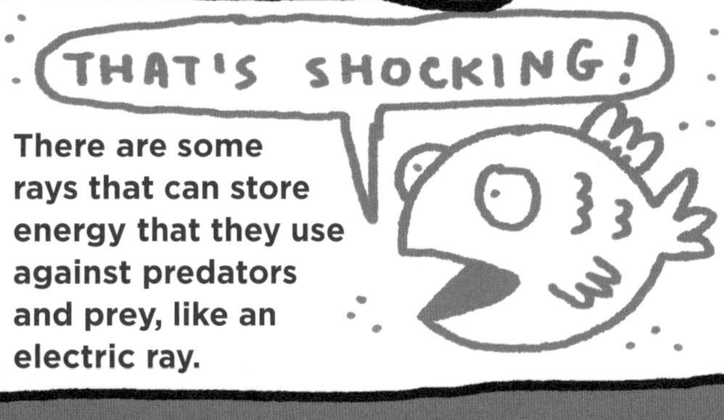
THAT'S SHOCKING!

There are some rays that can store energy that they use against predators and prey, like an electric ray.

# SEA JELLIES

They're 98% water.

They evolved MILLIONS of years before the dinosaurs.

Don't call them fish! Scientists now call jellyfish "sea jellies" to avoid someone mistakenly thinking they are a type of fish. (It's also why we've started calling starfish "sea stars!")

A group of sea jellies is called a BLOOM or a SWARM.

Some can have tentacles up to 98 feet long.

NASA has been sending sea jellies into space since the 1990s to study how zero gravity might affect them.

They have one opening that they eat and poop with.

It's estimated that at least 100 people die a year from their stings, which means they kill more people annually than sharks.

SEA JELLY CANDY?! In a town called Obama, Japan, one group is fighting a massive sea jelly invasion by harvesting them, boiling them down, and turning them into CANDY.

# I'M NOT A SEA JELLY!

PORTUGUESE MAN O' WAR

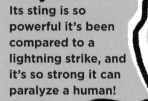

Its sting is so powerful it's been compared to a lightning strike, and it's so strong it can paralyze a human!

They can be found in warm water all over the world, sometimes swarming in groups of up to 1,000!

This might look like a sea jelly (and it gets confused for one a lot), but it's actually a floating

**SUPERORGANISM**

of thousands of little individual creatures. They can't survive on their own so they team up.

Tentacles can be up to 165 feet long

## OUCH!!

Even after a tentacle has been detached for several days, it can still sting you.

# BLUE WHALE

IT'S THE BIGGEST ANIMAL THAT'S EVER LIVED ON THIS PLANET!

Its tongue can weigh as much as an elephant!

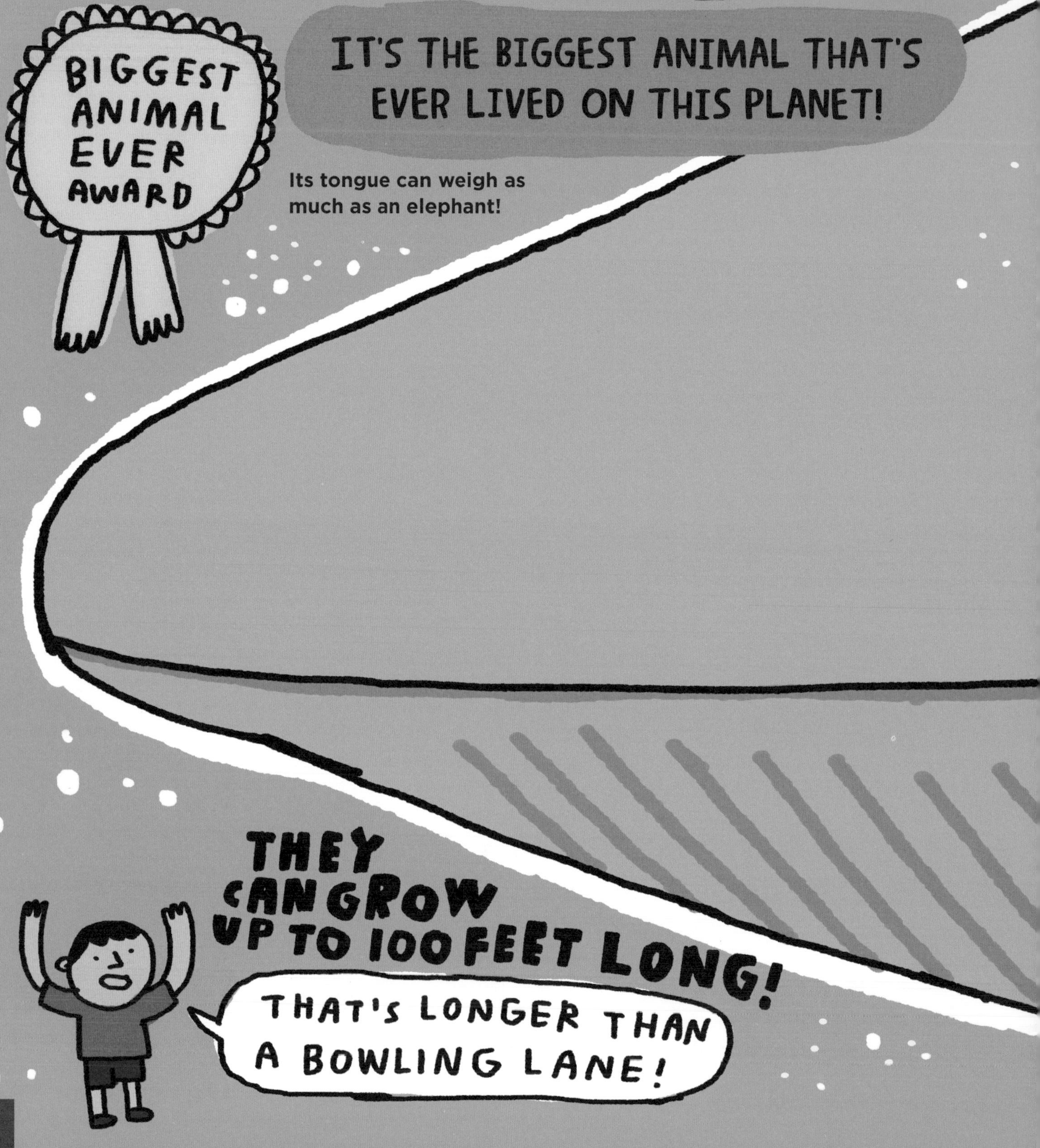
BIGGEST ANIMAL EVER AWARD
THEY CAN GROW UP TO 100 FEET LONG!
THAT'S LONGER THAN A BOWLING LANE!

They can swim up to 20 miles per hour!

# THEY'VE GOT A LOT OF HEART!

A blue whale's heart is 5 feet long and 4 feet wide and weighs a whopping 400 pounds. It only beats 8–10 times per minute!

They can live up to 100 years!

They can weigh up to 144,000 pounds!

# MORE WHALE FACTS!

## UNDERWATER NOISES.

Did you know that sound travels four times faster underwater?

This is how some animals are able to call each other even when they're really far apart.

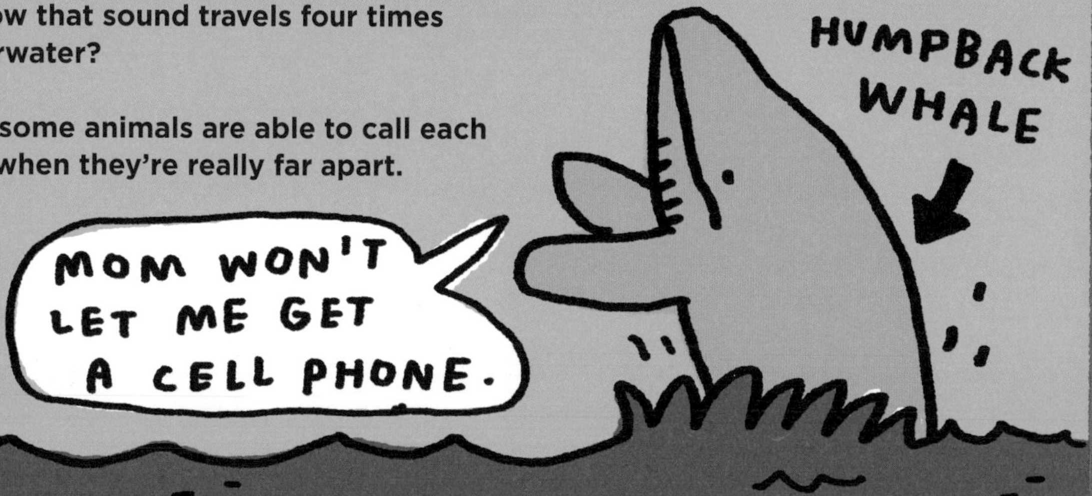

HUMPBACK WHALE
MOM WON'T LET ME GET A CELL PHONE.


Some humpback whales can even hear each other up to 15,000 miles away! That's about 3/5 of the way around the Earth OR more than 2.5 times the length of the Great Wall of China. (Or 5.5 times the distance from Los Angeles to New York!)

## WHALE VOMIT PERFUME?

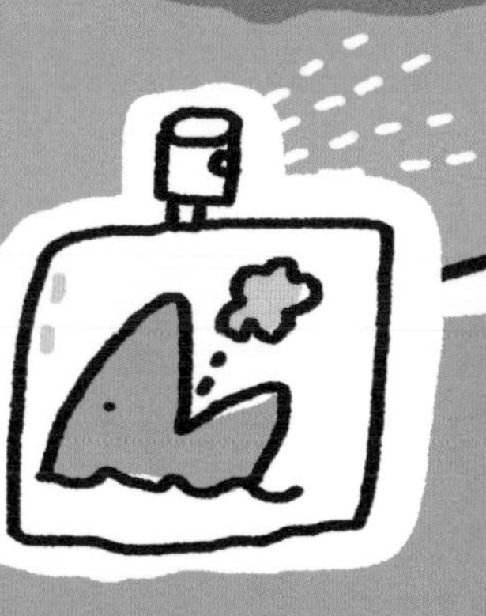

When sperm whales vomit, what comes out is a stinky, gray wax called ambergris. When it first comes out, the smell has been compared to "fecal matter." Aka poop! However, as the ambergris floats around at sea, or when it dries out, it starts to take on a nicer, sweeter smell. It has been collected and used in some perfumes, though that rarely happens now.

# FANCY TEETH.

Back in the 1700s sailors started passing the time on their long sailing trips by drawing on whale teeth! The art form is called scrimshaw, and it's done by scratching a design into a hard surface (like a sperm whale tooth) with something sharp like a knife or a nail. It's hard to see the design until it's covered with India ink and then the extra ink is wiped off to reveal the image. They often showed scenes of ships and other sailing stuff. At the time, whale teeth were easily available, but today it's illegal to sell them. But now you can buy plastic (fake) whale teeth to make legal scrimshaw art!

Blue whales have a relative that lives on land. They're distantly related to HIPPOS!

THIS IS THE BLUE WHALE CONTINUED FROM THE LAST PAGE!

HE'S WHALEY BIG!

I WISH I WAS THAT BIG. OH WHALE!

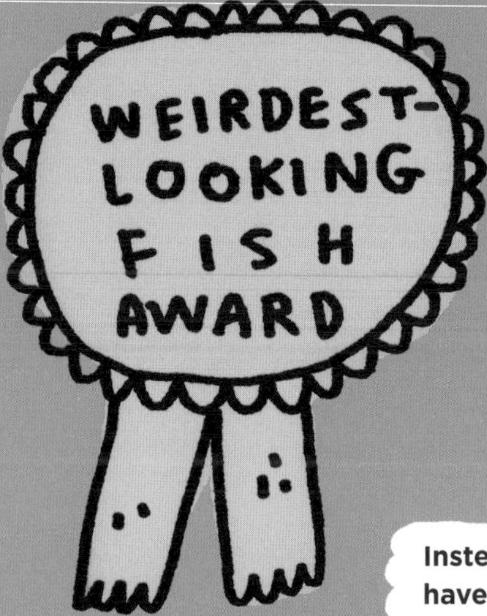
WEIRDEST-
LOOKING
FISH
AWARD

# BLOBFISH

## SQUISHY SKIN!

They like to live 2,000–4,000 feet deep, and way down there they don't look as weird and squishy as they do on the surface.

Instead of a swim bladder, which is an organ a lot of fish have to help them float, they've got skin with a lot of fat that sort of feels like jelly to keep them buoyant.

Mostly eat crabs and other shellfish, but because they don't have bones or teeth they don't actively hunt. They wait for unsuspecting prey to swim by!

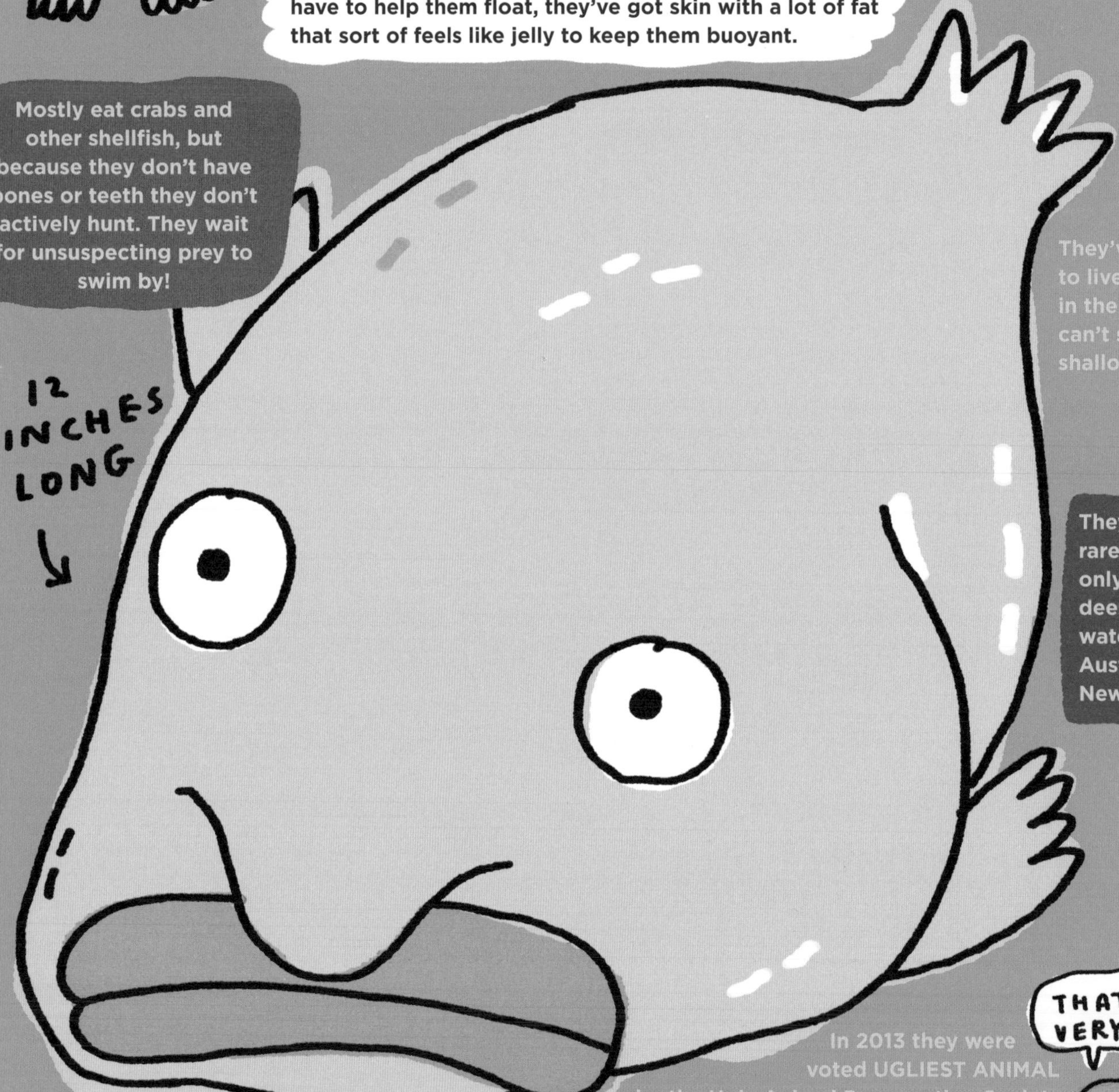
12 INCHES LONG

They've adapted to live really deep in the ocean and can't survive in shallow water.

They're very rare and are only found deep in the water near Australia and New Zealand.

In 2013 they were voted UGLIEST ANIMAL by the Ugly Animal Preservation Society.

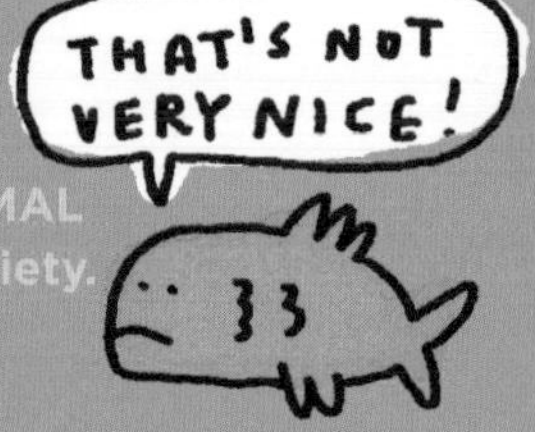
THAT'S NOT VERY NICE!

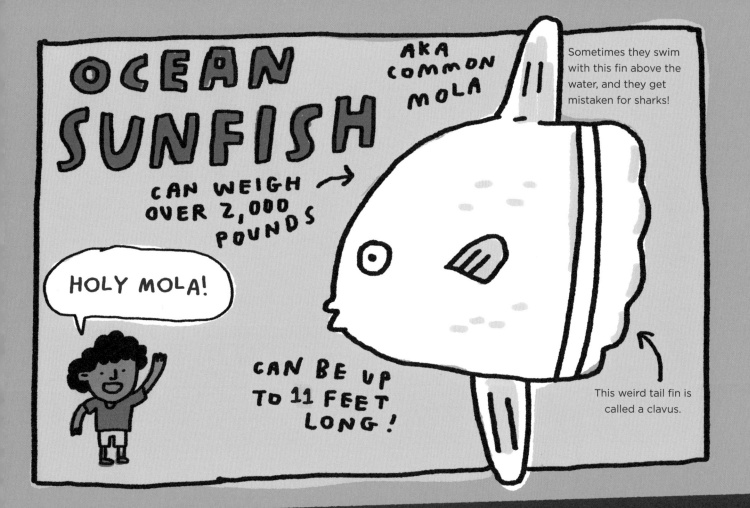

# OCEAN SUNFISH

### AKA COMMON MOLA

Sometimes they swim with this fin above the water, and they get mistaken for sharks!

CAN WEIGH OVER 2,000 POUNDS →

**HOLY MOLA!**

CAN BE UP TO 11 FEET LONG!

This weird tail fin is called a clavus.

# PISTOL SHRIMP

## AKA POPPING SHRIMP

Blue whales are really loud, but that's not very surprising since they're HUGE. But they've got a competitor for the Loudest Living Thing in the Ocean Award, and it's something that's a little unexpected.

**BANG!**

The pistol shrimp is a tiny, 1–2-inch-long arthropod that has one large claw. Inside that claw the shrimp can form a bubble, and when it pops, it makes an incredibly loud BANG and lets out a burst of heat that can be up to 18,000 degrees! They do this to stun prey.

# FRESHWATER FRIGHTS!

Okay, so most of the animals in this book so far have been found in salty oceans and seas, but I don't want to leave out some other awesome (and terrifying) marine animals that live in fresh water.

## DIVING BELL SPIDER

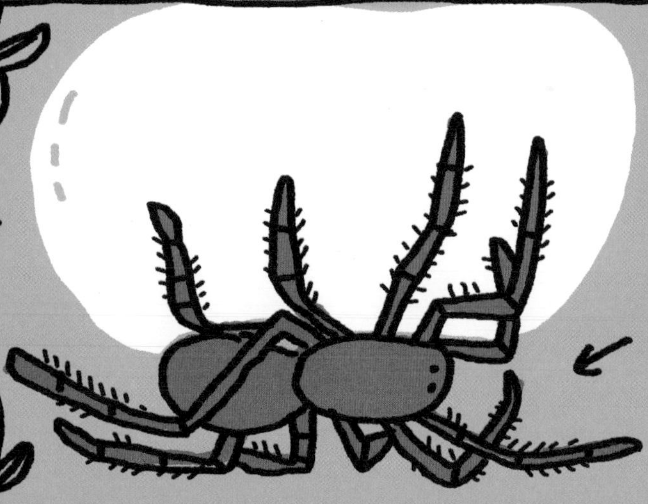

Found in mainland Europe, Asia, and the British isles.

IT'S THE ONLY KNOWN SPIDER THAT LIVES COMPLETELY UNDERWATER.

It gets air by going up to the surface of the water, capturing a little bubble with the hairs on its body, and then bringing it back down with them.

Its bites are really painful and give you fever-like symptoms.

## MATA MATA

Found in South America

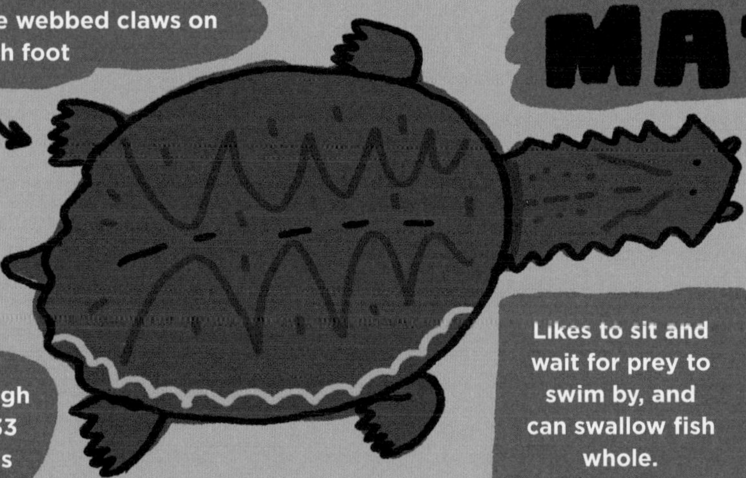

Five webbed claws on each foot

This fully aquatic turtle looks like some fallen tree scraps, which gives it great camouflage from predators.

Likes to sit and wait for prey to swim by, and can swallow fish whole.

Can weigh up to 33 pounds

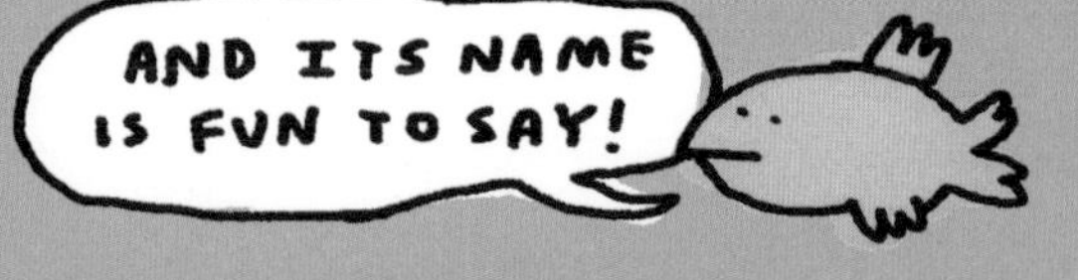
AND ITS NAME IS FUN TO SAY!

# PIRANHA!

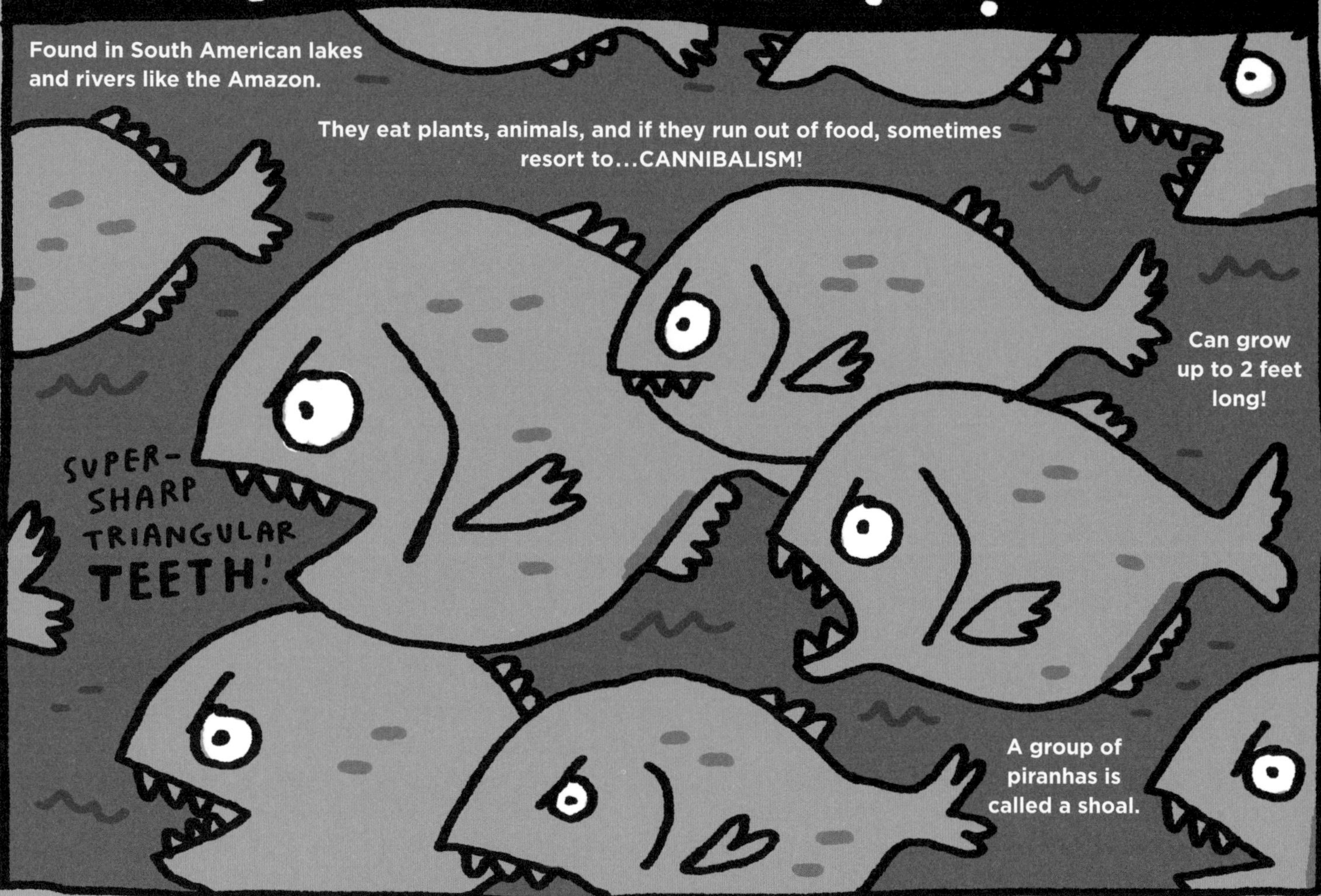

SUPER-SHARP TRIANGULAR TEETH!


Found in South American lakes and rivers like the Amazon.

They eat plants, animals, and if they run out of food, sometimes resort to...CANNIBALISM!

Can grow up to 2 feet long!

A group of piranhas is called a shoal.

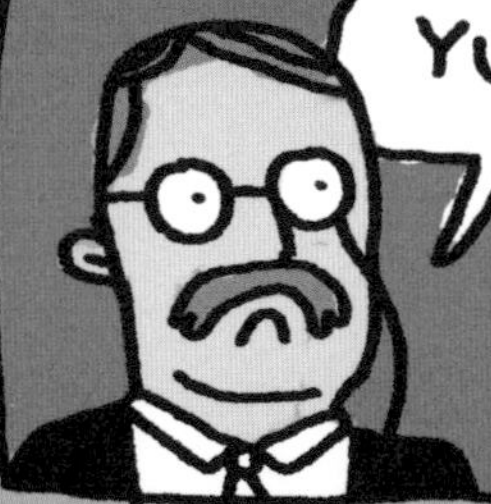

Yuck!


## DON'T HAVE A COW, MAN!

Theodore Roosevelt once saw an entire cow eaten by piranhas on a trip to South America. It turned out to be an event planned by a fisherman who blocked off an area in the river, filled it with piranhas, and didn't let them eat for a few days!

# PAYARA

AKA VAMPIRE FISH

THEY EAT PIRANHAS!

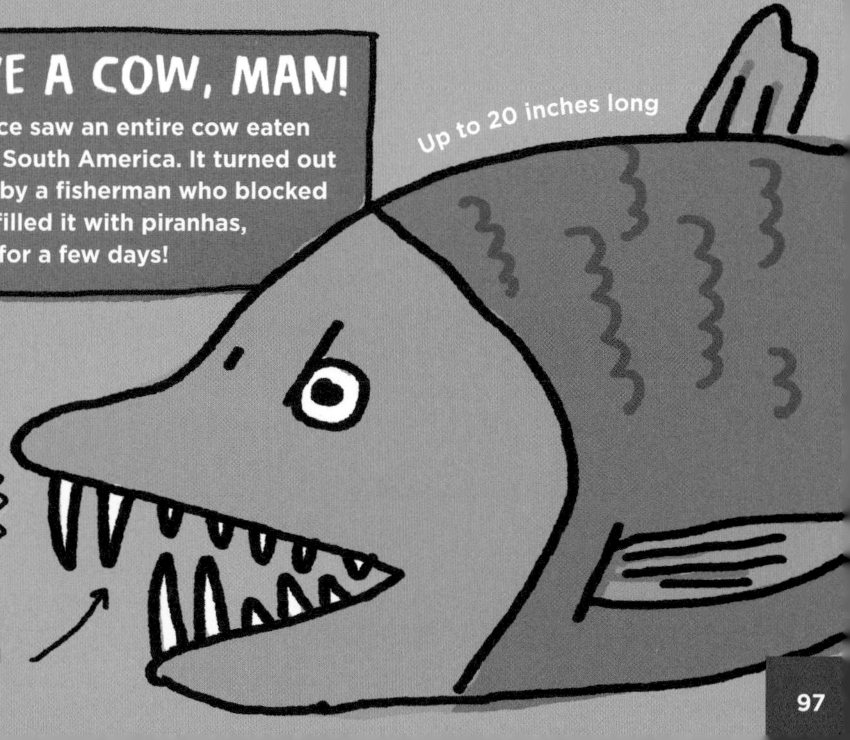

Up to 20 inches long
LONG, SHARP TEETH

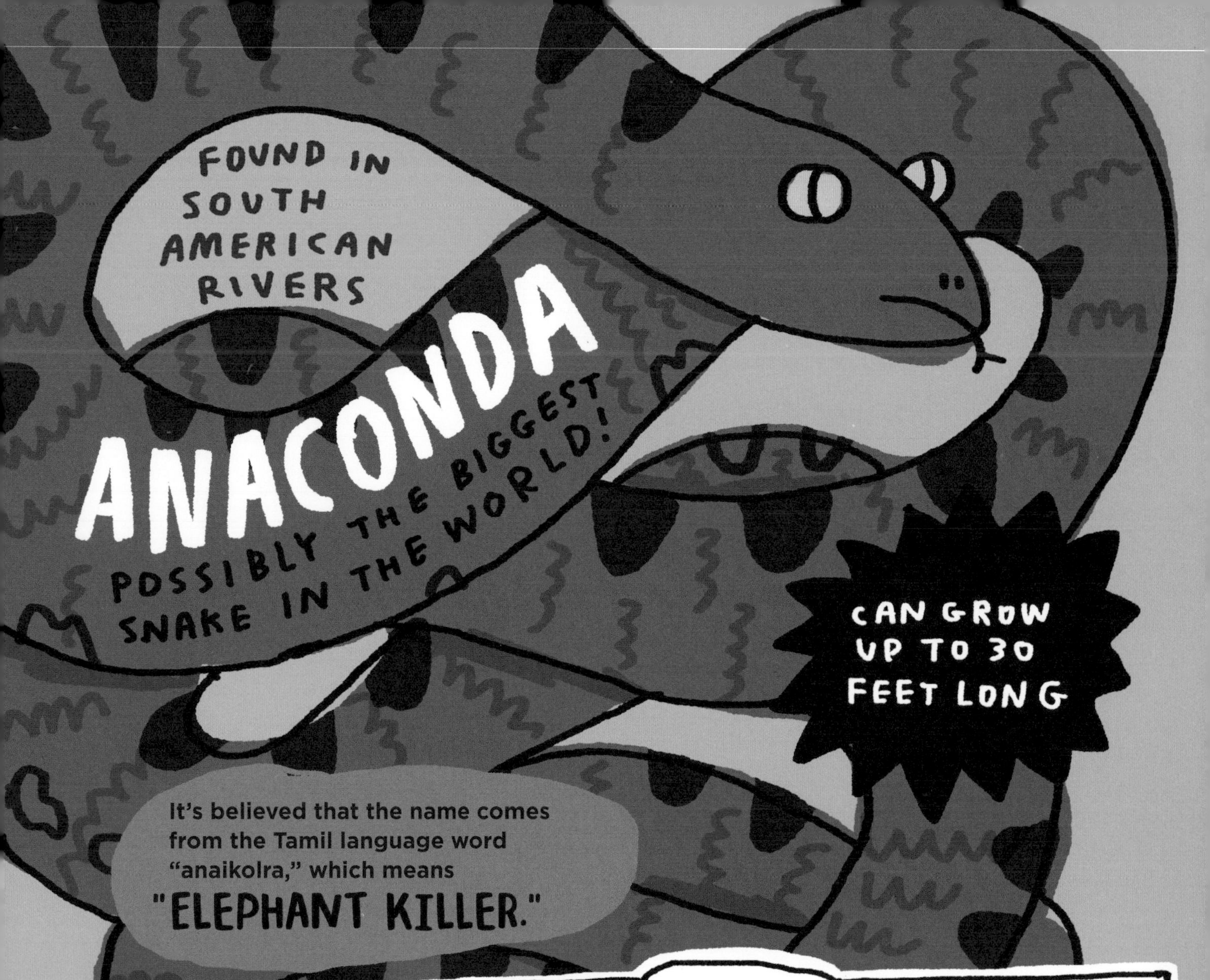
FOUND IN SOUTH AMERICAN RIVERS
ANACONDA
POSSIBLY THE BIGGEST SNAKE IN THE WORLD!
CAN GROW UP TO 30 FEET LONG

It's believed that the name comes from the Tamil language word "anaikolra," which means
**"ELEPHANT KILLER."**

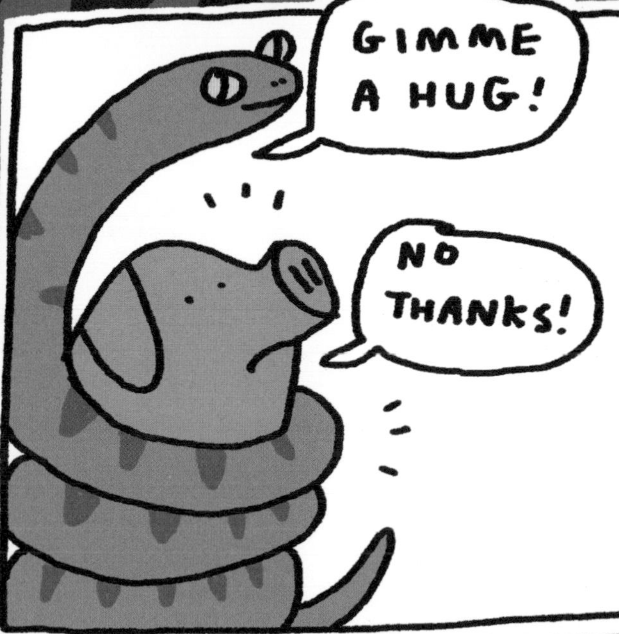
GIMME A HUG!
NO THANKS!

**They don't have venom; instead they squeeeeze their prey to death.**

**They've been known to eat pigs, deer, crocodiles, rodents, fish, smaller snakes, and even jaguars!**

# PART FIVE

# SAVE THE SHARKS

THE OCEAN NEEDS YOUR HELP!

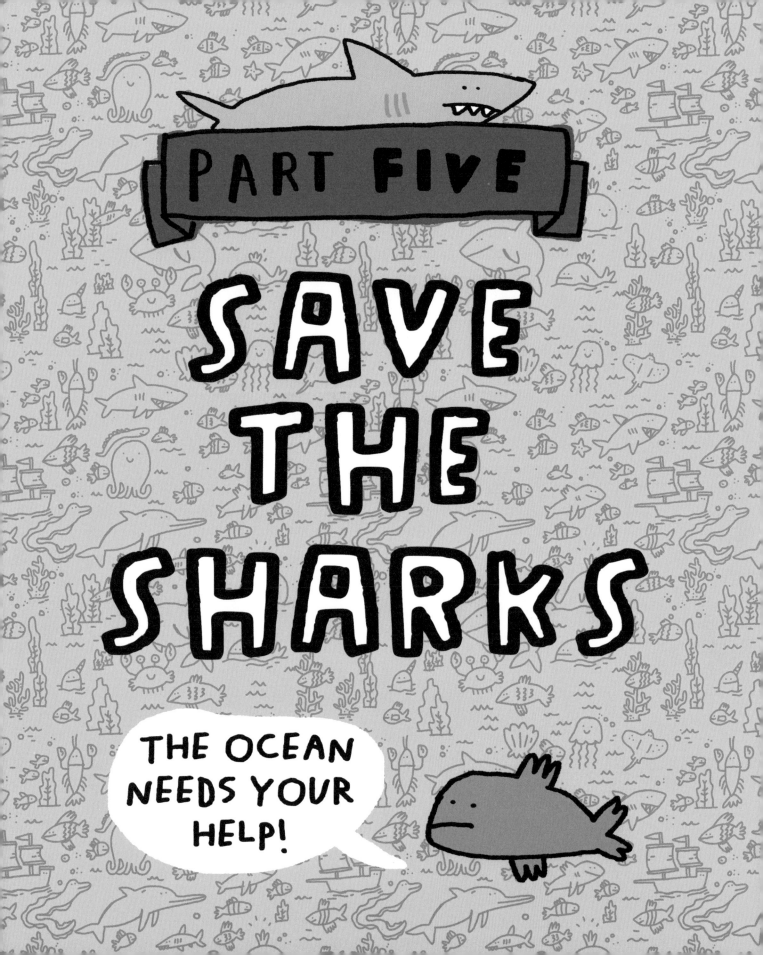

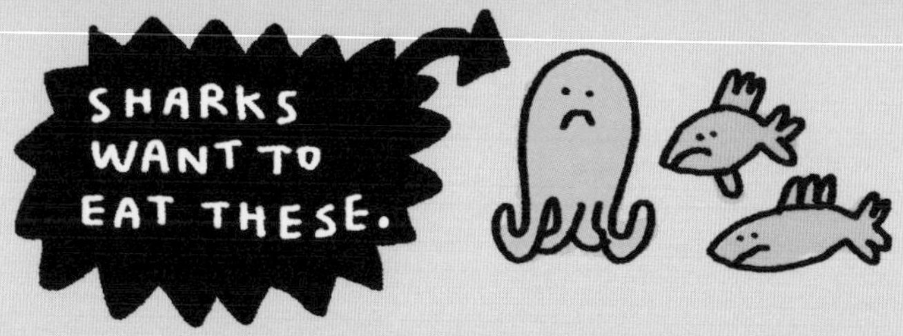
SHARKS WANT TO EAT THESE.

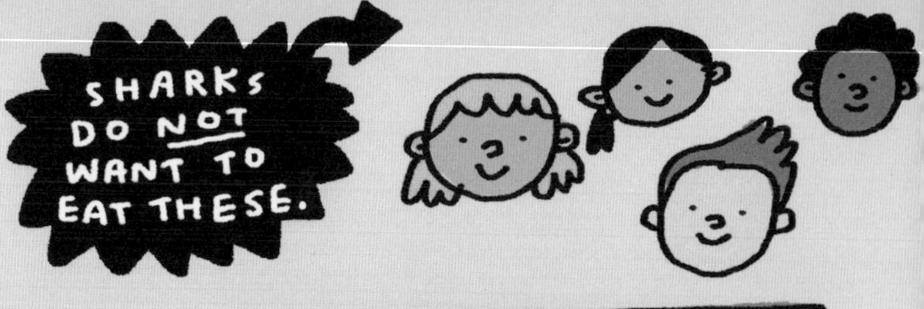
SHARKS DO NOT WANT TO EAT THESE.

If you've been following along, you've learned that sharks are pretty dangerous but only to other fish and the creatures they eat in the ocean. They're not very dangerous to humans. Attacks do happen, but they're rare and typically only occur when the sharks are provoked or when it's a case of mistaken identity.

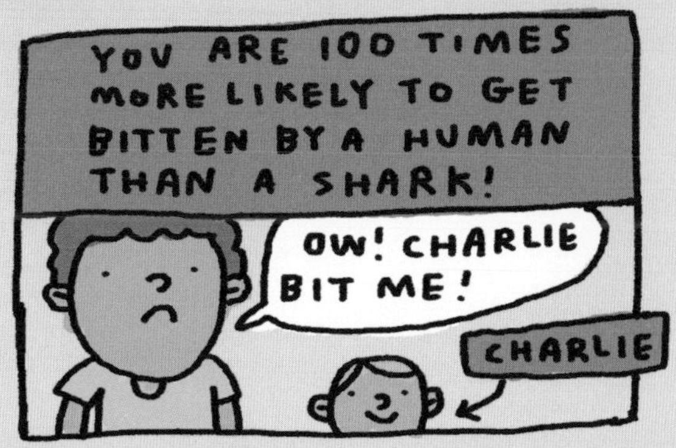
YOU ARE 100 TIMES MORE LIKELY TO GET BITTEN BY A HUMAN THAN A SHARK!
OW! CHARLIE BIT ME!
CHARLIE

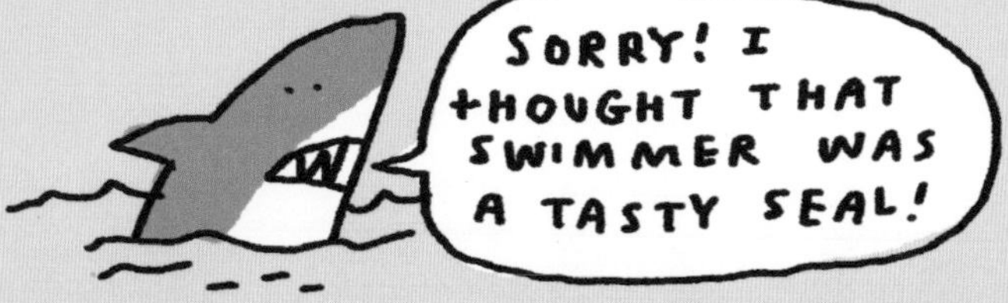
SORRY! I THOUGHT THAT SWIMMER WAS A TASTY SEAL!

When it comes to sharks versus people, sharks are actually the ones that are in danger. They have been overfished and hunted for so long they could even go extinct! Some sharks that are currently threatened include white sharks, makos, basking sharks, whale sharks, and many others. And sharks aren't the only sea creatures in trouble.

**THE OCEANS AND THE CREATURES THAT LIVE IN THEM ARE SUPER AWESOME, BUT THEY NEED OUR HELP!**

# THE BIG PLASTIC PROBLEM!

One of the biggest dangers to ocean life is pollution, and sadly there is lots of trash in the oceans. Single-use plastics (like yogurt cups or shampoo bottles that are meant to be used and then thrown out) are one of the biggest problems facing our oceans because they don't decompose like paper or wood.

The Ocean Conservancy found that plastic has been found in more than 60% of seabirds and 100% of all sea turtles. Fish eat bits of plastic thinking it's food, and since humans eat fish, fragments of plastic have been found in humans, too. Some fish will accidentally ingest up to 11,000 fragments of plastic a year.

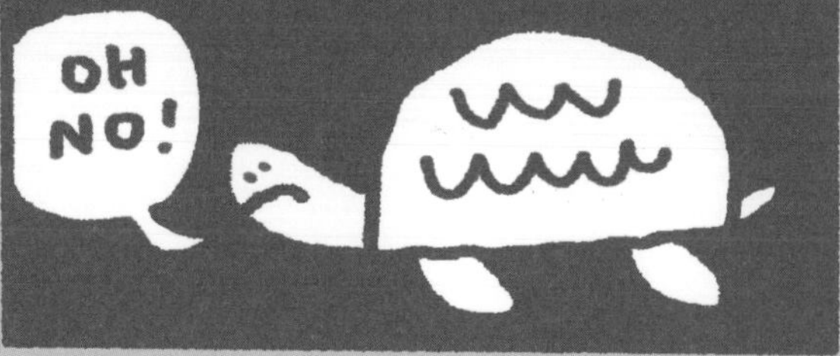
OH NO!

Plastic water bottles take about 400 years to break down!

**How many plastic water bottles do you think are sold every day all over the world? 5,000? 10,000? 50,000?**

It's more like 1 MILLION. EVERY. SINGLE. MINUTE. That's right, one million non-reusable plastic water bottles are sold EVERY MINUTE. And only about 9% of them get recycled. It's estimated that half a trillion bottles will be sold in one year. The world is making almost 300 million tons of plastic every year.

It's also estimated that by 2050 the ocean will contain more plastic than fish!

# BUT WE CAN CHANGE THINGS!

# HERE'S WHAT YOU CAN DO TO HELP!

1

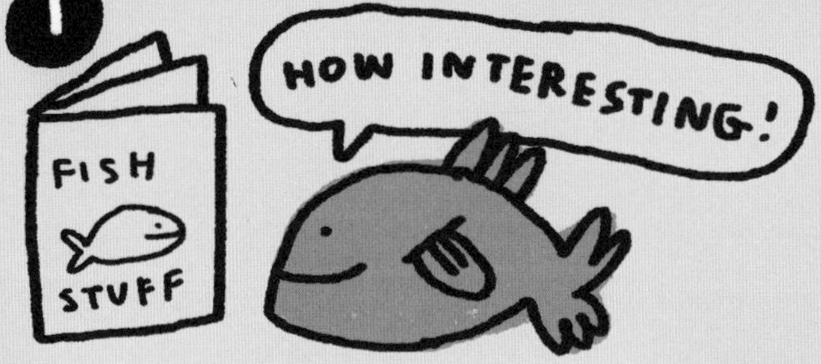
HOW INTERESTING!
FISH
STUFF

You've already started! Getting educated by reading books (like this one!) about the oceans and the animals that live in them is a great place to start.

2

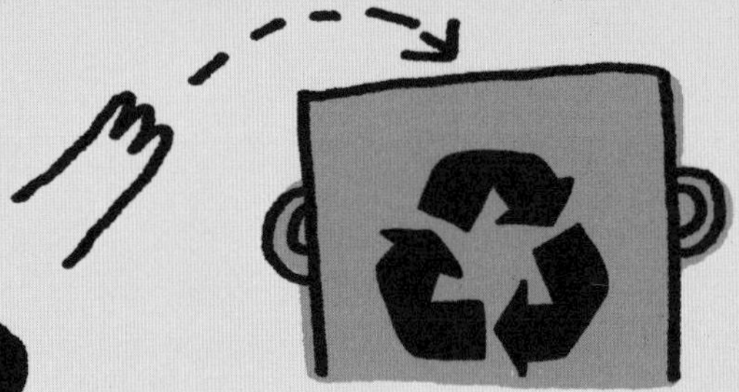

Recycle. Recycling helps to keep plastic out of the oceans.

3

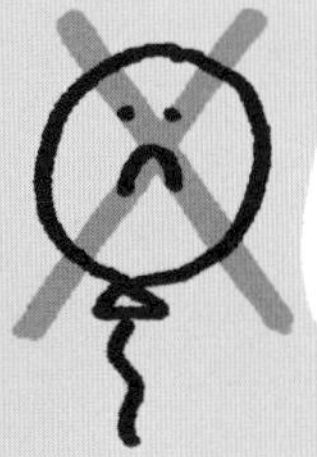

Skip the balloons! Balloon pollution is a huge problem. They can be a choking hazard when they're swallowed by marine life who mistake them for food. Their strings can even get wrapped around small animals and the necks of birds.

4

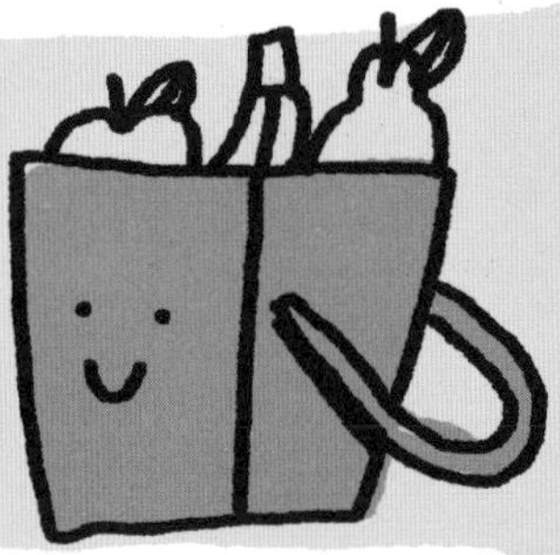

Bring reusable bags to the grocery store.

5

Volunteer for a beach cleanup! If you live near a beach, check out oceanconservancy.org with a parent to see if there's a cleanup event near you.

6

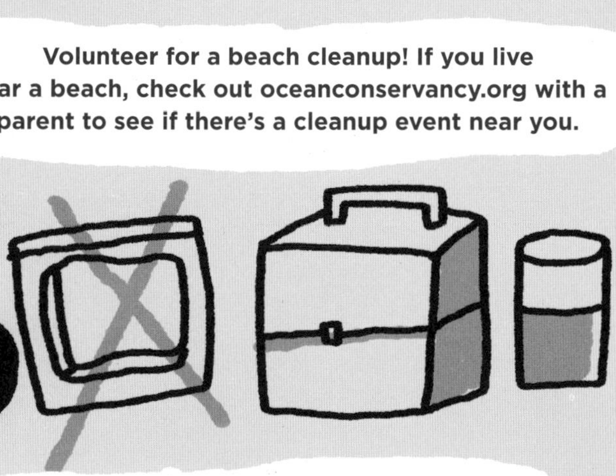

Get a lunchbox and reusable water bottle instead of using sandwich bags every day!

7

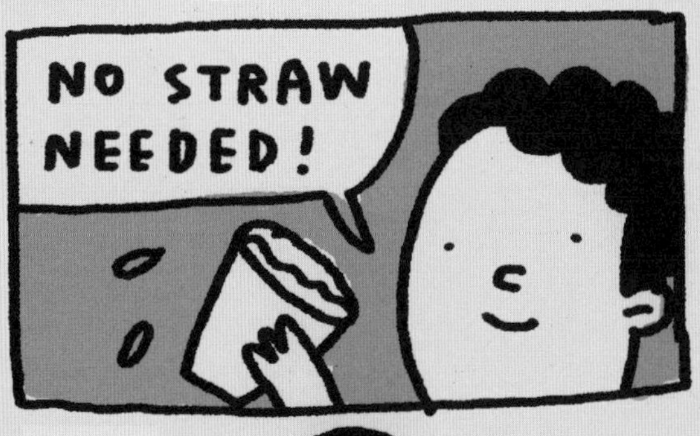
NO STRAW NEEDED!

Ditch the straw! It's estimated that up to 390 million plastic straws are used every single day. That's up to 140 BILLION a year!

And there's a really FUN thing you can do to help.

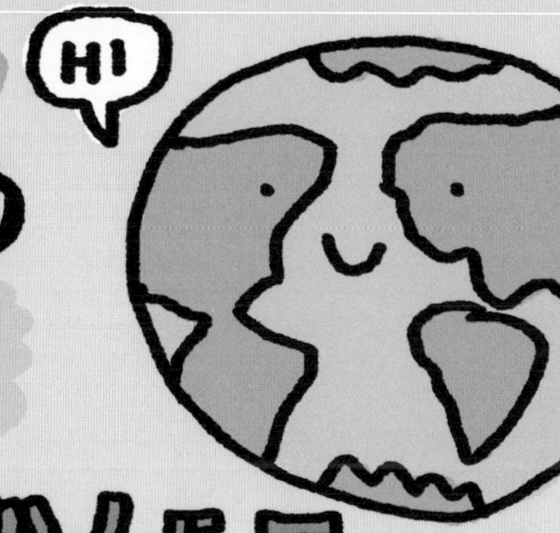
HI

# GO OUT AND EXPLORE YOUR PLANET!!!

Jacques-Yves Cousteau (a world-famous oceanic explorer and conservationist) was a big believer that

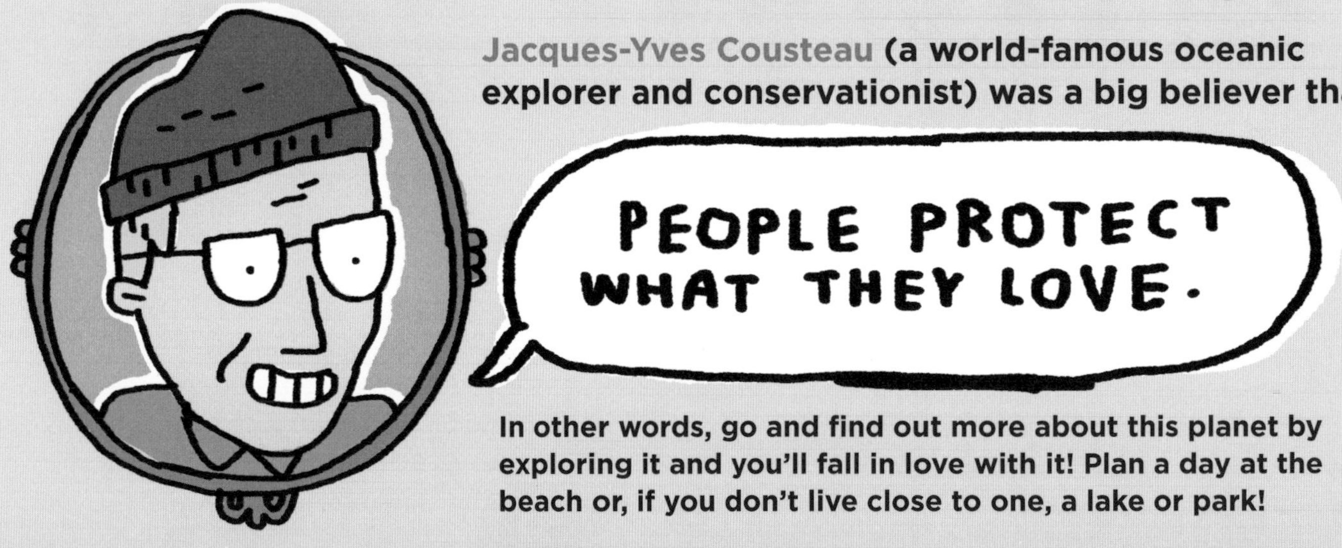
PEOPLE PROTECT WHAT THEY LOVE.

In other words, go and find out more about this planet by exploring it and you'll fall in love with it! Plan a day at the beach or, if you don't live close to one, a lake or park!

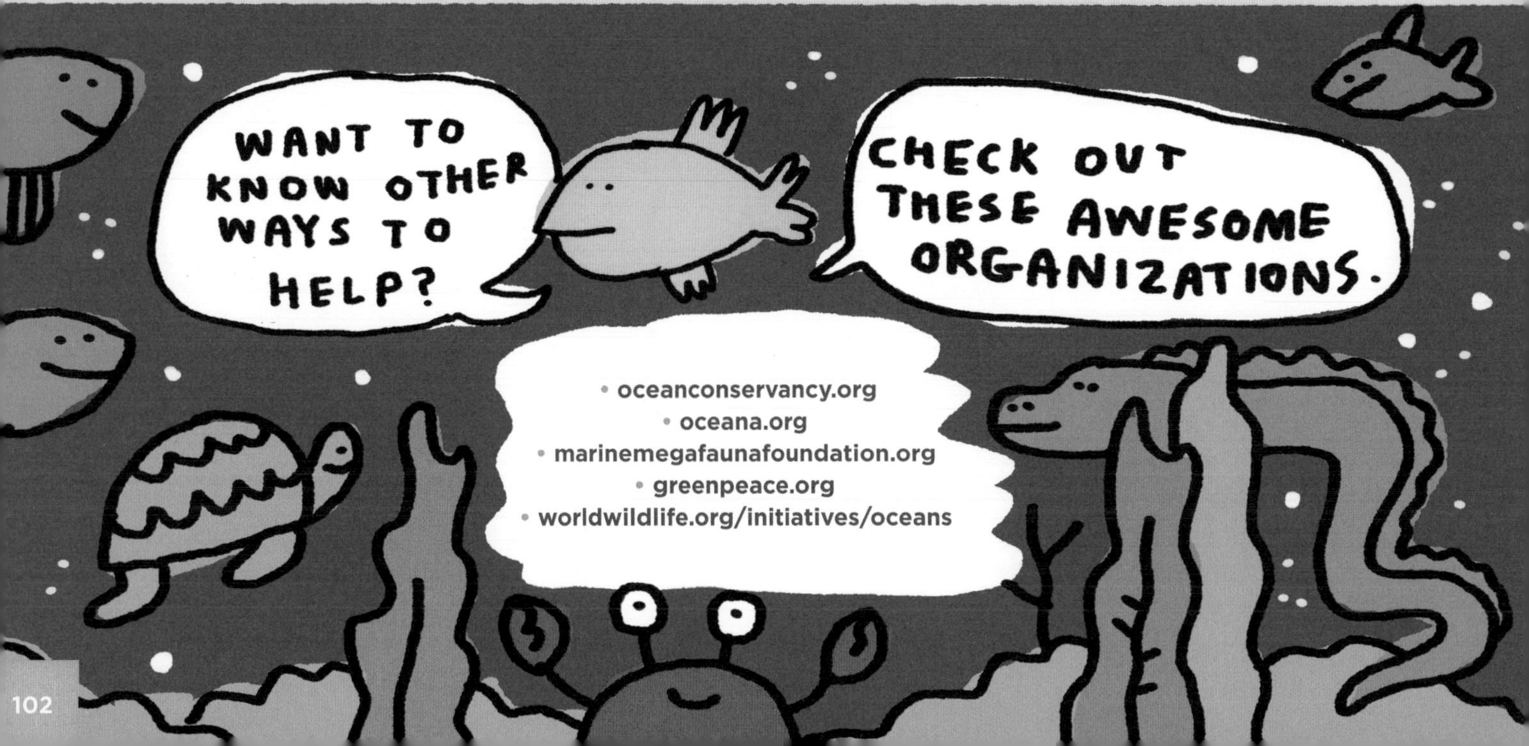
WANT TO KNOW OTHER WAYS TO HELP?
CHECK OUT THESE AWESOME ORGANIZATIONS.

- oceanconservancy.org
- oceana.org
- marinemegafaunafoundation.org
- greenpeace.org
- worldwildlife.org/initiatives/oceans

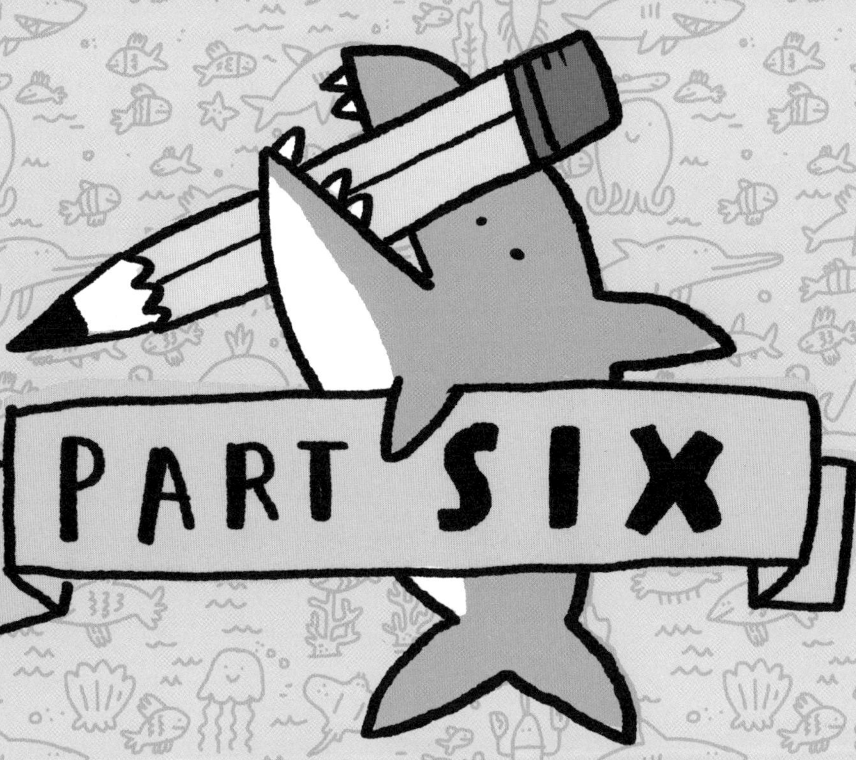

# PART SIX

# LET'S DRAW SHARKS!

## (AND OTHER SEA CREATURES)

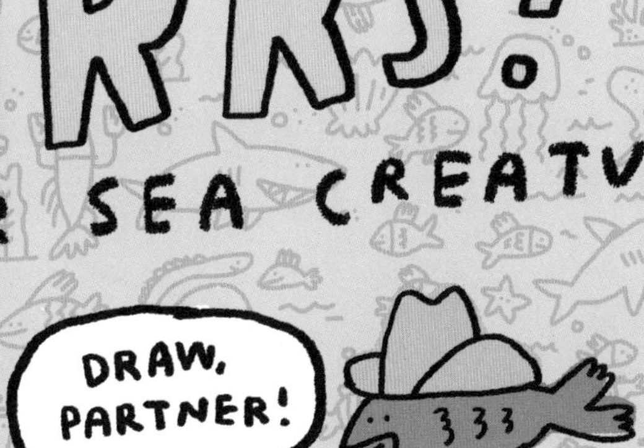
DRAW, PARTNER!

# LET'S DRAW SHARKS!
## (AND OTHER SEA CREATURES)

## SUPPLIES:

You don't need fancy art supplies to draw sharks! Here are a few things that I like to draw with, but you can use whatever you've got.

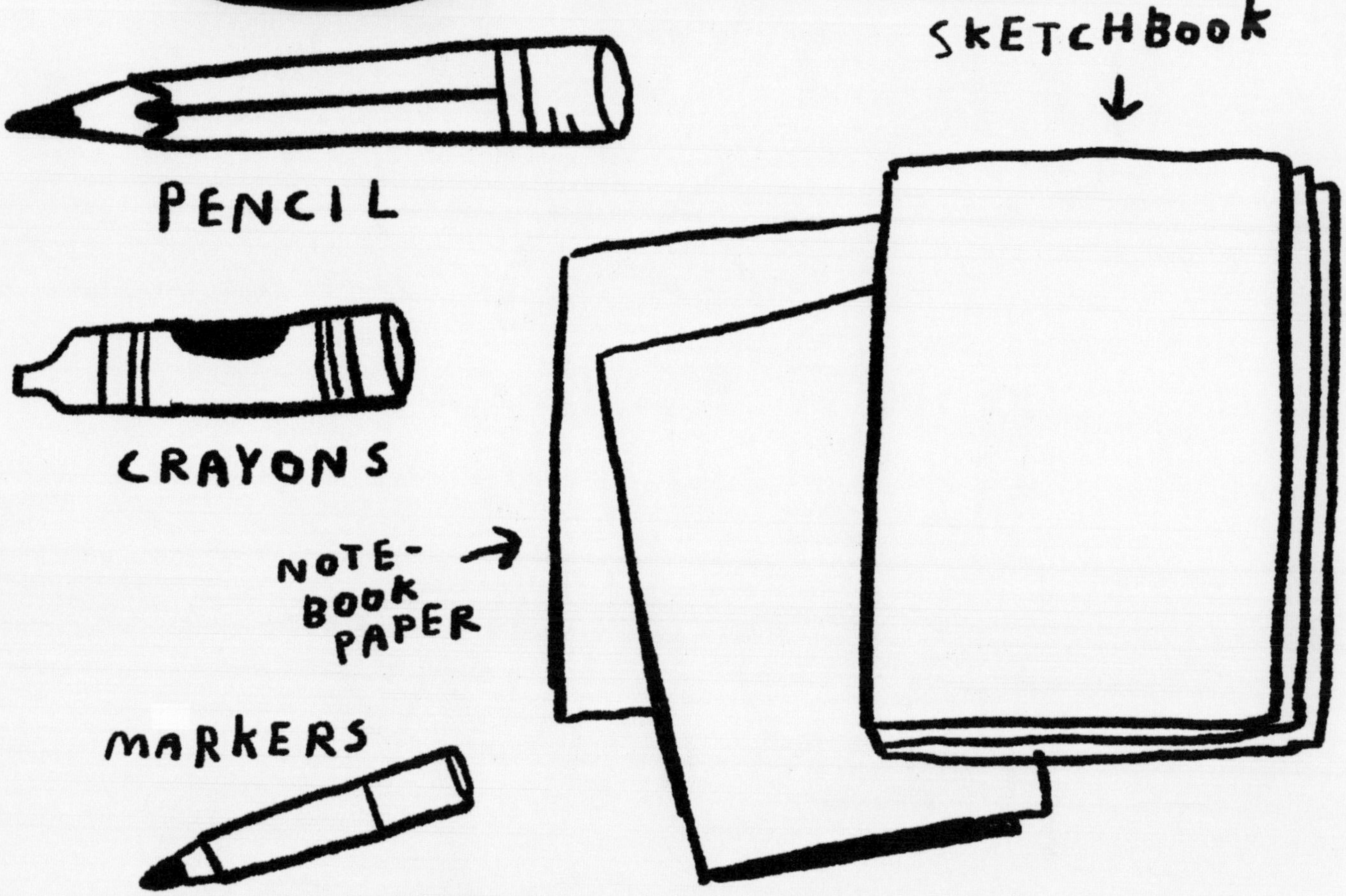

SKETCHBOOK
PENCIL
CRAYONS
NOTE-BOOK PAPER
MARKERS


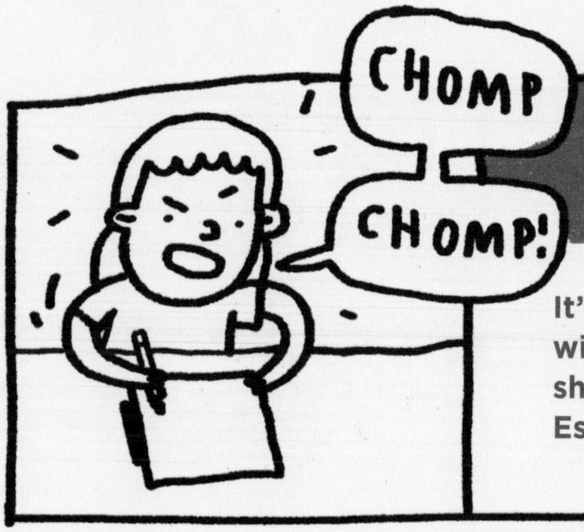

CHOMP
CHOMP!


## IMPORTANT!

It's important to know that your drawings will be significantly better if you make shark sounds and faces while drawing them. Especially if you are in a crowded, quiet area.

# WHITE SHARK

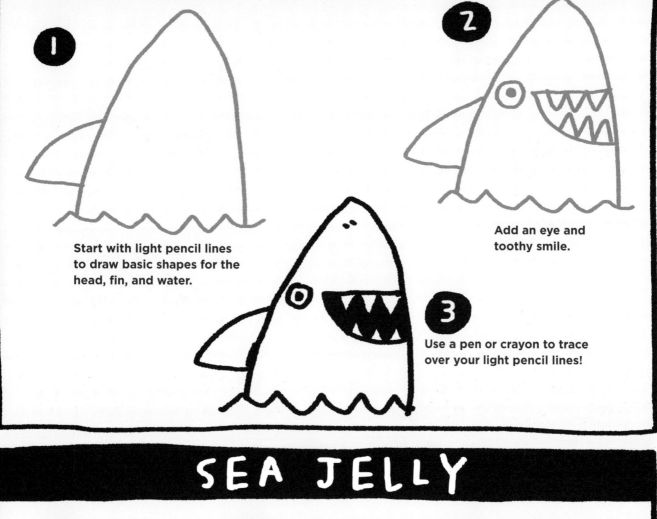

**1** Start with light pencil lines to draw basic shapes for the head, fin, and water.

**2** Add an eye and toothy smile.

**3** Use a pen or crayon to trace over your light pencil lines!

# SEA JELLY

**1** Start with light pencil lines to draw the body outline.

**2** Add a face.

**3** Use a pen or crayon to trace over your light pencil lines and add lots of tentacles!

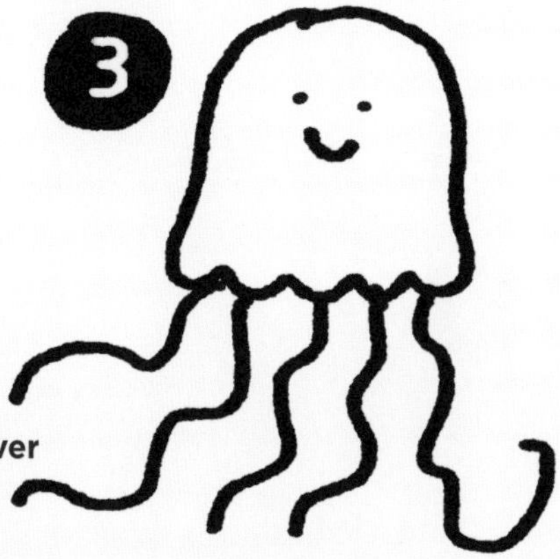

# OCTOPUS

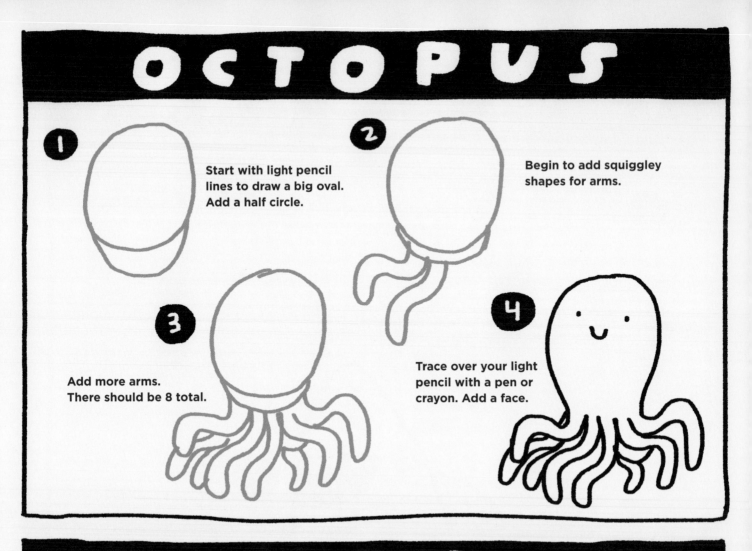

**1** Start with light pencil lines to draw a big oval. Add a half circle.

**2** Begin to add squiggley shapes for arms.

**3** Add more arms. There should be 8 total.

**4** Trace over your light pencil with a pen or crayon. Add a face.

# WHALE

**1** Start with light pencil lines to draw the body. Add a tail.

**2** Add a fin and water coming out of the blowhole.

**3** Add water line and face.

**4** Trace over your light pencil with a pen or crayon.

# NARWHAL

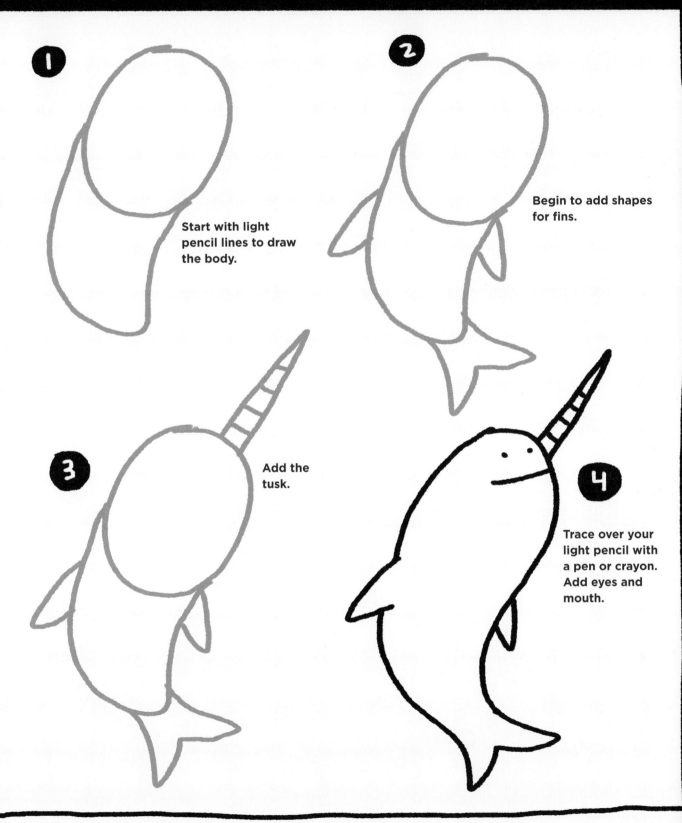

1

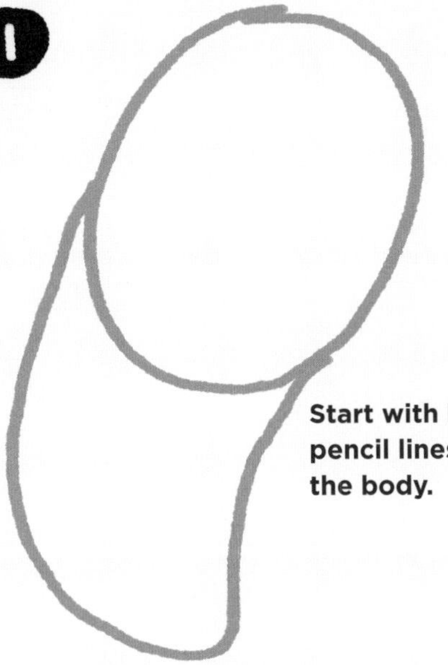

Start with light pencil lines to draw the body.

2

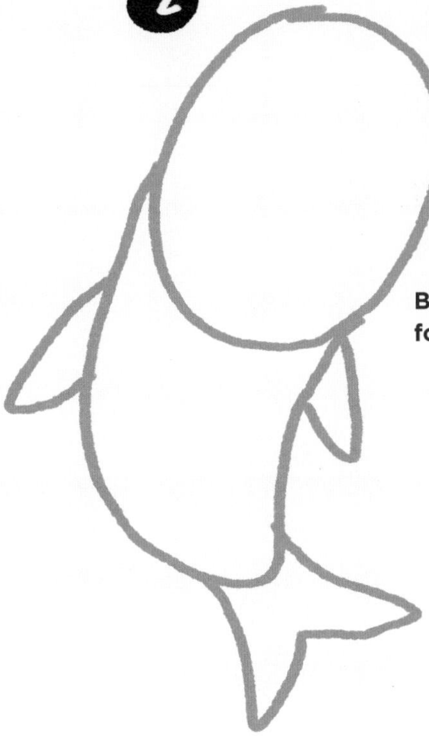

Begin to add shapes for fins.

3

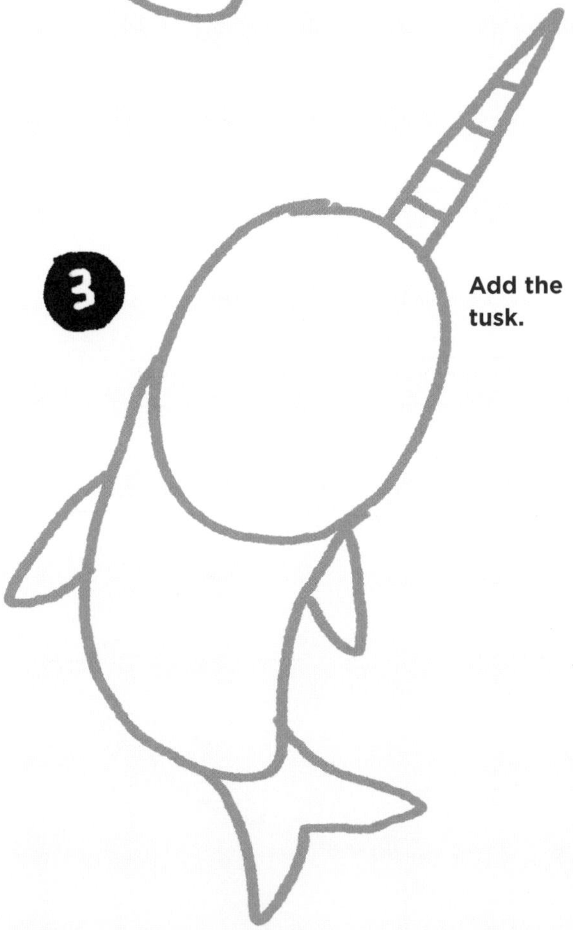

Add the tusk.

4

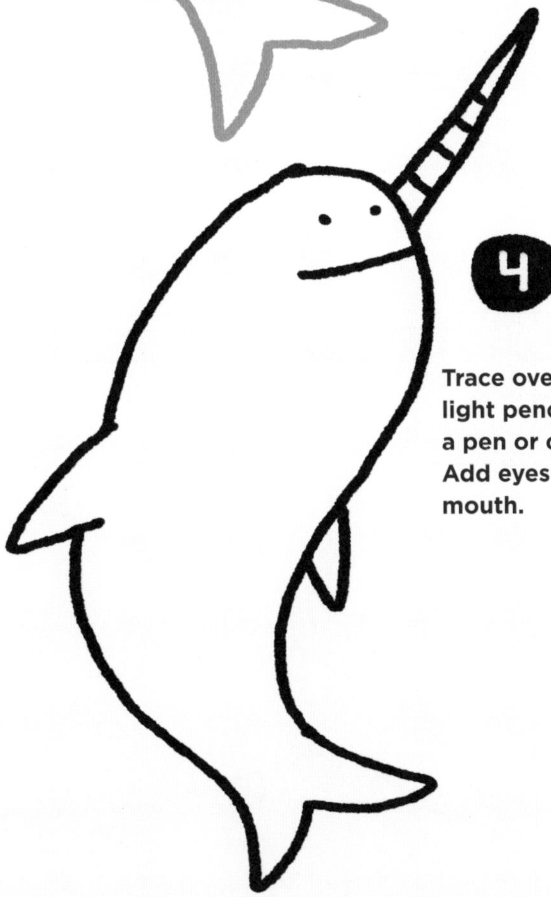

Trace over your light pencil with a pen or crayon. Add eyes and mouth.

# TIGER SHARK

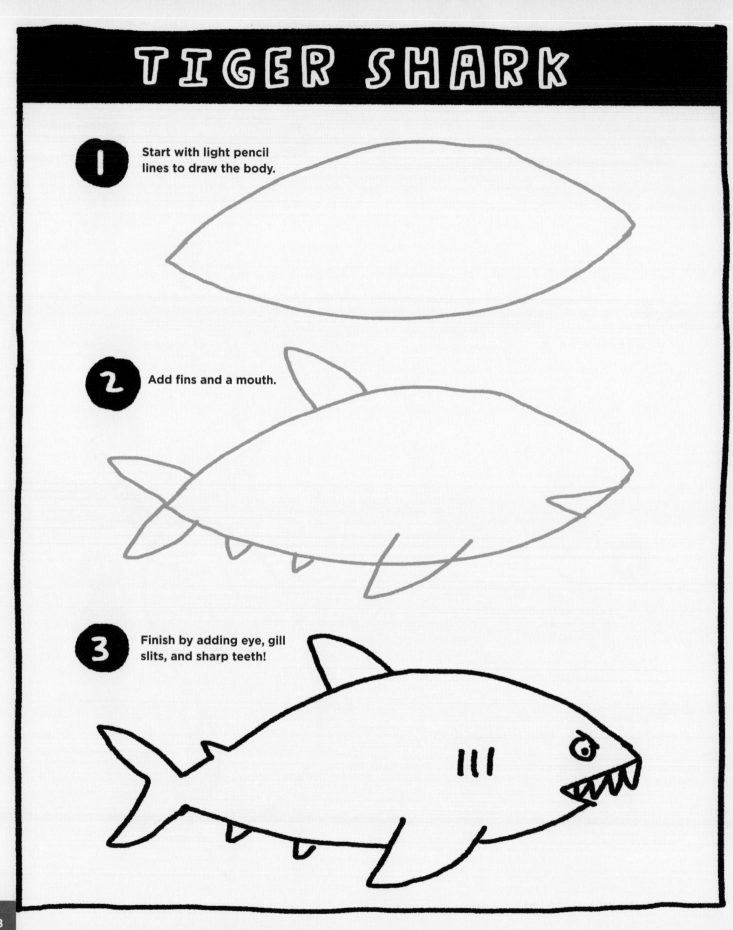

1 Start with light pencil lines to draw the body.

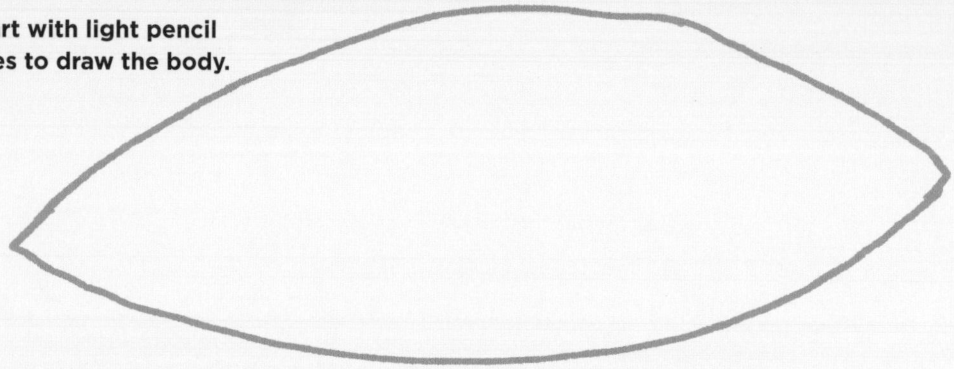

2 Add fins and a mouth.

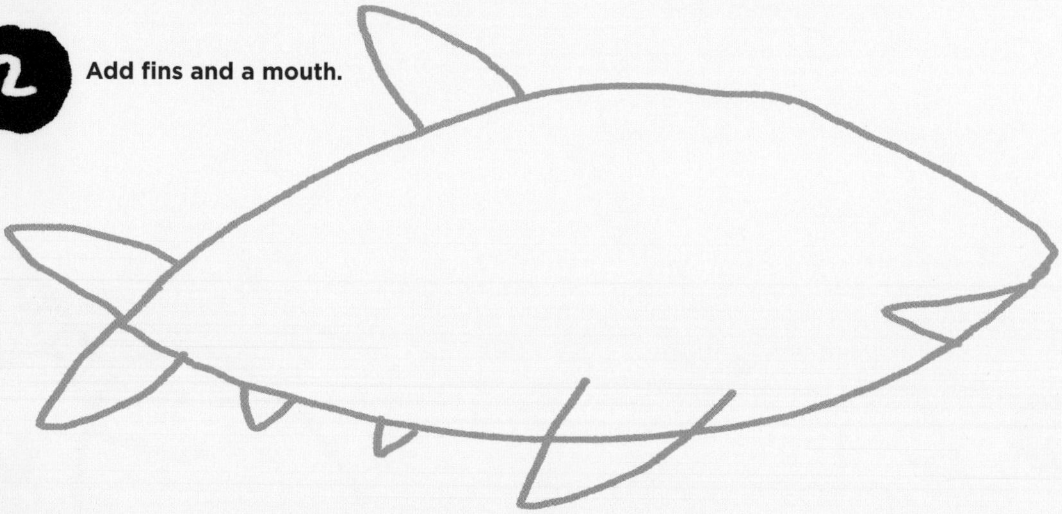

3 Finish by adding eye, gill slits, and sharp teeth!

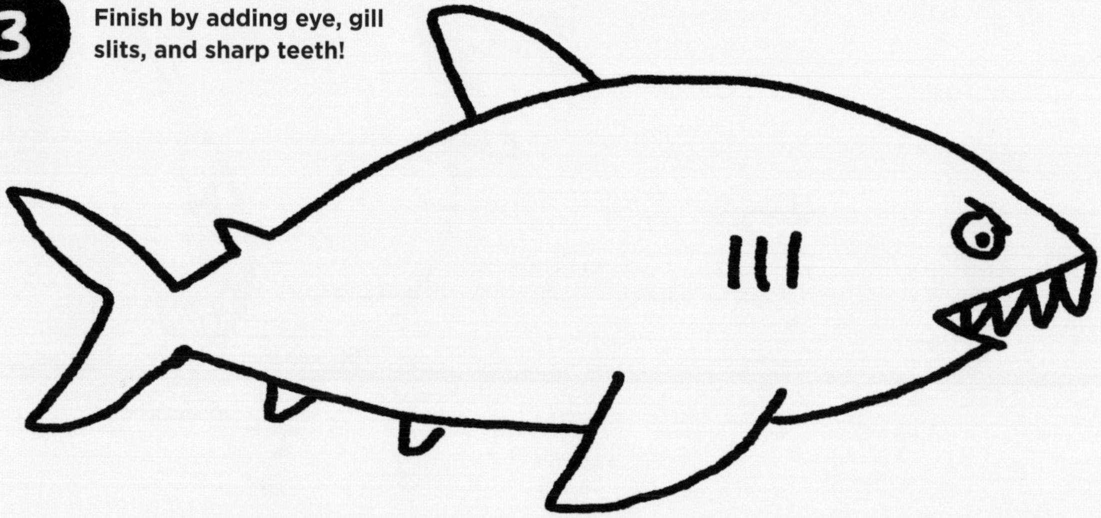

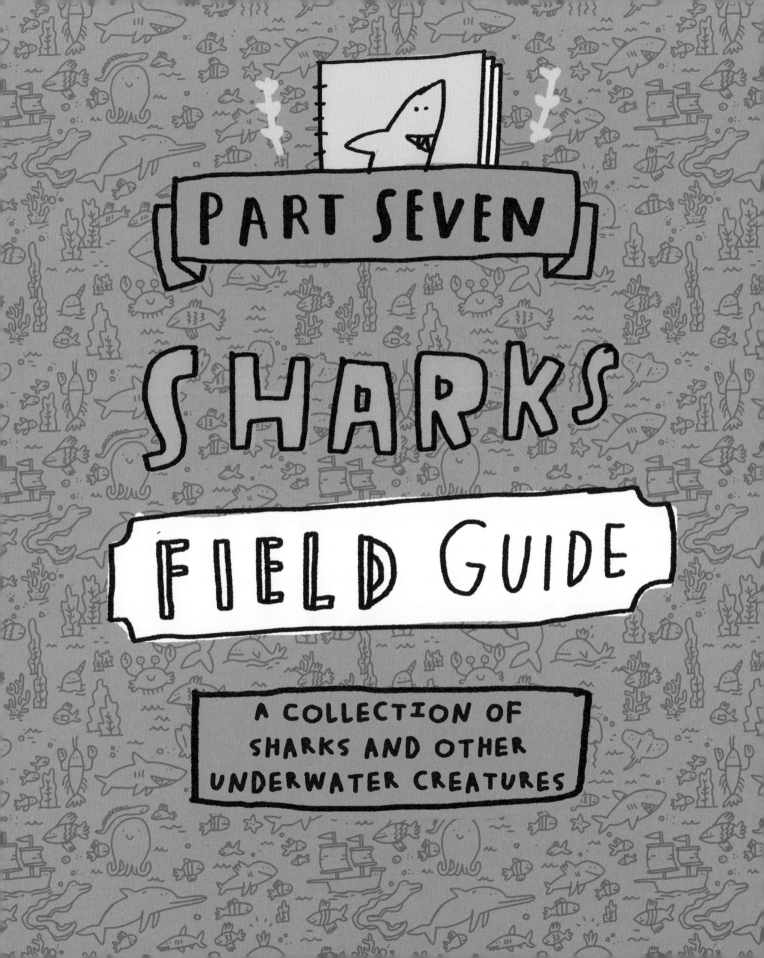

# PART SEVEN

# SHARKS

## FIELD GUIDE

A COLLECTION OF
SHARKS AND OTHER
UNDERWATER CREATURES

# SHARKS OF THE WORLD

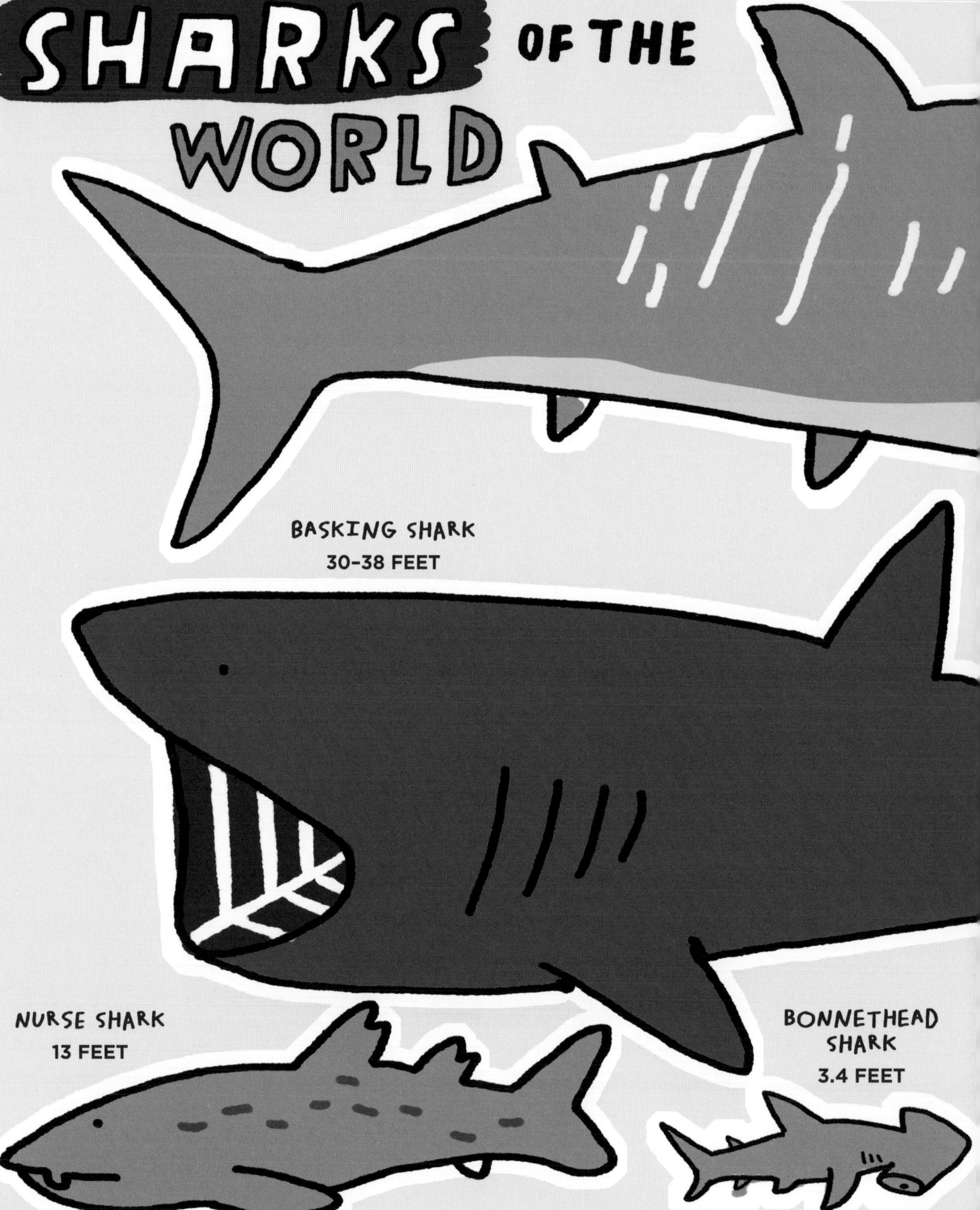
BASKING SHARK
30–38 FEET
NURSE SHARK
13 FEET
BONNETHEAD SHARK
3.4 FEET

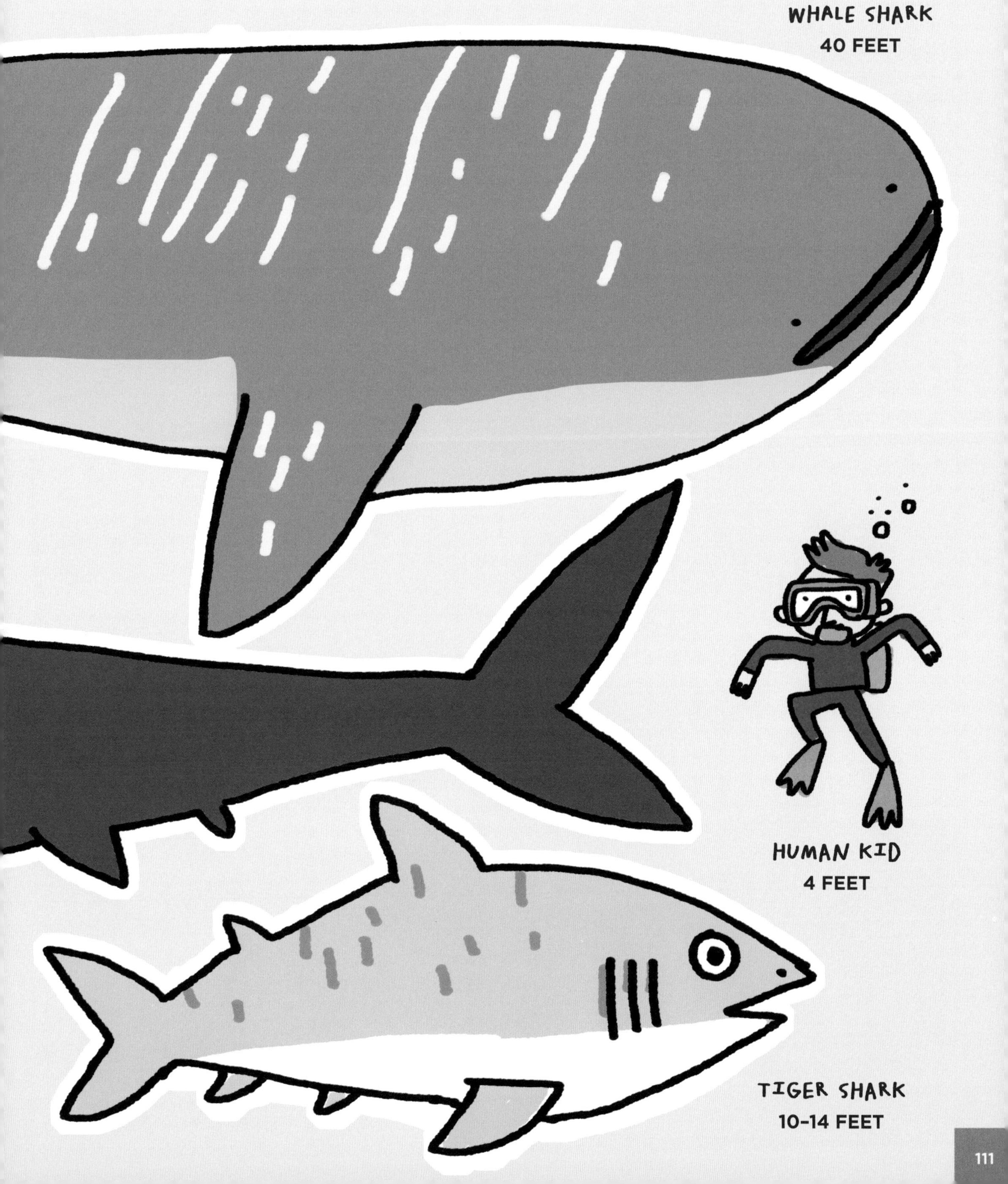
WHALE SHARK
40 FEET
HUMAN KID
4 FEET
TIGER SHARK
10–14 FEET

PORTUGUESE DOGFISH
3 FEET

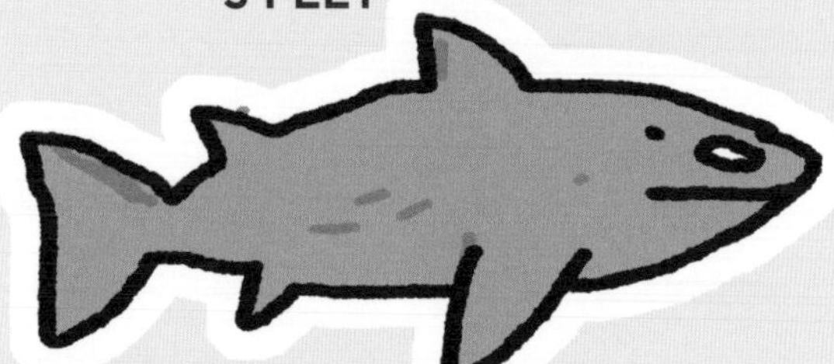

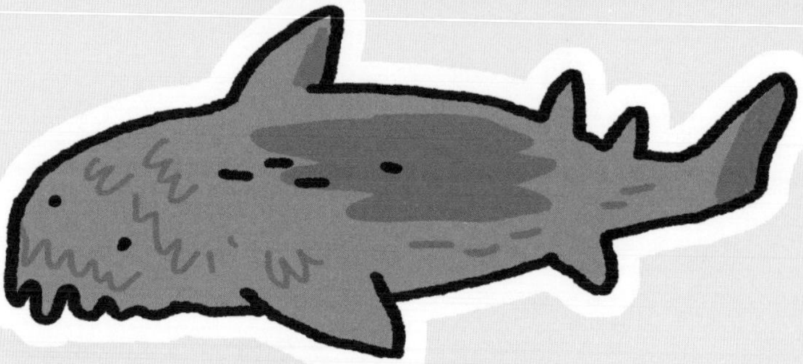

TASSLED WOBBEGONG SHARK
4 FEET

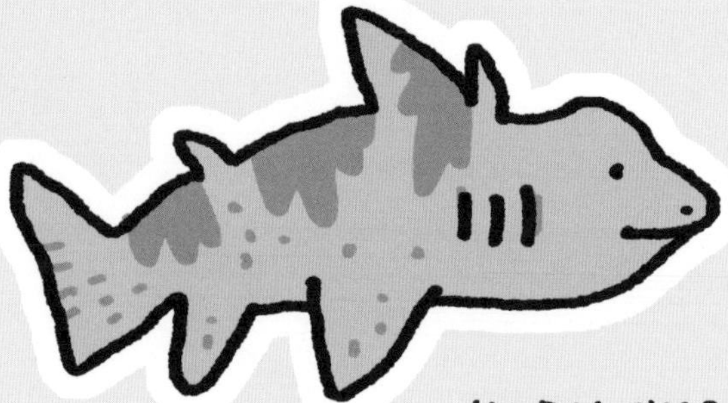

HORN SHARK
2-4 FEET

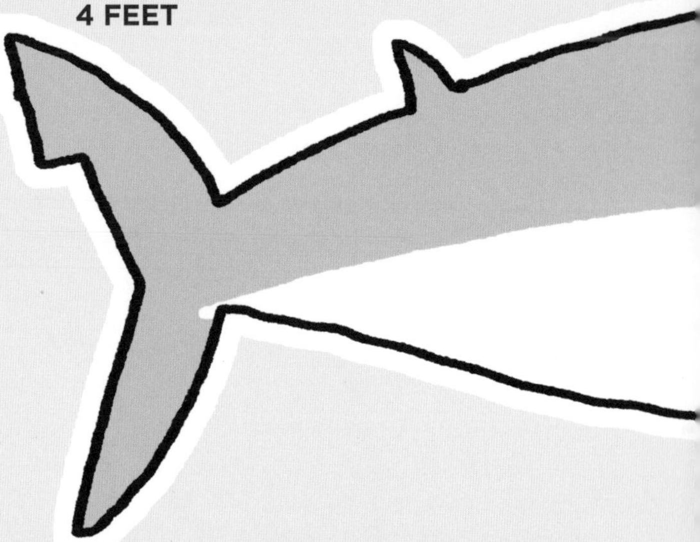

FRILLED SHARK
6 FEET

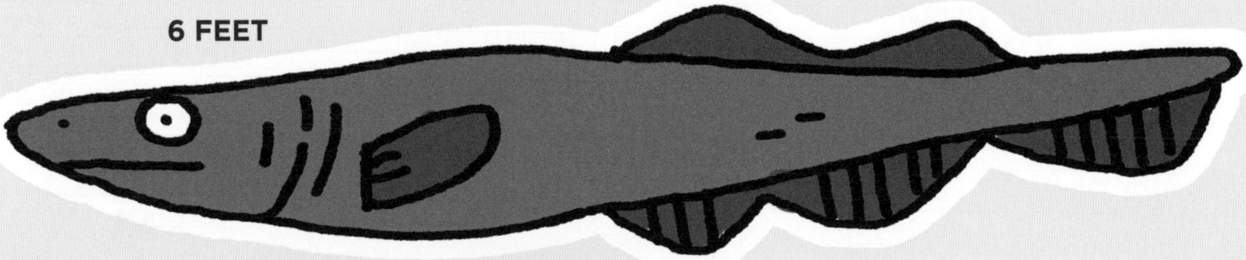

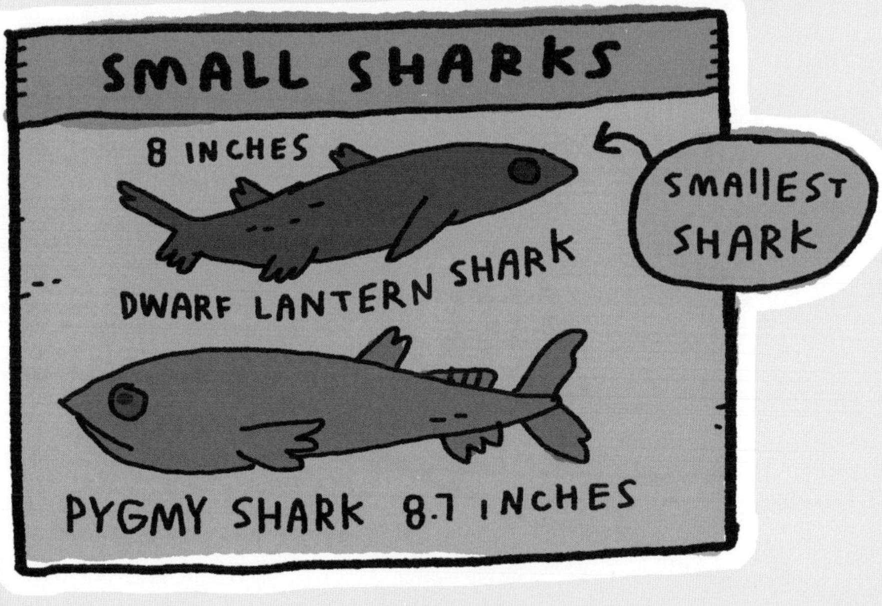
SMALL SHARKS
8 INCHES
DWARF LANTERN SHARK
SMALLEST SHARK
PYGMY SHARK 8.7 INCHES

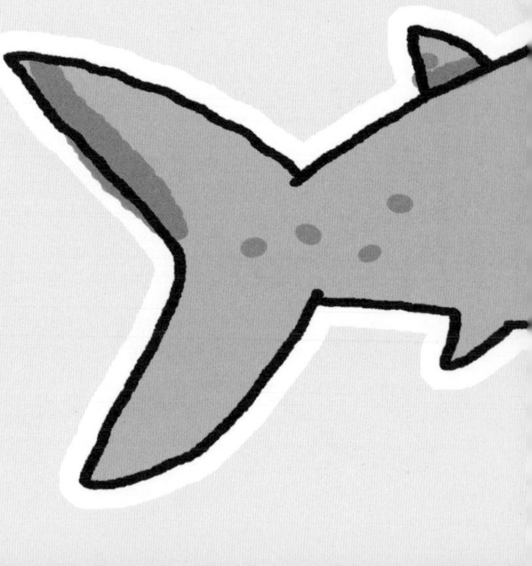

# SHARKS OF THE WORLD

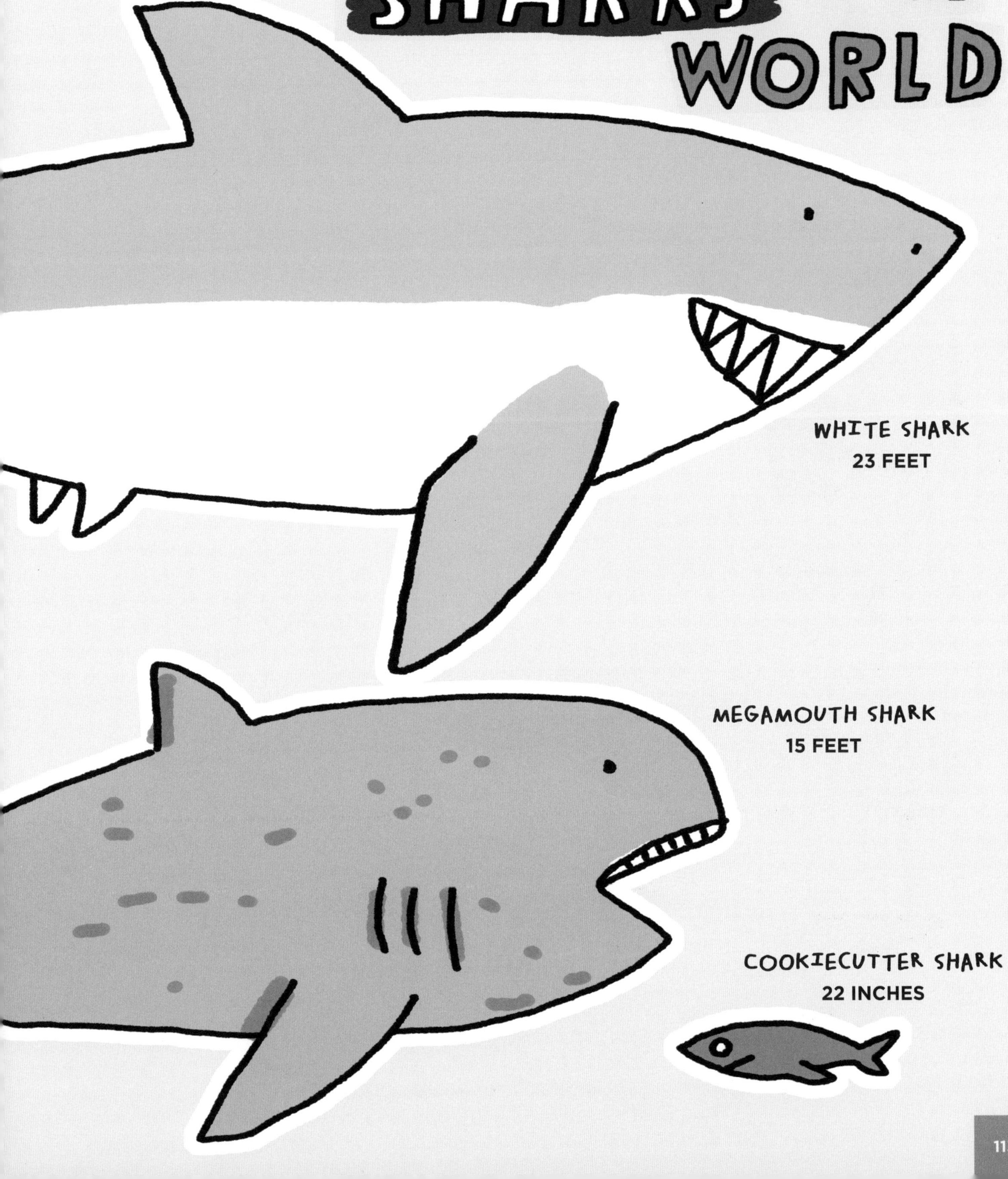
WHITE SHARK
23 FEET
MEGAMOUTH SHARK
15 FEET
COOKIECUTTER SHARK
22 INCHES

# SHARKS OF THE WORLD

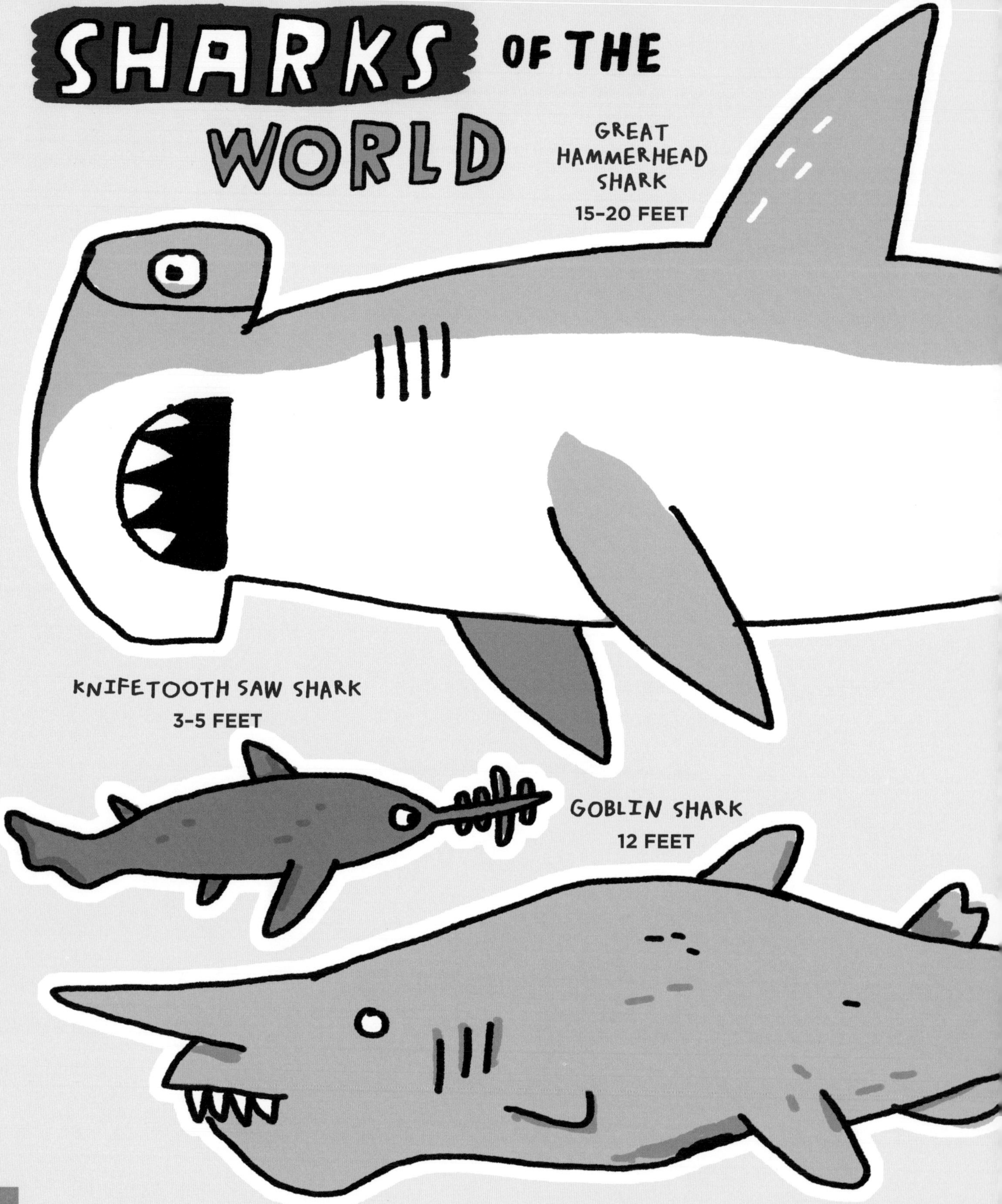
GREAT HAMMERHEAD SHARK
15–20 FEET
KNIFETOOTH SAW SHARK
3–5 FEET
GOBLIN SHARK
12 FEET

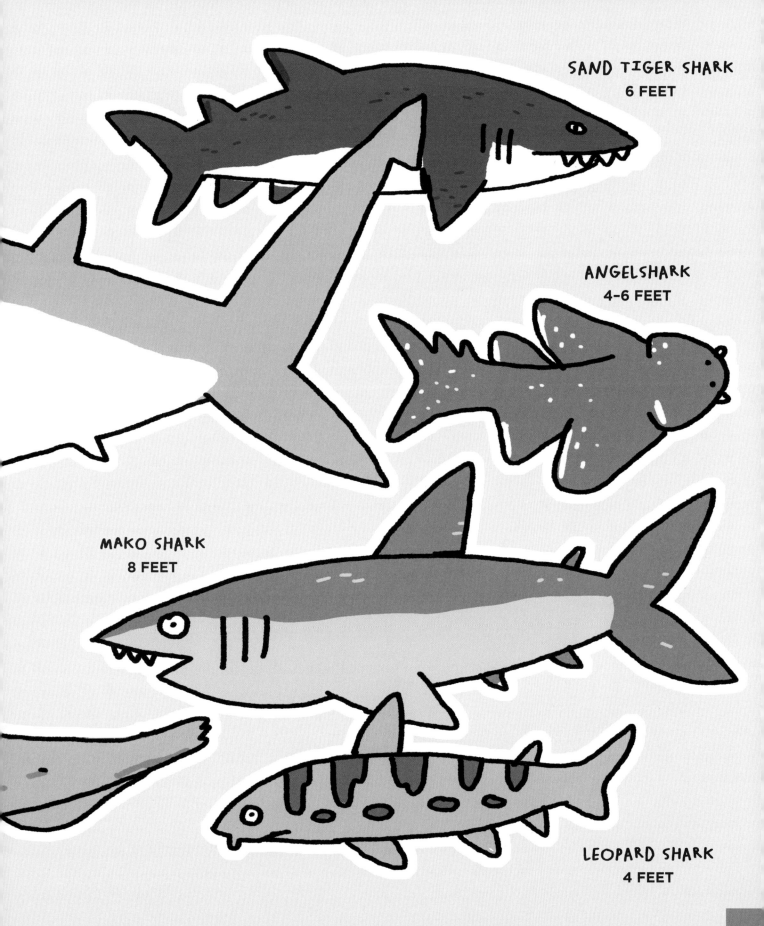

SAND TIGER SHARK
6 FEET

ANGELSHARK
4-6 FEET

MAKO SHARK
8 FEET

LEOPARD SHARK
4 FEET

# WHALES!

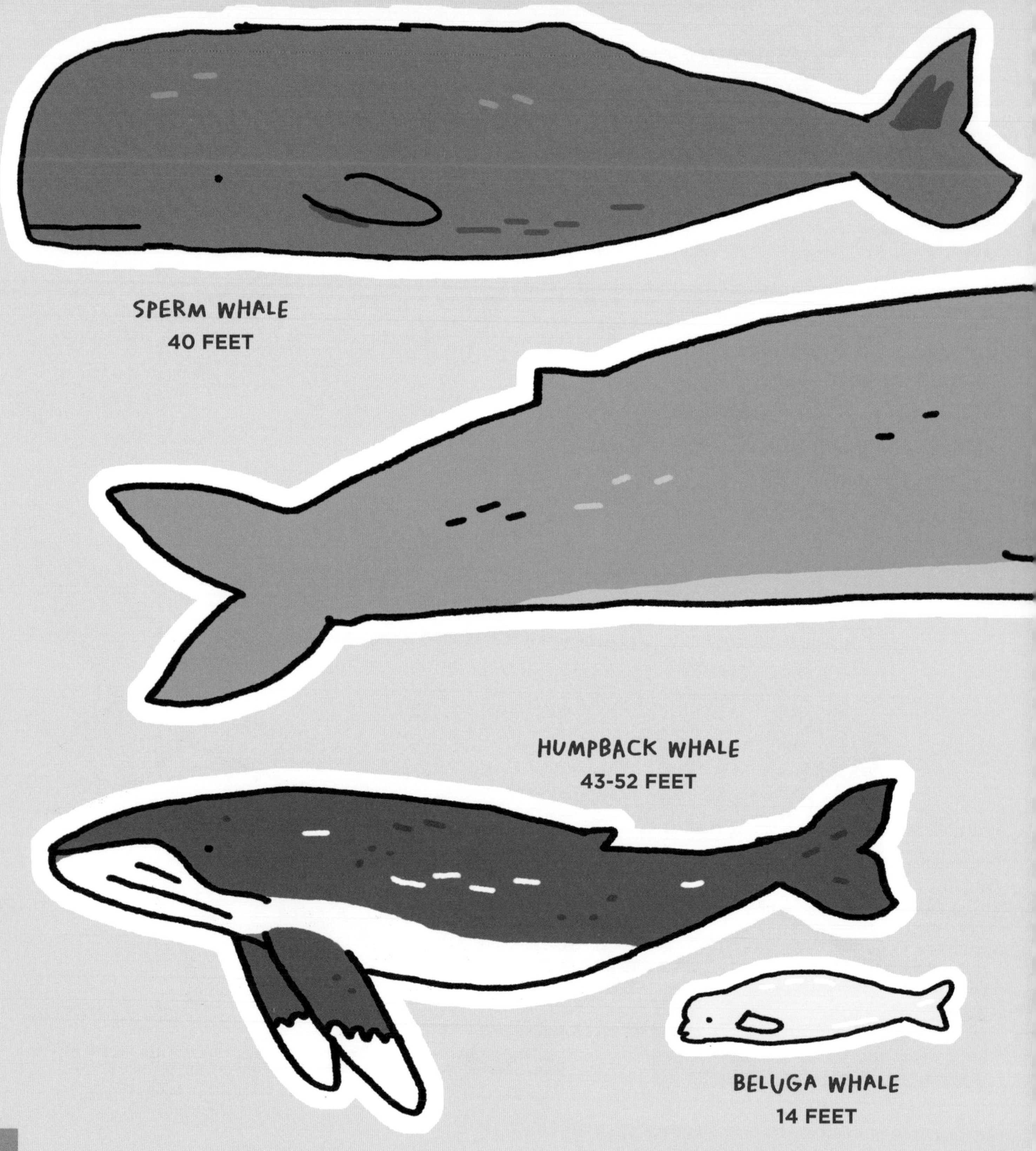
SPERM WHALE
40 FEET
HUMPBACK WHALE
43-52 FEET
BELUGA WHALE
14 FEET

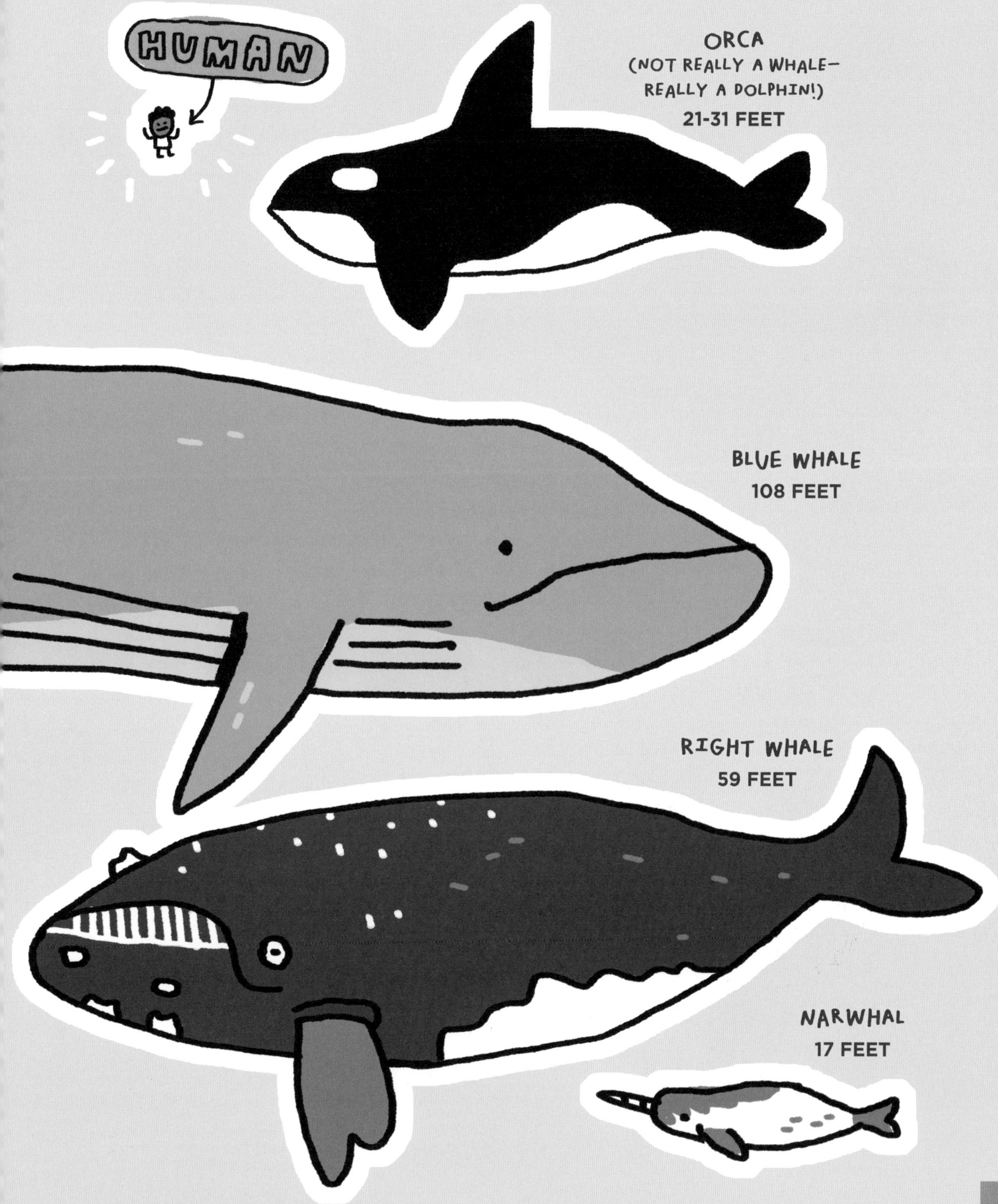
HUMAN
ORCA
(NOT REALLY A WHALE—
REALLY A DOLPHIN!)
21-31 FEET
BLUE WHALE
108 FEET
RIGHT WHALE
59 FEET
NARWHAL
17 FEET

# MORE GIANTS OF THE OCEAN!

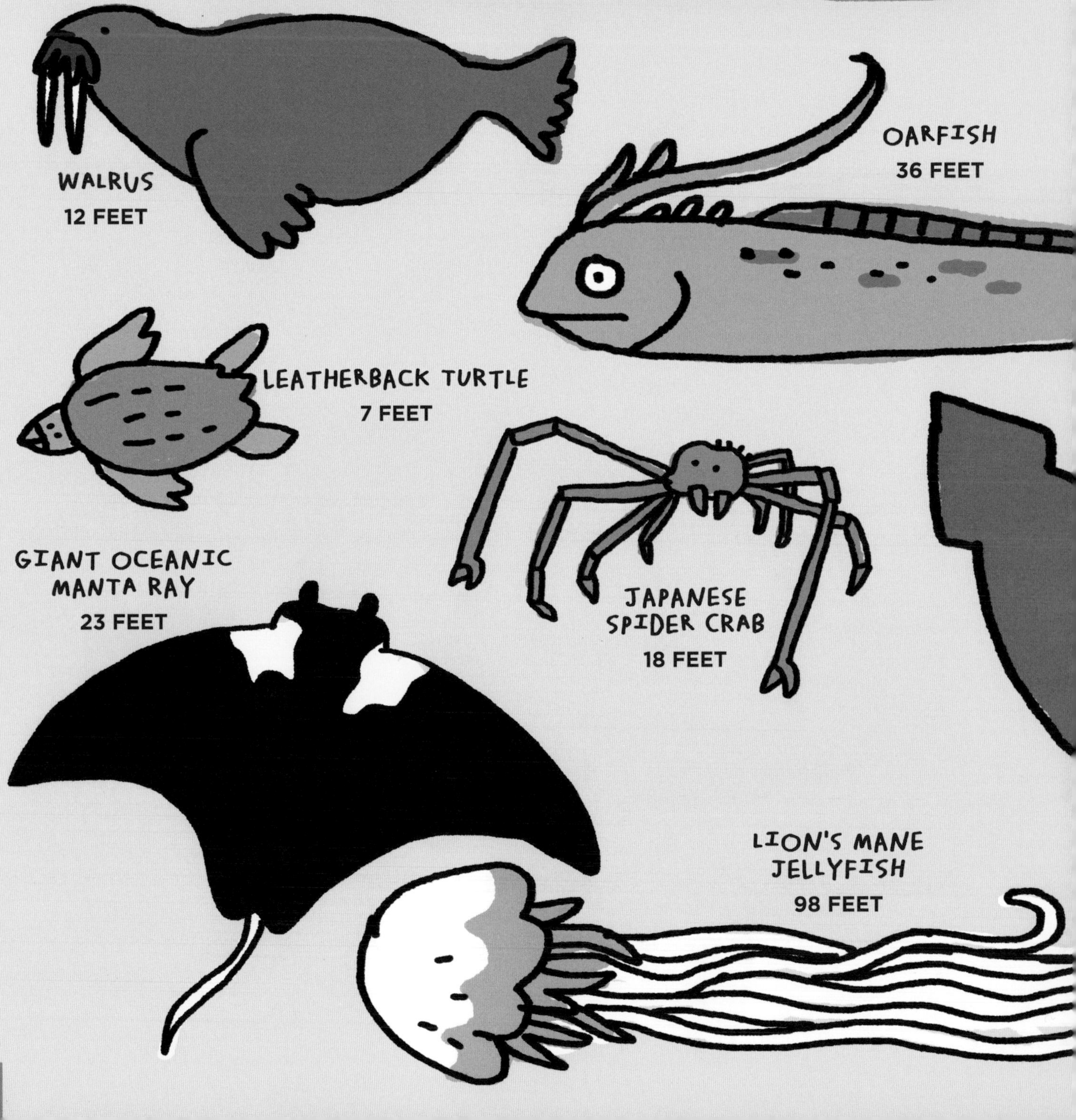
WALRUS
12 FEET
OARFISH
36 FEET
LEATHERBACK TURTLE
7 FEET
GIANT OCEANIC MANTA RAY
23 FEET
JAPANESE SPIDER CRAB
18 FEET
LION'S MANE JELLYFISH
98 FEET

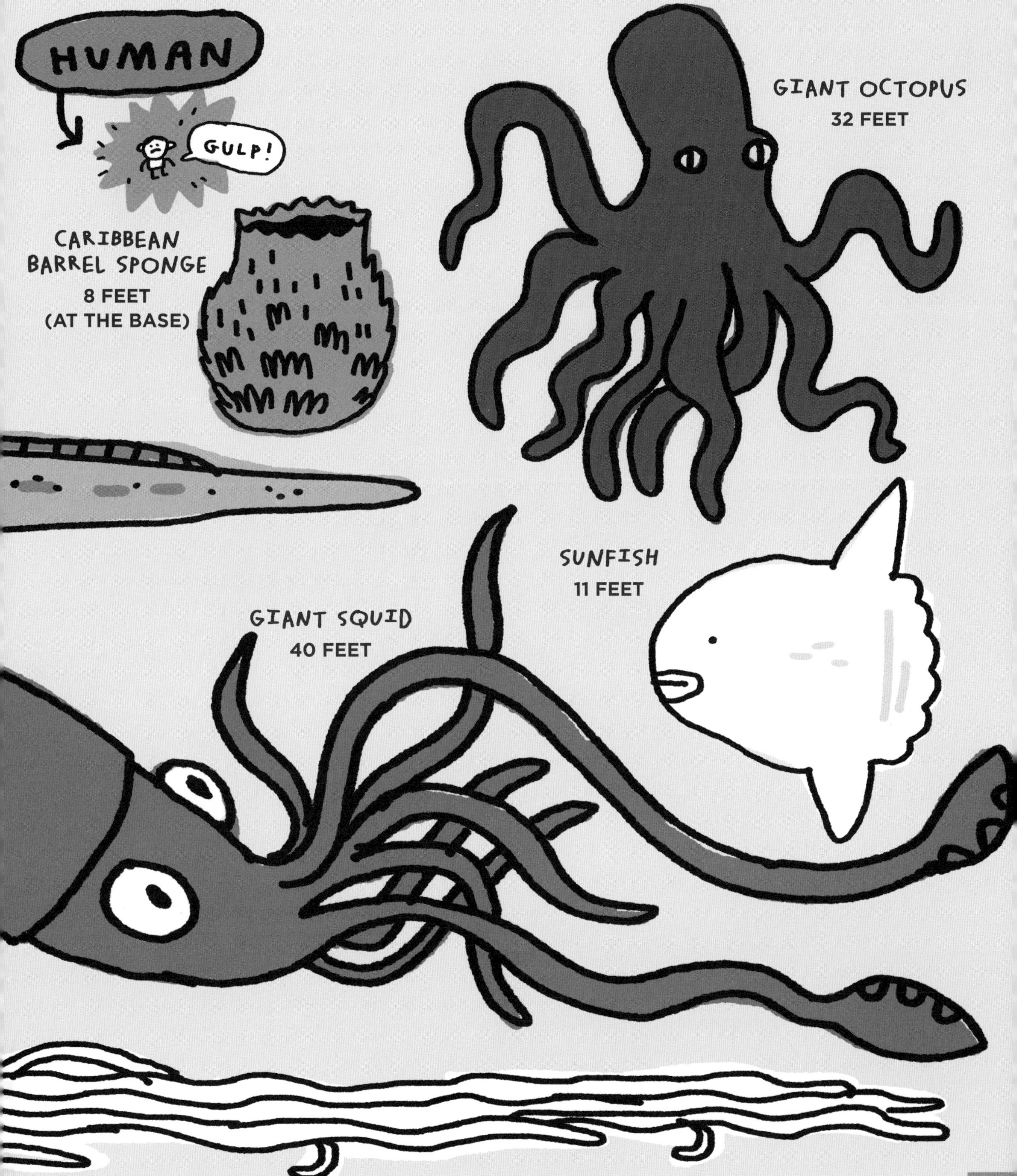
HUMAN
GULP!
CARIBBEAN BARREL SPONGE
8 FEET
(AT THE BASE)
GIANT OCTOPUS
32 FEET
SUNFISH
11 FEET
GIANT SQUID
40 FEET

# DEEP SEA JOKES!

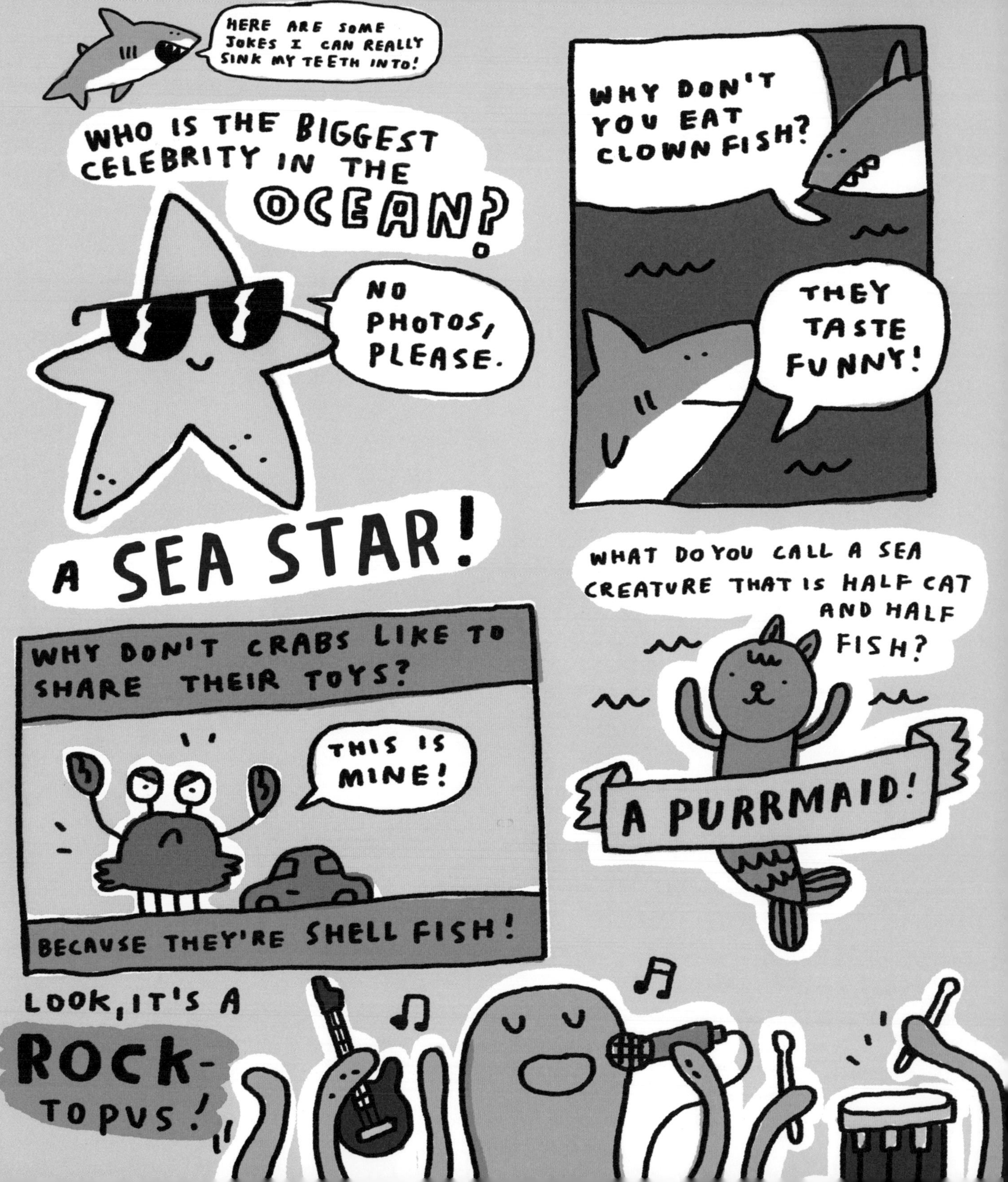
HERE ARE SOME JOKES I CAN REALLY SINK MY TEETH INTO!
WHO IS THE BIGGEST CELEBRITY IN THE OCEAN?
NO PHOTOS, PLEASE.
A SEA STAR!
WHY DON'T YOU EAT CLOWNFISH?
THEY TASTE FUNNY!
WHY DON'T CRABS LIKE TO SHARE THEIR TOYS?
THIS IS MINE!
BECAUSE THEY'RE SHELLFISH!
WHAT DO YOU CALL A SEA CREATURE THAT IS HALF CAT AND HALF FISH?
A PURRMAID!
LOOK, IT'S A ROCK-TOPUS!

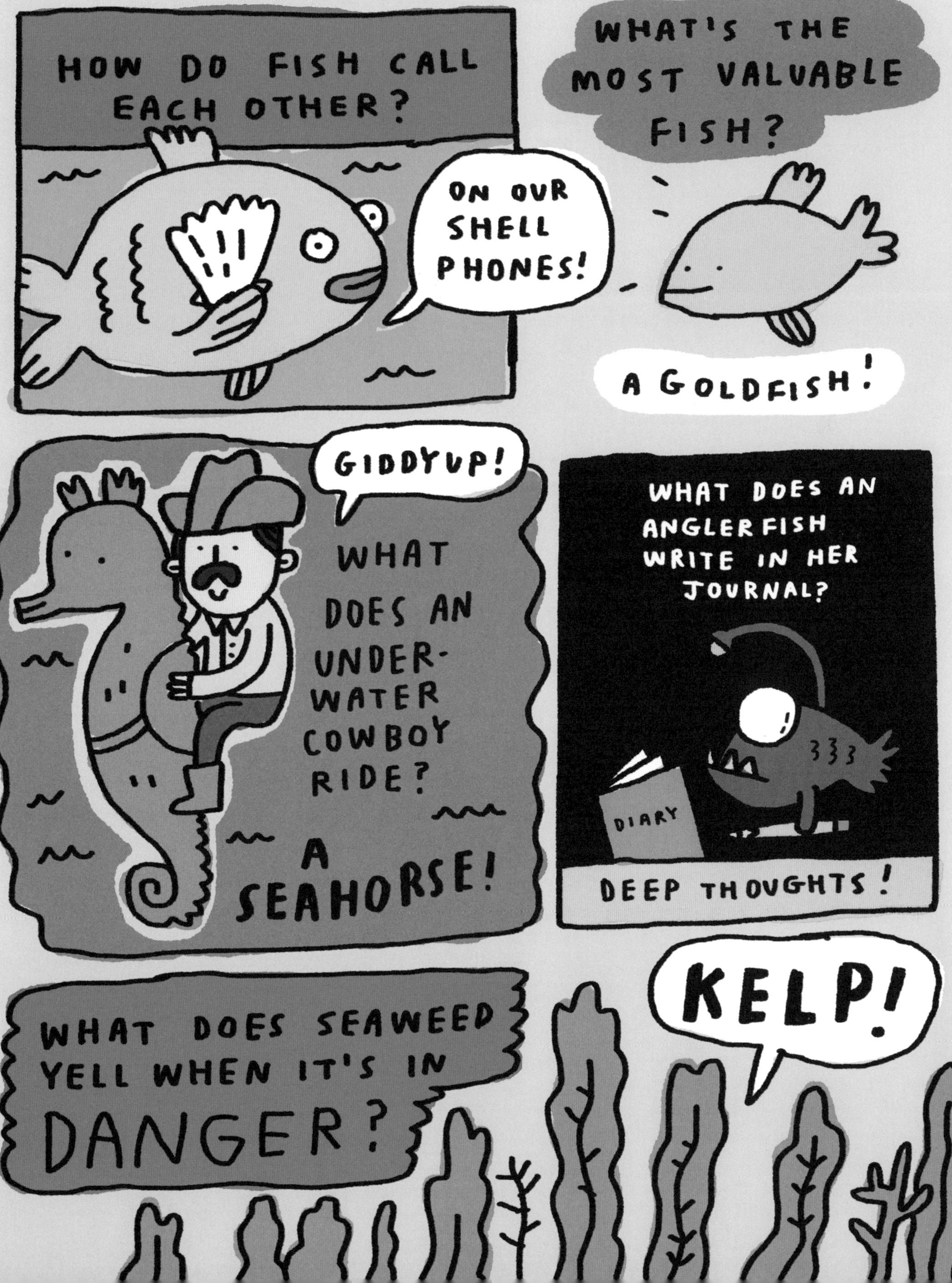
HOW DO FISH CALL EACH OTHER?
ON OUR SHELL PHONES!
WHAT'S THE MOST VALUABLE FISH?
A GOLDFISH!
GIDDYUP!
WHAT DOES AN UNDER-WATER COWBOY RIDE?
A SEAHORSE!
WHAT DOES AN ANGLERFISH WRITE IN HER JOURNAL?
DIARY
DEEP THOUGHTS!
WHAT DOES SEAWEED YELL WHEN IT'S IN DANGER?
KELP!

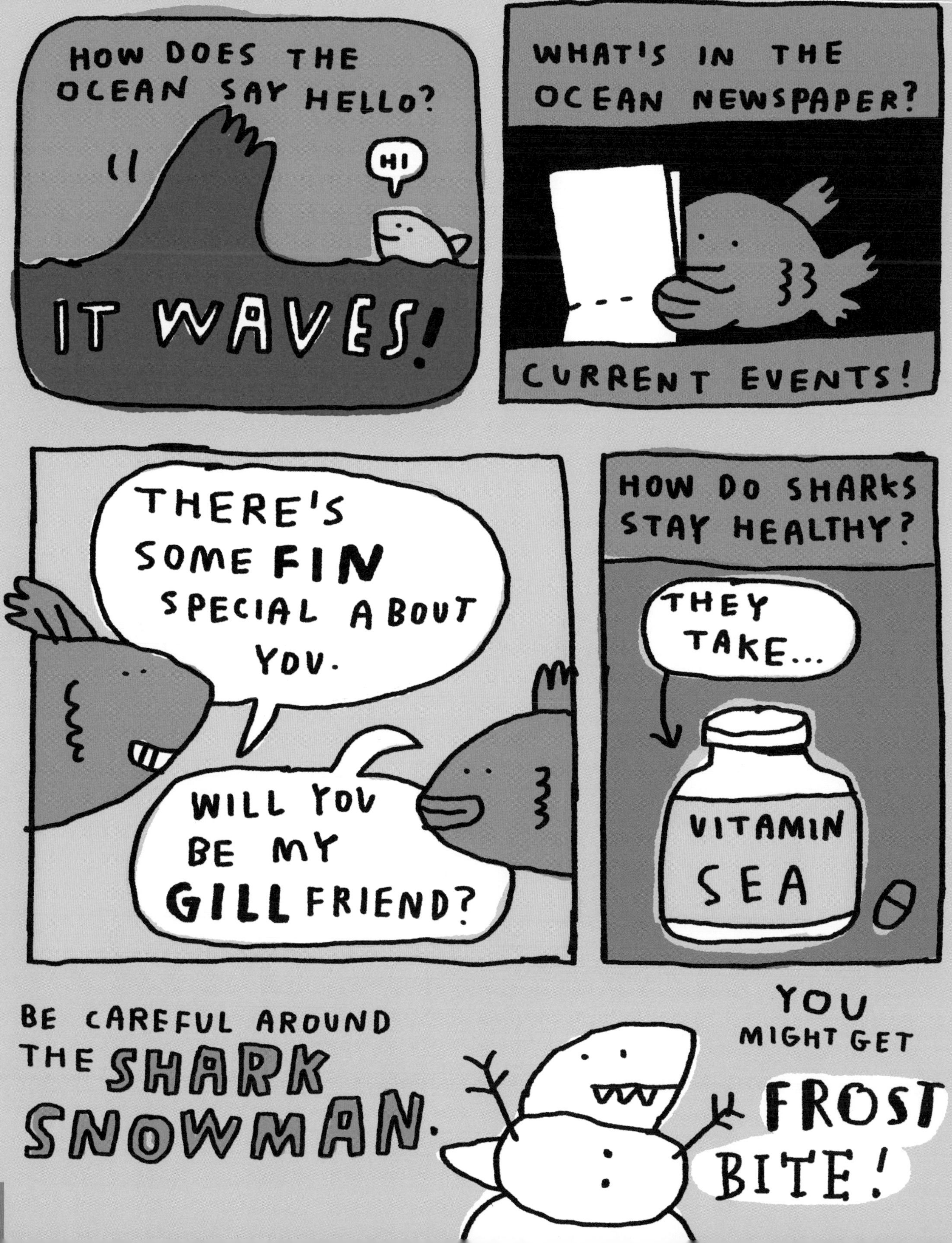
HOW DOES THE OCEAN SAY HELLO?
HI
IT WAVES!
WHAT'S IN THE OCEAN NEWSPAPER?
CURRENT EVENTS!
THERE'S SOME FIN SPECIAL ABOUT YOU.
WILL YOU BE MY GILL FRIEND?
HOW DO SHARKS STAY HEALTHY?
THEY TAKE...
VITAMIN SEA
BE CAREFUL AROUND THE SHARK SNOWMAN.
YOU MIGHT GET FROST BITE!

Here are a few awesome books I devoured while working on this book!

Castro, Peter, and Michael Huber. *Marine Biology*. New York, NY: McGraw-Hill Education, 2015.

DK Publishing. *Super Shark Encyclopedia*. New York, NY: DK Publishing, 2015.

Earle, Sylvia. *The World Is Blue: How Our Fate and the Ocean's Are One*. Washington, D.C.: National Geographic, 2010.

Ebert, David, and Sarah Fowler, Marc Dando. *A Pocket Guide to Sharks of the World*. Princeton, NJ: Princeton University Press, 2015.

Jackson, Jack. *Dive Atlas of the World: An Illustrated Reference to the Best Sites*. United Kingdom: IMM Lifestyle Books, 2016.

Kelly, Richard. *Encyclopedia of Sharks*. Thaxed, England: Miles Kelly Publishing, 2017.

Skerry, Brian. *The Ultimate Book of Sharks*. Washington, D.C.: National Geographic Kids, 2018.

Wilsdon, Christina. *Ultimate Oceanpedia: The Most Complete Ocean Reference Ever*. Washington D.C.: National Geographic Kids, 2016.

Woodward, John. *Ocean: A Visual Encyclopedia*. New York, NY: DK Publishing, 2015.

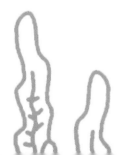

NEED MORE FACTS?

THEN CHECK OUT: EVERYTHING AWESOME BOOK 3!

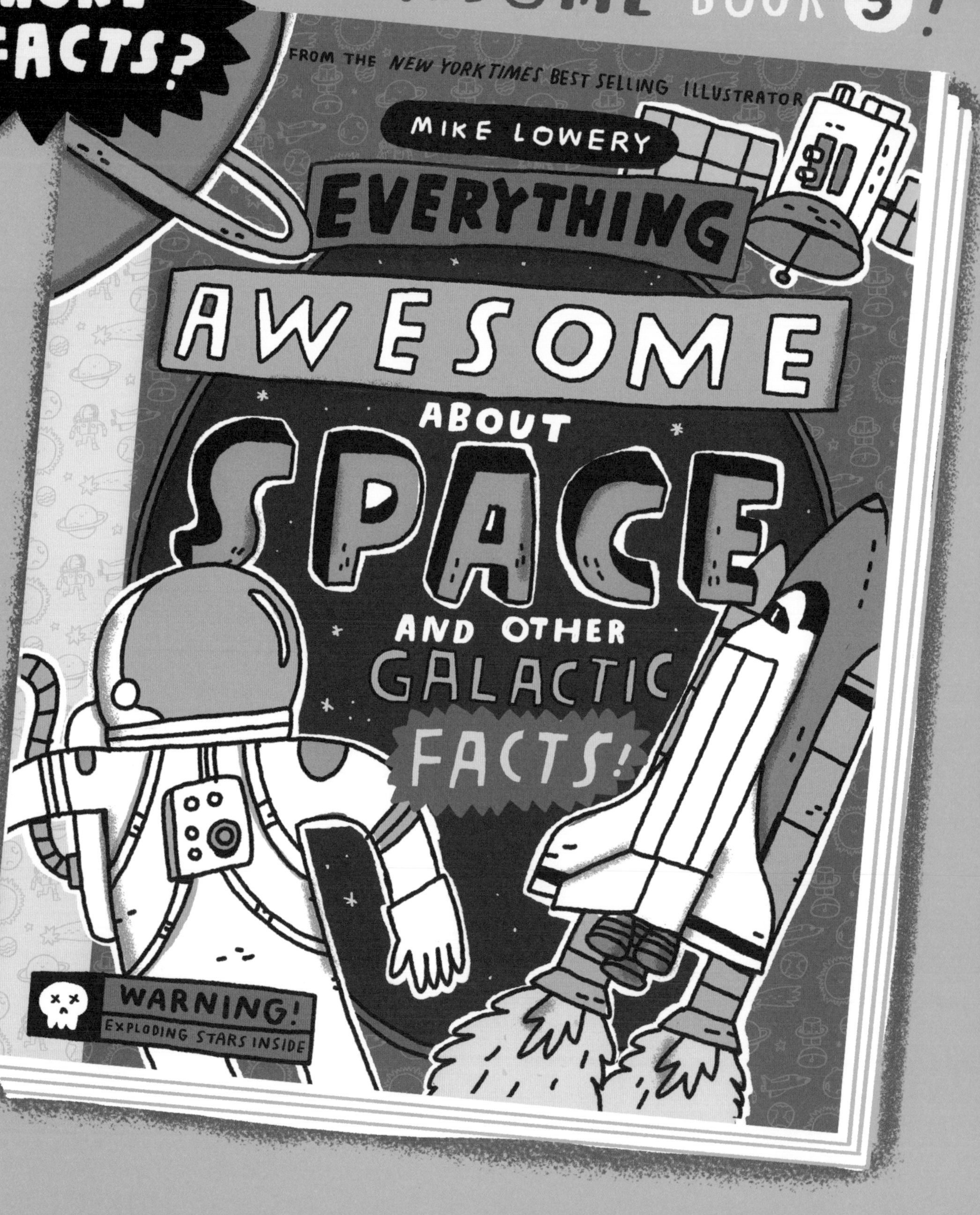
FROM THE NEW YORK TIMES BEST SELLING ILLUSTRATOR
MIKE LOWERY
EVERYTHING AWESOME
ABOUT SPACE
AND OTHER GALACTIC FACTS!
WARNING!
EXPLODING STARS INSIDE

MORE THAN ONE **MILLION** EARTHS COULD FIT INSIDE THE **SUN!**

HI

THE SUN MAKES UP 99% OF ALL OF THE MASS IN OUR SOLAR SYSTEM.

THERE'S A VOLCANO ON MARS THAT IS **THREE TIMES** THE SIZE OF MT. EVEREST!

ALL ASTRONAUTS HAVE TO BE FLUENT IN **RUSSIAN!**

Привет

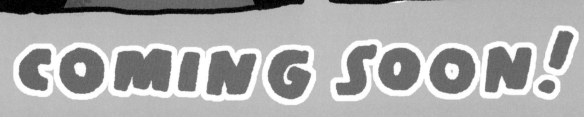

COMING SOON!

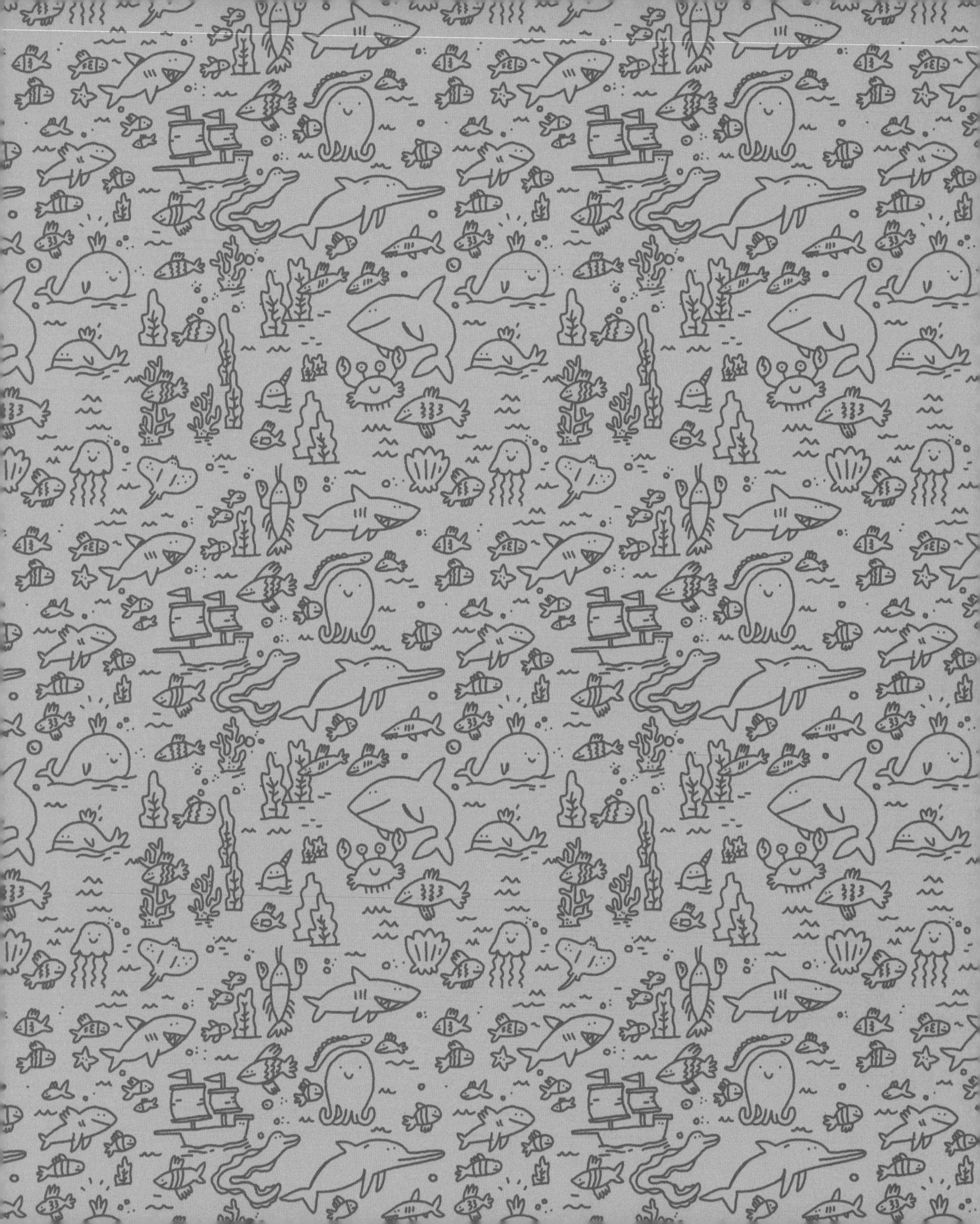